THE PSYCHOLOGY
OF COGNITION

THE PSYCHOLOGY OF COGNITION

Second Edition

Gillian Cohen

Faculty of Social Sciences
The Open University

ACADEMIC PRESS
Harcourt Brace Jovanovich, Publishers
London   San Diego   New York
Boston   Sydney   Tokyo   Toronto

ACADEMIC PRESS LIMITED
24–28 Oval Road, London NW1 7DX

United States Edition Published by
ACADEMIC PRESS, INC.
San Diego, CA 92101

British Library Cataloguing in Publication Data
Cohen, Gillian
    The psychology of cognition.—2nd ed.
    1. Cognition
    I. Title
    153.4   BF 3111

ISBN 0-12-178760-5
ISBN 0-12-178762-1 Pbk

Printed in Great Britain by
St Edmundsbury Press Limited, Bury St Edmunds, Suffolk

Preface to the Second Edition

In this second edition, *The Psychology of Cognition* has been extensively re-written. It has been updated so as to include new materials, and to take account of new developments and approaches. Like the first edition, it is arranged as a set of tutorial essays, each of which can be read on its own, although I have tried to show the connexions between the different topics and to refer the reader to relevant sections of other chapters. This book is designed for students and those who already have a basic knowledge of the subject. It does not aim to provide a comprehensive survey of the whole of cognitive psychology, but reviews some central topics in the study of thinking. In presenting an account of research methods and findings, I have tried to show what kind of evidence is relevant to a given problem, and how to evaluate it. The purpose is to give an idea of how to think about problems in psychology. The book also reflects my own preference for an interdisciplinary approach to problems in cognitive psychology. Evidence from animal studies, from child development, from clinical psychology, computer modelling, neurophysiology, philosophical analysis and common sense is collated (as far as my own ignorance permits), and converging trends are noted. I should point out that although I have chosen, unfashionably, to use "he" throughout the book, where other writers substitute "she", or "he and she", this is due to stylistic preference rather than an anti-feminist stance.

I am very much indebted to the staff of Academic Press for advice and encouragement. I would also like to thank my research assistant, Dorothy Faulkner, who made it possible for me to devote time to re-writing this book by taking on so much of my research work; Susan Digby-Firth who made a splendid job of typing the final draft; and Tony Morris for his drawing of Nim signing to his teacher (Fig. 19).

January, 1983   G.M.C.

Preface to the First Edition

The Psychology of Cognition examines some central topics in the study of thinking, and tries to evaluate, and set in perspective, the developments of the last decade or so in these areas. The common theme is the role of concepts, words and images in thought. The aim has been to extricate the main issues and problems from the steadily accumulating mass of data; to reveal the shape of the wood, and not to leave the reader lost among the trees. The emphasis is on the overall patterns of evidence that are discernible when we try to correlate the results of different methods—experimental testing, computer simulation, clinical studies and observation of everyday behaviour. An attempt is made to assess the relative power and scope of different methods, to discuss their limitations, and to show how models of cognitive processes gain support when the evidence from different sources converges. The book is designed to provide an intelligible introduction to cognition for readers not familiar with the subject, and an overview for those who already know the ground.

I am indebted to colleagues and students of the Department of Ex perimental Psychology in the University of Oxford for many helpful discussions; to my husband, who eliminated much that was unclear and awkward in the writing of earlier drafts; and to Anne Bell, who typed the final draft.

October, 1977   G.M.C.

Contents

1 TRENDS *and* ISSUES *in* COGNITIVE PSYCHOLOGY

In recent years there have been substantial and important changes in the way that psychologists approach the study of human thought. It is easier to understand the theories, issues and controversies described in later chapters with reference to particular areas of cognition, if some of the current trends are first outlined. These trends reflect changes in aims and emphases, in methods and in points of view. More importantly, they reveal the conceptual framework that currently guides attempts to describe and explain the mechanism of thinking. A brief account of the background to current developments helps to give a better idea of what cognitive psychologists are trying to do, and why. The six trends that are listed below are clearly inter-related. Some of them are offshoots or logical consequences of others. So they should not really be considered as separate trends but rather as elements within a more general change in the study of thinking.

Strategies and Structures, and Related Distinctions

Strategies and structures

The distinction between strategies and structures is only one of a set of distinctions that are frequently encountered in current theories. These distinctions are not identical, but nevertheless resemble each other quite closely. Besides strategy and structure, the group includes distinctions between performance and competence; habits and capacities; cognitively penetrable and cognitively impenetrable functions; and software and hardware. What all of these have in common is that some aspects of the cognitive system are seen as fixed, while other aspects are flexible, dynamic and variable. An adequate cognitive theory must not only distinguish which parts of the mechanism are fixed and which are flexible. It must also specify the control processes that govern the selection and operation of the optional elements in the system. These distinctions are necessary because it is quite clear, as anybody who runs a simple cognitive experiment in the laboratory will soon find, that different people are doing the experimental task in different ways. It is also often true that the same person may shift from one strategy to another over a period of time. The need to account for this variability has forced psychologists to pay much more attention to optional strategies. So, instead of the kind of box and arrow models common in the early days of information theory, which represented mandatory patterns of information flow through a set of fixed structures, we are concerned to try to describe different possible strategies which employ different sets of processes in variable orders, and utilize different structures. Ask any group of people to describe carefully how they add 621 and 734. Some will report adding the hundreds first; others the tens or the units. Some may retain the subtotals in working memory by means of overt or covert verbal rehearsal; others rely on visualization. External aids such as paper and pencil, fingers, an abacus or an electronic calculator may be employed. The same basic rules and symbols may be involved in each version, but the number, type and sequence of operations may vary widely.

The word strategy tends to imply a deliberate choice of method and conscious control, but this implication is misleading here. Although in the example of arithmetic calculation a strategy may be consciously selected, in other tasks optional variations may be switched in without conscious control or even awareness. In reading, for example, the pattern of eye movements may shift without the reader being aware of it.

Habits and capacities

Experimental data often reflect habits rather than capacities, norms rather than limits. Studies may show how people habitually solve problems or read text, without establishing the limits of their capacity. Sometimes the psychologist may be primarily interested in determining norms or habitual modes of cognitive processing. This is often the case when the study has some practical aim. If the object is to design an advertisement so as to attract attention and be memorable; or to devise an educational method that will make material interesting and easy to learn, then cognitive habits are of primary relevance. Habits represent preferred strategies. Capacities or limits are set by constraints arising from fixed aspects of the mechanism, such as the size of the memory store, the maximum speed of processing, or the extent to which different forms of representation are inter-convertible. These constraints come into play when performance is pushed to its limits. Most of the time we operate well inside our cognitive limits, just as we seldom stretch to anywhere near the limits of our physical capacities. But with practice and effort cognitive performance may approach its limits. The performance of a skilled reader may hit a ceiling when speed can increase no further without a fall in the amount comprehended and remembered. The psychologist who is aiming to construct a theoretical account of reading, and to understand the nature of the mechanisms involved in reading needs to establish the limits as well as the norms.

Software and hardware

The software–hardware distinction, borrowed from computer science, is similar, corresponding roughly to structure and process. Hardware refers to fixed, wired-in structures. In the human brain, these structures are usually described in neurological or biological terms instead of electronic ones, but it is possible to formulate a description at a level of abstraction that is applicable to both human and machine systems. Software is the term used to refer to computer programmes. In the brain these are equivalent to cognitive processes, or sets of cognitive processes which are explained in computational terms. These processes can also be characterized at a level of abstraction that allows them to be realized in different kinds of system. Rather confusingly, cognitive scientists may sometimes refer to a set of processes normally considered as part of the software, as being "hard-wired", meaning that they are mandatory, rather than optional.

Cognitive penetrability

Cognitive penetrability is a concept introduced into cognitive theories by Pylyshyn (1980). He distinguishes cognitively impenetrable fixed capacities of the mind (which he sometimes calls the functional architecture), from the particular representations and processes used in specific tasks, which are cognitively penetrable in that they can be affected by other factors such as goals, beliefs and tacit knowledge. Pylyshyn maintains that any satisfactory model of the mind must make this distinction. However, it proves difficult in practice to identify the fixed impenetrable elements in the system. Even capacities that would seem to be physiologically determined, such as sensory thresholds turn out to be cognitively penetrable. For example, the threshold for detecting just noticeable differences in weight can be influenced by tacit knowledge of size–weight relations. Although it is obviously desirable to be able to specify the fixed, hard-wired, invariant, impenetrable aspects of the cognitive system, in order to produce a general theory, the enormous flexibility of human thought makes this a very difficult undertaking. The problem is particularly apparent in, for example, the study of hemisphere differences described in Chapter 9. Both structural models and dynamic models have been proposed to explain the specialized abilities of left and right brains. Neither is satisfactory on its own, and it is clear that both kinds of model will need to be combined to produce an adequate account.

Performance and competence

The distinction between performance and competence runs into similar difficulties. Performance is there to be observed, measured, manipulated or analysed; but competence is by definition not directly observable. The distinction was emphasized by Chomsky (1967) in the context of his syntactic theory, to explain the way in which the language user's speech and comprehension may deviate from the predictions of the model. "Competence" describes the structural model and the rules whereby it functions in a pure and ideal form. "Performance" refers to the way it actually functions in practice, when it is contaminated by many other factors which are extraneous to the competence model. Competence represents an underlying abstract system which is general and invariant, but this system is only very indirectly reflected in performance, which is individual and variable. The psychologist is faced with the double task of characterizing the underlying competence, and also identifying the factors that cause actual performance to deviate from the ideal standardized form which would be predicted on the basis of competence alone. The distinction is relevant in many aspects of cognitive functioning. A person's mathematical competence may be obscured by errors, lapses of memory or by the adoption of different strategies when he comes to carry out a particular calculation. Or linguistic competence may be obscured by speech difficulties. Performance data do not reflect cognitive competence at all purely. Many other variables including familiarity, context, errors, ignorance and the preoccupations and emotions of the individual intrude and influence the pattern of responses on which the experimenter tries to build a theory. It is his formidable task to parcel out these extraneous factors and isolate the underlying structure and mechanism. Experimental methods have limited power. A competence model gains corroboration when it predicts the empirical findings, but is not necessarily invalidated when the results fail to conform to the model, since the discrepancy may always be due to performance factors. While positive results can lend support to a competence model, negative results provide no reliable evidence for or against, so the competence–performance distinction is both a stumbling-block and a safety net for the experimenter.

Chomsky's claim that linguistic competence can exist in the absence of ability to use the language for communication has been challenged (Schank, 1980). To Schank, it does not make sense to credit people with possessing the rules and representations of language unless they have the ability to produce and comprehend it. To some extent, such differences of opinion reflect a difference in approach. Applied psychologists with practical aims are necessarily mainly concerned with performance, habits, strategies; theoretical psychologists must necessarily be more concerned with competence and fixed structures.

Automatic and attentional processes

A further distinction that permeates much of cognitive psychology today is that between automatic and attentional processes. Automatic processes do not require conscious control, and are inaccessible to conscious awareness. Processes become automatic with prolonged practice, and cease to make demands on the limited capacity attentional system. Automatic processes are relatively more fixed, and are run off as a precompiled sequence. In contrast, attentional processes are under continuous conscious control and monitoring, and can be changed and modified. The distinction is important, empirically as well as theoretically, since predictions about performance in a given task must take into account whether the processes required in the task are automatic, or attentional (and therefore subject to capacity limitations).

Ecological Validity

A dominant trend in present day cognitive psychology is the demand for studies with greater "ecological validity". In part this is a reaction against the kind of rigorous but highly artificial laboratory experiments which proved sterile, in that they yielded little information about how people behave in everyday life outside the laboratory. Neisser (1978) has been one of the leading advocates of ecological validity. Surveying the lack of real progress in memory research after nearly 100 years of laboratory experimentation, he urged the need to study actual uses of memory in everyday life. The result has been a marked change of direction. Where memory researchers once studied subjects' ability to learn nonsense syllables, and to reproduce lists of digits in reverse order, many are now examining eye witness testimony (Loftus and Palmer, 1974); what kind of information students retain from lectures and texts (Kintsch and Bates, 1977); absent-mindedness (Herrman and Neisser, 1978); and how people remember old school mates (Bahrick *et al.*, 1975), recipes, shopping lists and town plans. The return to real life is not limited to memory research, but is evident in other areas of cognition as well. In problem solving, studies of chess playing and of the reasoning underlying medical diagnosis have superseded the study of syllogistic reasoning. In concept learning experiments, natural concepts like chairs and bicycles have replaced the geometrical shapes that were used in the earlier style of laboratory experiment. All this new work is of great interest and relevance, but it has certain obvious disadvantages. Rigorous control, strict standardization of material and procedure, and precise measurement of responses may all be sacrificed, so that findings are bound to be less reliable. Naturalistic methods of studying behaviour allow us to describe, and perhaps to predict, but not to explain. Ecologically valid studies produce performance data and reveal habits and strategies. They tell us little about the underlying mechanism, its functional capacities and limitations, and the causal role of structures and processes. Some researchers also maintain that ecological validity cannot be achieved simply by studying behaviour in its social and cultural context. The ontogenic and evolutionary antecedents of the behaviour should also be studied.

Individual Differences

Another trend is toward increasing recognition of the existence of wide-ranging individual differences in cognitive functioning. This factor has been much neglected by cognitive psychologists in traditional studies of learning and memory. Experimenters have been content to make comparisons between groups, and to ignore quite glaring differences between the performance of individual subjects. Indeed, it is common practice to select subjects of similar age and educational background in order to avoid too great a disparity in results. This policy can result in models of performance which reflect the average performance of deliberately homogenized groups, but do not characterize any single individual. Currently, there is a growing awareness of the inadequacy of an approach which fails to take account of the rich variety of intellectual strategies and cognitive styles (Hunt *et al.*, 1973, 1975) that are exemplified in the performance of individuals. Memory is also, to a considerable extent, personal and idiosyncratic. Because each individual's life experience is unique, the contents of his store of knowledge will be unique. We do not all know the same facts or relate them together in the same ways. Although education imposes some degree of uniformity, in some areas of knowledge, we can be thankfully confident that the memories of individual humans must be very diverse. This diversity of the knowledge structures is one factor which makes experimental results variable, and renders attempts to construct general models peculiarly problematic.

It has been a common experimental practice to express results in terms of the group average, but a great deal of potentially informative data are suppressed if this is done. Like the average family of 2·5 children, the group average is something of a mythical beast. Averaging across individuals can produce a distorted and unrepresentative pattern of results.

The effort toward greater ecological validity and the practical spirit of contemporary psychology has induced greater attention to individual differences. In real life it is the behaviour of individuals we want to understand and predict. However, there is no great merit in simply recording the different patterns of behaviour of different individuals. We need to be able to classify individuals into types, and to find correlations between these types and performance in cognitive tasks. We need to know what characteristics of an individual influence his pattern of cognitive abilities and how. Individual differences only become theoretically interesting if we can specify the causal mechanism that relates individual characteristics to cognitive abilities.

Attempts to correlate psychometric measures with performance on information processing tasks have shown that, with multicomponent tasks, it is necessary to adopt a procedure similar to R. J. Sternberg's componential analysis of information processing tasks in order to examine individual differences in each stage separately. This approach is exemplified in the work of MacLeod *et al.* (1978), and Hunt (1978). They studied a sentence verification task. Subjects were presented with a sentence such as "Plus is above star", or "Star is not below plus". This was followed by a pattern (either $\overset{+}{*}$ or $\overset{*}{+}$), and the subject was required to respond "True" or "False" according to whether the sentence matched the pattern or not. In this task some subjects tend to read the sentence and visualize the corresponding pattern. The pattern actually presented can then be matched to the visualized one. MacLeod *et al.* found a correlation between psychometric measures of spatial ability and use of a visualizing strategy. Individuals with high verbal ability tended to use a verbal strategy. For the visualizers, performance on the task correlated with spatial ability scores. For verbalizers, performance correlated with verbal activity. Individual differences show up when the task is decomposed, rather than in overall scores. Chiang and Atkinson (1976) adopted a similar approach and found that female subjects with high verbal ability scores had a slower than average rate of search in a visual search task (deciding if a target letter was present in a display), and also in a memory search task (deciding if a target letter was in a memorized list). Presumably a tendency to verbalize the tasks slowed down the search for these subjects. Preference for verbal or nonverbal strategies appears to be one of the major sources of individual differences in cognitive tasks. Besides classifying individuals according to their scores on psychometric tests such as verbal or spatial ability, researchers often attempt to establish relationships between the age and sex of an individual and performance on cognitive tasks. Fairweather (1976) reviews studies of sex differences in cognition, but in spite of the many claims linking sex with particular cognitive abilities, he finds little evidence of reliable correlations, due largely to failure to control other factors such as age, culture, education, birth order and family size, all of which may exert an influence on cognition. Another factor contributing to individual differences is handedness. Efforts to link left-handedness with specific patterns of cognitive ability have a long history (Herron, 1980), although again the findings are not very consistent.

Although the use of interviews, intelligence test scores and examinations for job selection rests on the assumption that individual differences can be evaluated, and used to predict performance, the theoretical justification for these assumptions lags behind their application. A cognitive theory which ignores individual differences is considered too simplistic, but as yet we are far from understanding how the many characteristics of the individual interact to constrain or influence performance.

Methodological Changes

Along with the changes in aims and emphases already described, there have been changes in methods. New methods have been developed, and old methods, previously discredited, have been rehabilitated. There has been a tendency to admit the limitations of a purely experimental approach, and to seek additional or alternative methods for studying human thought processes.

Obviously a major difficulty for the experimental investigation of cognitive operations is the inaccessibility of the phenomena being studied. The workings of the human mind occur on the innermost loop of a chain of processing of which only the two ends, the stimulus or input end, and the response or output end, are observable. In consequence, experimental conclusions are necessarily inferential and results of even the best designed experiments need to be interpreted.

Naturalistic psychology

Besides being indirect, experimental techniques may be irrelevant or inappropriate. The shift toward topics and issues of greater ecological validity has produced a new methodology advocating the study of real life situations which will take in the whole context in which behaviour patterns occur. This approach necessarily entails the abandonment of much experimental control and a move toward an observational, descriptive methodology since strict control procedures are incompatible with natural behaviour. This reaction against the artificiality of rigorous laboratory experiments can be a valuable corrective. Many experimental paradigms involve requirements so remote from everyday life versions of the task that there may be little overlap between the processes employed in the laboratory and in the outside world. But real life psychology is not without its own disadvantages. Once we move psychology out of the laboratory, and into the real world, the number of variables that influence behaviour escalates, and once we abandon the attempt to limit and manipulate them, it becomes correspondingly more difficult to determine their relative importance and how they operate.

Philosophical criteria

Experimental methods have been criticized by some psychologists as lacking the power to resolve some current issues. Chapter 3, for example, reviews the controversy between those who believe that visual information is mentally represented as images, and those who believe it is represented in the form of abstract descriptions. Some of the participants in this debate, such as Anderson (1978), believe that it is impossible to confirm or refute either theory by experimental tests. He maintains that although the two theories are conceptually distinct, they are not empirically distinguishable. Similar problems arise in finding experimental evidence to distinguish unequivocally between models of serial and parallel processes (Townsend, 1973). It may be difficult to derive clear predictions about behaviour from a particular model; or patterns of behaviour may be consistent with more than one model.

In the face of problems that arise when different models do not predict different patterns of behaviour, other methods may be brought to bear. Experimental testing may be supplemented by philosophical analysis. Some of the philosophical criteria which are usually proposed for the evaluation of models are economy or parsimony, universality, completeness and precision or rigorousness. The usefulness of these criteria has too often been accepted as a matter of faith, although their relevance for psychological models is sometimes questionable. For example, it is not enough to say that a mechanism should be economical without specifying whether this constraint applies to storage space, to durability or to power consumption. Lacking this information, we cannot construct an ideal model of memory any more than an engineer could plan a heating scheme without a specification of temperature required and of constraints on the cost of running it. A memory which stores multiple copies is wasteful of storage space, but more resistant to damage and decay. We need to know which is the more important consideration. Similarly, a mechanism which consumes more time and effort may achieve greater accuracy, but reduce the organism's capacity to carry out other ongoing functions.

The requirement of universality implies that, although the content of the system might vary, all individuals should have the same basic structure, and function according to the same general principles. But strict adherence to this criterion can end in triviality. When we have stripped our models of all the differences that exist between members of different cultures, between infancy and old age, between the stupid and the intelligent, the ignorant and the well-informed, and abstracted what is common to them all, we are liable to end up almost empty-handed.

.The criterion of completeness is much more acceptable as a guiding principle in psychological research. The model which fits more of the data is a better model. A model is more complete, and therefore more valid, if it fits not only with the available experimental results, but also with clinical and physiological findings, and with our logical assumptions and common-sense intuitions as well. Evidential support for a theory is greater when it comes from several converging sources, since although one alone might be flawed, they are unlikely to share the same biases. A model which is more rigorously and precisely specified is preferable to a model which is only formulated in vague general terms, since it will generate more specific testable predictions which can be confirmed or falsified, and the model can then be retained, modified or discarded accordingly.

A model may also be preferable on grounds of coherence and plausibility. A model is more coherent and more plausible if the characteristics of the mechanism hang together and arise logically out of each other. For example, it may be considered an inherent property of a visual image that it is difficult to represent very tiny details clearly. Theorists who claim that visual information is stored as descriptions, and not as images, have some difficulty in explaining why this should be so. To attribute this kind of limitation to an abstract description additional *ad hoc* assumptions have to be made. So in this particular case, the application of rational criteria favours the imagery model. Problems in cognitive psychology are now, after an interval of many years, arousing considerable interest among philosophers, and philosophical methods of analysing the problems are making an important contribution to the study of, for example, reasoning, semantics, concepts and imagery.

Introspective evidence

Introspection, long considered as a disreputable and unreliable method, has also made a come-back. Self-ratings, self-reports and verbal protocols are now quite extensively used. Subjects are asked to describe their images, to rate confidence in their decisions, and to provide running commentaries on their own thought processes while solving problems (see Chapter 7 for a detailed discussion). Such evidence is usually invoked to support conclusions or interpretations based on more objective measures, but it is also sometimes used as the primary source of evidence for the nature of mental processes. Of course, the utility of introspection is limited, not only by doubts about its reliability, but because many mental processes are not accessible to consciousness. It is not much good asking a speaker how he constructed the sentence he has just uttered, or asking a listener how he recognizes the voice on the other end of the telephone. Neither of them will be able to describe their mental processes. On the other hand, getting subjects to describe the strategies they used in solving a problem can provide useful pointers to the underlying processes, and may show up individual differences within the group.

The current trend is to combine different methods and different kinds of evidence including philosophical analysis; real life observations; experimental testing; developmental and evolutionary trends; introspective reports and common-sense intuitions; clinical findings and physiological facts. In trying to understand the human cognitive system, the functioning of the normal brain, the developing brain and the damaged brain are compared and taken into account.

The Computational Metaphor

In cognitive psychology the adoption of the computer as an analogy or metaphor for the human brain has come increasingly to dominate our theorizing, and to influence our thinking. A theoretical account of mental structures and processes needs to be pitched at a certain level of abstraction if general principles are to be apparent. It turns out to be possible to describe any system that processes information in such a way that, in spite of differences in physical structure, similar general principles emerge. Information storage and retrieval systems exist both in machines and in the human brain, and the same software may be used in each. At this level of abstraction differences in the hardware, whether electronic or neurophysiological, are irrelevant. This "functionalist" approach (Fodor, 1981) treats the mind as a device for manipulating symbols. The computational metaphor provides a detailed account of the rules and processes required for carrying out these manipulations.

There is nothing new about the use of machine metaphors in psychology. Marshall (1977) provided a historical review to support his claim that since at least 430 BC, the mind has been likened to machines of one kind or another. Hydraulic models of the mind characterized mental processes and motivation in terms of ebbs and flows, reservoirs and pressures. Metaphors for memory have included the wax tablet, the storehouse, the well-indexed library and the hologram. Brain activity has been compared to a telephone exchange, to weaving on a loom, and to a servomechanism like that in a guided missile. The computational metaphor is simply the latest in a long line of quasi-mechanical analogies.

Whether it is helpful to view the mind as a computer is a question discussed at length in Chapter 8. In general, the analogy is useful in that expressing mental processes in terms of computer programs produces an account that is necessarily detailed, precise, unambiguous and logical. Moreover, a theory of mental functioning that is in the form of a computer program can be tested to find out whether it actually works or not. Computer science supplies us with a powerful experimental methodology as well as with models of the mind. The analogy becomes useful and illuminating insofar as it suggests what type of computational processes, and what forms of symbolic representation the brain might use, and how these are organized and controlled. Work in Artificial Intelligence generates discoveries about different ways of representing knowledge and different processes acting on it. It is concerned with the design of possible mechanisms, and the properties of these complex mechanisms are revealed by actually constructing them and seeing what they do—how they perform. So the computational metaphor suggests theories of human brain functioning, and provides the means to test them. Building models capable of visual scene analysis, of playing games and solving problems, of storing scientific knowledge and using it to generate scientific hypotheses, of understanding and using language, has entailed confronting problems of mechanism, problems about how the system works, at a level of detail which cognitive psychology, at least until recently, has traditionally glossed over.

A major difficulty in applying the computational metaphor lies in deciding the criteria for functional equivalence. What degree and kind of similarity is required for us to conclude that man and machine work in the same way? The man–machine analogy is not a perfect one. It is arguable that it is misleading to theorize about software divorced from hardware. According to this argument, the metaphor breaks down because the biological structure of the human brain endows it with properties, and constrains its performance, in ways that are significantly different from the ways in which a computer is constrained by its electronic embodiment. Indeed, computers are often specifically designed to complement human abilities rather than to mimic them, so computers do well the things we do badly and vice versa. The human brain computes relatively slowly; it makes errors; it is easily distracted, and it tends to lose or mislay information from store. The computer, on the other hand, is fast and accurate, and retains whatever is stored. The human continues to perform reasonably well when damaged, and can cope with novel problems and questions, and seek out new knowledge. These characteristics are not typical of computers. Physical factors like drugs, fatigue and stress affect the efficiency of human processing. Hunt (1980) has suggested that we need the concept of a mental fuel supply to explain the variations in human performance that result. There is no counterpart in the computational metaphor for this kind of fuel supply fluctuation. The computer analogy applies better to an abstract competence model of human thought, and is rather less appropriate for a performance model.

Certain general principles that emerge from Artificial Intelligence may have parallels in the human brain. One such general principle is that the basic mechanism of thought is pattern matching. Large numbers of Artificial Intelligence systems are organized in terms of a basic mechanism whereby sets of rules (production systems) each consist of a procedure or *action* that is invoked when a given *condition* is recognized. When a pattern of symbols that is present in the data base matches the condition, the rule is activated. This simple form of organization is capable of expansion to form a highly complex system with interacting sets of production rules, and of generalizing to many different tasks.

The computational metaphor also provides some insight into the problem of systemic organization. The fundamental problem for designing (or for understanding) a complex system is how the individual components are co-ordinated and integrated. The control structure that governs these interactions is the crux of the system.

Numerous models in Artificial Intelligence, and in psychology, represent the human cognitive system as a richly interconnected interacting set of specialist subsystems which are essentially modular. Modular systems are defined by the fact that each component consists of specific structures operating according to their own specific principles. The modules are functionally separable: each has a separate identity and a degree of independence, so that a modular system can be described as "nearly decomposable". In nonmodular systems components are not functionally separable, and depend on shared central executive processes. Modular systems have many advantages. Elements within one module can be modified or added to without affecting other modules. A modular system is easier to extend than a nonmodular one, in which any changes are liable to affect the whole system. Similarly, in a modular system, damage can be confined to the damaged module, and need not affect the functioning of other parts. For these reasons, a modular system is especially suitable for the human brain which is subject to continuous modification in development (while abilities and knowledge are evolving), and to deterioration and injury. Studies of brain injuries provide support for the view that the brain is organized as functionally separable component subsystems, since local damage which selectively destroys or disconnects a particular subsystem can have highly selective effects on cognitive function. For example, language skills may be seriously impaired, while musical ability and visuospatial ability remain intact. Or, more strikingly, particular aspects of language ability may be affected so that patients can speak or write, but not read; or can name objects that are held in the hand, but not objects that are only seen. Selective deficits of this kind point to a modular system. On the other hand, some computer scientists have rejected a modular approach on the grounds that, in some Artificial Intelligence models, the components are not functionally autonomous. Schank (1980) argues that a theory of language is vacuous and pointless unless it includes perception and production, and comprehension and memory and motivation. Artificial Intelligence models of language processing have notoriously failed to get off the ground unless they incorporate a store of general world knowledge. Similarly, in most programs designed to recognize three-dimensional objects the system relies on a store of higher order knowledge about the properties of the objects, which is brought to bear on the earliest stages of analysis, guiding the pick-up of information as well as its interpretation. An exception to this generalization is Marr's (1976) model of early visual processing whereby a "primal sketch" is computed autonomously from the image. The role of higher order knowledge is restricted to later, attentive processes of recognition and categorization. In general, however, it is true to say that the degree of functional separability shown by the human brain in the course of disintegration is not present in the machine system in the course of development.

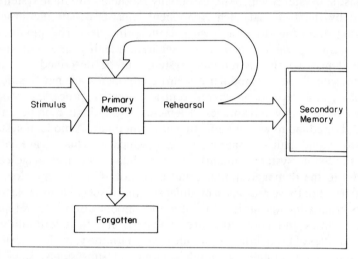

FIG. 1. *A sequential stage model of memory (adapted from Waugh and Norman, 1965).*

Whatever conclusions are reached about modular organization, the performance of the system depends on co-operative interaction between the subsystems. Whether or not the components are functionally separable in principle, in practice the system is highly interactive. Early information processing stage models (like the one shown in Fig. 1) represented mental operations as a linear sequence of stages, with only a very limited amount of interaction, mostly unidirectional, between the stages. Such simple models have now been largely superseded by systems with multidirectional connexions between components. Control is heterarchical rather than strictly sequential, so that interactive relationships between component subsystems operate between as well as within levels. Figure 2 shows a model of this kind. Models of language comprehension exhibit similar complex interactive relationships. Comprehension is controlled and facilitated by processes operating from the top-down, as well as from the bottom-up. High level processes and low level processes interact with each other. People understand stories, written texts and conversations by using their prior knowledge, both factual information about the topic, and knowledge of linguistic rules. They use this prior knowledge to fill gaps, to interpret, to edit, and to disambiguate the information that their senses pick up. Prior knowledge also guides the initial uptake of the input, selecting the crucial elements in the message. When prior knowledge is lacking, as for the young child, the foreigner in an alien culture, or the student confronting an unfamiliar subject, comprehension is difficult and defective. In the normal intact system, efficient performance depends on co-operative interaction.

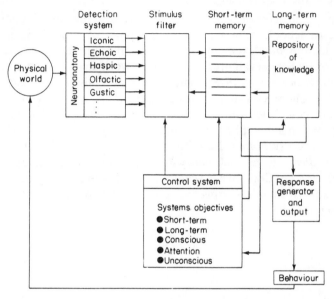

FIG. 2. *Memory as part of a highly interactive cognitive system (adapted from Solso, 1979).*

The way in which these interactions between subsystems are scheduled and constrained so as to produce coherent co-operation, rather than chaotic competition, is one of the major problems for computer scientists and for psychologists alike.

Summary

When the various trends reviewed in this chapter are summarized, two opposing forces are apparent. On the one hand, the drive toward a more applied and practical psychology entails an emphasis on the importance of norms and habits of behaviour; on studies of everyday behaviour in natural settings; on individual differences and the influence of subjective factors. On the other hand, the computational metaphor focusses attention on more universal and invariant aspects of performance; on underlying competence and capacity limitations; and on theories constructed at a high level of abstraction. Although the two approaches are not mutually exclusive, and, ideally, ought to be combined, the likelihood is that these two different kinds of cognitive psychology will tend to diverge.

Recommended reading

Fodor's paper in *Scientific American*, 1981, is a readable introduction to the functionalist school, from a philosophical point of view. Neisser's book *Cognition and Reality* exemplifies the interactive approach, and makes out the case for ecological validity. Hunt reviews work on individual differences in *Psychological Review*, 1978. Some of the issues raised in this chapter are discussed in Chomsky's *Rules and Representations*, and the commentaries that follow in the *Behavioral and Brain Sciences*, 1980. Good discussions of the computational metaphor can be found in Allport's chapter in Claxton's book *Cognitive Psychology*: New Directions and another chapter by Allport in Nilsson's *Perspectives on Memory Research*. For an interesting discussion of the objectives of Cognitive Psychology, read Norman in *Cognitive Science* **4**, 1980, and Norman's *Perspectives on Cognitive Science* contains many interesting papers.

2 SEMANTIC MEMORY *and the* STRUCTURE *of* KNOWLEDGE

Definitions of Semantic Memory: Scope and Function

Semantic memory is concerned with the structure of knowledge; with how knowledge is represented, stored, cross-referenced and indexed so that it can be accessed and retrieved on demand. The models of semantic memory discussed in this chapter are concerned rather more with the organization of the system, than with the nature of the concepts represented in it, although these two aspects of knowledge storage are obviously inter-related.

The contents of the knowledge store: different kinds of knowledge

The dictionary and the lexicon. A distinction is commonly made between memory systems that correspond to an internal dictionary or lexicon, and those that constitute a mental encyclopaedia. According to this distinction, the dictionary stores information about word meanings as linguistic definitions. The encyclopaedia includes a wider range of real world factual knowledge. So the dictionary would contain a definition of "cat", while the encyclopaedia would contain everything known about cats. Semantic memory is not equivalent to the dictionary. The elements of semantic memory are abstract concepts, not words. While most of these concepts have verbal labels, some may be nonverbal. There are some concepts, such as "cats living in London suburbs" which have no name, and other concepts which may have several different names. The knowledge represented in semantic memory can exist in the absence of language, or be linked to different languages. The conceptual system and the dictionary are related, but the relationship is not necessarily a one-to-one mapping. If semantic memory is not equivalent to the dictionary, does it correspond to the encyclopaedia? The answer must depend on the kind of knowledge that is stored, and not all the models are in agreement on this issue.

Episodic and semantic memory. Nickerson (1977) uses the term Archival Memory, and includes within this system all the knowledge an individual acquires during the course of a life-time, including events, facts, faces, places, skills, rules and procedures. Some psychologists, such as Tulving

(1972), prefer to make a distinction between two different kinds of knowledge, semantic and episodic. These two kinds of knowledge have been variously characterized as type and token, lexical and topical, permanent and temporal–contextual, or necessary and accidental. The precise nature of the distinction being made varies somewhat with the terminology. The term semantic memory is used to refer to a store of more or less permanent knowledge, of facts that are true independently of context, such as that cats are animals, that leopards have spots, that roses are red, and that two and two make four. Episodic memory refers to a store of personal experiences, and knowledge that is relative to a given context, such as what X had for breakfast today, and that Y's shirt is blue. The models of organization in memory discussed in this chapter are mostly concerned with semantic memory. Episodic memory has received less attention although it must obviously play a large part in everyday cognitive functioning. In practice there is no sharp dividing line between semantic memory and episodic memory. Any model which proposes to make a distinction of this kind must also supply an interface between the two kinds of knowledge, and must tell us something about how items of information are classified and allocated to one or other of the two knowledge systems. How many leopards do we have to see before we know that spots are a defining characteristic, and not an accidental episodic feature? How does information get transferred from the semantic store to an episodic store when we find out that not all roses are red? It is clear that a semantic memory system must be dynamic. It must be capable of constant modification as new information is acquired. Some models, such as HAM, described on page 34, are able to represent the interplay between novel episodic inputs, and permanent stored knowledge; other models are restricted to semantic information, and make no attempt to deal with episodic knowledge.

However, even if episodic knowledge is excluded, the contents of semantic memory must still vary considerably from one individual to another. Although there is a common core of culturally shared knowledge, semantic memory is personal because each individual's knowledge and experience differs. It is not just a static mental encyclopaedia, but a working system, in which new facts are constantly being incorporated, stored knowledge is being updated and re-classified, and particular items of information are being sought, located, assembled and retrieved. Semantic memory models are not pure competence models, but include performance factors as well. The content and organization of the system reflect the user, his experience, needs, emotions and the way he uses his knowledge.

Another distinction is sometimes made between procedural knowledge and declarative knowledge. Procedural knowledge (or "knowing how") includes skills, rules, procedures and plans. Declarative knowledge (or "knowing that") is restricted to facts. Most of the models described here are concerned to represent declarative knowledge.

The computational metaphor and semantic memory

Theories of human semantic memory are often based on computer systems for information storage and information handling, but some psychologists (such as Lachman and Lachman, 1979) believe that the computational metaphor is misleading. They emphasize that the human system differs from the computer in many important ways. Semantic memory in adult humans is the product of evolutionary and ontogenetic development. While the information represented in a computer is, for the most part, detailed, precise and logical, human knowledge has quite different characteristics. Human knowledge is fuzzy, approximate and vague. A good deal of our knowledge is relational rather than quantitative. We may know that Leeds is north of London, but not know by how many miles. Similarly, we know the order of events in history but not the dates; and we know the relative sizes of different objects without knowing the magnitude of any of them. In computers, knowledge is permanently stored, but can be deleted from the store. Human knowledge is not eraseable in the same way. We forget a great deal, but it is difficult to forget to order. Humans also have a mysterious faculty known as "metamemory", or "metaknowledge", which enables us to know, with a fair degree of accuracy and confidence, what is in the store, and what is not in the store, apparently without carrying out an exhaustive search. When we are asked a particular question, we can usually say right away whether the answer is readily accessible; whether we could dredge it up given time; or whether there is no hope of coming up with it at all. So far, computer models lack this useful facility. Computers also lack the ability to access information needed to answer a question that was not anticipated at the time of acquisition.

Search and Retrieval Processes. The human system is characterized by great flexibility, such that information in the store can be accessed by way of many different routes. Some of Nickerson's studies (1977) of search and retrieval processes provide striking illustrations of this ability. His subjects were able to produce lists of words that spelled other words backwards (time, loop); one word palindromes (tenet, deified, level); words containing a set of specified letters such as "i", "b" and "t". The search process successfully located such words in the store, although it is very unlikely that they were prestored under these headings. Nickerson also studied the introspective reports of people attempting to recall forgotten names, which again demonstrated the versatility of the search strategies used. In one case, the subject could not remember a street name, but knew that it was also the name of a person, that someone he knew had that name, and that it had two syllables with the stress falling on the first. Eventually, by searching through names with these characteristics, he succeeded in recalling it. Similar findings were reported by Brown and McNeill (1966) in their study of the "tip-of-the-tongue" or TOT state. Subjects were given dictionary definitions of rare words such as "a Japanese fishing boat" (sampan). Although unable to produce the required word, they typically produced a series of responses (shampoo, samurai) which reflected search paths through words that were structurally, associatively or semantically related. These search attempts do not always succeed, but it is interesting to note that people generally know that the related words turned up in the course of search are not the one they are looking for. When retrieval attempts fail, the sought-for item sometimes "pops up" hours or days later, after conscious search has been abandoned. So, human search processes are not always deliberate conscious strategies, but can go on automatically and unconsciously. The versatility of human search contrasts with the rigid and predetermined retrieval processes typical of current computer models.

Prestorage and Computation. Another way in which human and computer storage systems may diverge is in the extent to which information is prestored or computable. In any system, facts may be represented explicitly, prestored as a complete item. Or, they may be computable by application of inferential procedures to the prestored information. So, for example, "The First World War began in 1914" may be prestored. From this, and from the year of his birth, the fact that "My father was twelve years old at the outbreak of the First World War" is computable. In all information storage systems there is a trade-off between prestorage and computation. Prestorage is expensive in space, and requires very efficient search and access procedures. Computation needs rapid error-free processing. Since constraints of space and speed do not apply to human systems and computer systems in the same way, it is unlikely that the prestorage/computation trade-off operates in the same way. It follows that the kind of knowledge storage optimal in a computer is unlikely to be optimal for a human.

It is also important to note that the kind of inferential processes that are typical of human reasoning are different from the inferences made by computers. Computer models generate strict logical deductions leading to conclusions that are necessarily true or false. Syllogistic inferences based on class inclusion relationships predominate. This type of inference plays a relatively small part in human computational procedure. In human cognition, inference-making is less logical and more pragmatic. Inductive inferences generating probabilistic conclusions are more common. Inferences tend to be plausible rather than strictly true or false. Fuzzy knowledge produces "best guess" conclusions. Inference-making is another factor that tends to blur the distinction between episodic and semantic memory. We frequently invoke semantic knowledge in order to make inferences and predictions about episodic information. When we interpret the episodic sentence "The postman did not call today" we infer "There were no letters" by reference to our semantic knowledge that postmen call if and only if bringing letters. The advice issued by the telephone company "Call us before you dig. You may not be able to after." requires semantic inference-making to interpret it. Episodic and semantic information interact in inference-making of this kind.

Units of knowledge. It is evident that a major problem for any semantic theory will be the choice of a basic unit. A familiar problem in the psychology of perception, it is equally crucial in cognition and linguistics. Many semantic models propose that the basic units or elements are defined by labelled relationships to other units (Quillian, 1968; Rumelhart *et al.*, 1972). The problem is that semantic relations hold over different sizes of unit. Individual words like "black" and "white" may be linked by the relation of opposition. A causal relation may hold between whole conceptual clusters such as "food" and "growth". Presuppositions and implications commonly apply to whole propositions. In "He succeeded in starting the car" it is the whole proposition that implies "the car was mechanically unreliable". Contextual effects may operate over even larger spans, so that the title of a chapter may affect the interpretation of a sentence in it, or the setting of a conversation govern the meaning of a remark. It is partly a consequence of the recent drive toward greater ecological validity that psychologists have become more interested in how a substantial body of information, such as a text or a story, is comprehended and remembered. It is arguable that studies in which the input consists of isolated sentences, taken out of context, are unrepresentative of normal functioning. In the real world, knowledge tends to come in larger chunks. Models of semantic memory that are capable of handling concepts and simple propositions should be extendable, so that the more complex relations between elements in these much larger configurations of information can also be modelled.

Experimental Findings

Methods

Quite a varied battery of experimental methods is available for studying semantic memory. We can present subjects with word lists, sentences or passages of text, and ask them to comprehend, to recognize or to recall. We can require them to answer questions; to judge propositions true or false; to scale pairs of words as semantically similar or different; to produce associates of designated words; and to classify sentences as nonsensical, ambiguous or metaphorical. Performance in all these kinds of task can be measured in terms of speed and accuracy. When the results of different experimental paradigms converge, and the same sort of patterns appear in the data from different tasks, then we can be more confident that they are a valid reflection of the cognitive structures and operations we are studying. By studying the effects of brain damage, and by studying young children, we can observe semantic memory in disintegration and in development.

Evidence for categorical organization

Recall and recognition experiments have provided some valuable clues to the working of semantic memory, and only a selection of those which seem to highlight the most important features of the memory system are discussed here. Many studies using different paradigms have shown that people have strong spontaneous tendencies to organize items into categories and subcategories, and to use imposed groupings of this kind to aid recall (Mandler, 1967). When subjects have learned lists of words, category clusters can be observed in the ordering of their responses, with, for example, food words and animal words grouped together. If the material to be learned lends itself to hierarchical grouping into categories and sub-categories, then recall is greatly improved. For example, a list which can be organized into categories of food and tools, and then subdivided into subcategories such as vegetables and meat, and gardening tools and carpentry tools, is much easier to learn than a list of unrelated items.

Similar clusterings occur in free association experiments (Deese, 1962). In these experiments the subject is presented with a single stimulus word and asked to respond by producing associated words. The nature and grouping of the elicited response words can reveal the underlying semantic organization. Typically, subjects respond with batches of words from the same category, and then pause before beginning to search another related category. Miller (1971) asked subjects to sort words into categories, and found that hierarchical structures emerged. The use of cueing techniques also reveals categorical organization in memory. Tulving and Pearlstone (1966) showed that forgotten items can often be recalled by category cues. A subject may remember that "kite" was on a list when he is given the cue "toy". Wickens (1970) showed that in learning successive lists of words there is less interference from prior lists when a new list is of a different class. If all the lists consist of similar items, recall of later list items is impaired by proactive interference or inhibition, the earlier lists inhibiting the recall of items in the later list. However, if the earlier lists consist of one semantic category (such as names of towns), and a later list is composed of a different category (such as animals), the phenomenon Wickens (1970) calls "release from proactive inhibition" occurs. The switch to a new category reduces interference, indicating that the different categories are functionally separated in memory. There is also evidence that category clustering is not just an experimentally induced phenomenon, not just a strategy adopted in the artificial situation of laboratory testing. Morton and Byrne (1975) recorded housewives' responses when they were asked to list the items required to equip a house, and found their responses were systematically grouped either by category (furniture, linen, china etc.) or by place (bedroom, kitchen etc.). When they were asked to recall ingredients for recipes these were clustered according to the temporal order of handling. For any material, more than one classification scheme is usually possible. If we consider how words can be elicited by crossword clues of very varied kinds, it is obvious that memory organization is a very complex cross-referencing system. Anderson and Ortony (1975) comment:

> The *a priori* arguments for a dynamic knowledge structure are also, we believe, compelling. Consider, for example, the case of "piano" in the two sentences "Pianos can be pleasing to listen to" and "Pianos can be difficult to move". . . . In one context "piano" is a member of the same category as "harmonica" . . . in the latter case "sofa" would be a cohyponym. . . . There are so many ways in which every object can be classified . . . there are cases in which only the context will help us to determine how to classify an object.

The experiments reported by Anderson and Ortony, and by Morton and Byrne (1975) confirm that the adoption of one classification rather than another can be manipulated by context.

The categorical organization of semantic memory is also strikingly revealed by the pattern of deficit that can sometimes occur following brain injury. Yamadori and Albert (1973) reported a case of a patient exhibiting specific word category aphasia, with inability to produce or comprehend names within a category corresponding to "parts of a room", including furniture and structural features like "floor", "ceiling" and "walls". McKenna and Warrington (1980), described a patient with a nominal deficit for a particular class of proper nouns, names of people, while other classes of proper nouns, such as names of towns were unaffected.

Organization of semantic memory in children

How far do children show the same tendency to organize items into categorical groupings in semantic memory? The evidence reviewed by Ornstein and Corsale (1979) suggests that categorical organization is gradually superimposed on earlier associative grouping. Clustering in free recall develops with age. In sorting tasks, young children tend to group items according to perceptual similarities such as colour, rather than by semantic category. In word association tests (Nelson, 1977) the responses made by children below the age of seven or eight are classed as syntagmatic, and reflect associations in experience. Typical responses are table–eat; dark–night; men–work. These contrast with the so-called paradigmatic responses of the adult which are usually antonyms, synonyms, or superordinates such as table–furniture; dark–light; difficult–hard. The young child's responses are episodic rather than semantic, and the shift toward an adult-style organization in terms of logical and conceptual relationships does not occur until around seven years. McCaulay, Weil and Sperber (1976) reached similar conclusions on the basis of a priming experiment. Children between five and eight years old were asked to name pictures. When a pair of pictures were associatively related (e.g. dog–bone), all the children showed a priming effect which reduced latency to name the second item of the pair. When the pictures were categorically related (e.g. dog–lion), only the older children showed a priming effect. It looks as if categorical organization becomes functionally effective around seven to eight years, although some categories and relationships between categories may be established earlier if they are particularly familiar or salient. Bowerman (1979) believes that formal tasks fail to reveal children's semantic organization, which can best be inferred from observation of spontaneously occurring semantic confusions in their speech. Sometimes initial usage is correct and confusions occur later. The onset of confusions such as give/put, and behind/after shows, according to Bowerman, the developing conceptual relationships.

Memory for texts and stories: restructuring and assimilation

Besides providing evidence for the organization of items into labelled clusters, experiments have also shown that passages of text and stories are extensively re-structured in memory. Bartlett (1932) studied subjects' ability to reproduce stories from memory. The reproductions exhibited certain typical transformations. Besides loss of detail, the original story was altered by processes of normalization and assimilation, so that it conformed more closely to the subjects' own prior experience and beliefs. When Europeans reproduced an American Indian folk tale "canoes" was changed to "boats" and "hunting seals" turned into "fishing". The reproduced story tended to be considerably distorted from the original, but internal coherence was preserved, if necessary by adding new elements. These observations led Bartlett to the view that new information is not just passively stored, but is actively re-structured to fit existing conceptual frameworks, which he called "schemata".

Bartlett's schemata have reappeared recently in a new version. Schank and Abelson's (1976) computer programme MARGIE illustrates the role of "scripts" in comprehension. Like Bartlett's schemata, these scripts consist of the relevant prior knowledge structures, and include a wide range of background knowledge of the topic, beliefs, associations, personal experience and cultural conventions. The scripts provide a conceptual framework which generates expectancies, and guides plans for actions. Given the correct script, new information can be interpreted and organized; gaps can be filled, and implications and presuppositions understood. Without the relevant script, information may be almost unintelligible. In one of his best known examples, Schank outlines a "restaurant script" which supplies a general framework of prior knowledge about what goes on in restaurants, about the variables (waiters, customers, menus, bills, etc.), and the relationships (choosing, eating, paying, etc.). An anecdote about an incident occurring in a restaurant can be understood by being mapped on to this script. A sentence like "The waitress recommended the duck" is interpretable if the listener possesses a restaurant script. In contrast, if an anecdote about a driving incident is related to somebody who has never driven a car, and so lacks a "driving script", the hearer is unlikely to understand and appreciate the story fully. McCartney and Nelson (1981) asked young children to generate scripts by describing the sequence of events involved in activities like having supper, going to bed, etc., and found evidence that recall of stories based on these themes was structured by the pre-existing script. Where the original story was distorted in recall, the distorted version conformed to the child's own experience. These studies underline the crucial importance of knowledge prestored in semantic memory in governing the way new information is understood and remembered. They fail, however, to shed much light on how new scripts are acquired in the first place.

Recent studies of memory for prose, stories or texts have revealed the internal structural characteristics of the memory representations. A global representation is constructed, with the constituent propositions of the story linked in a network. Propositions are not verbal, but consist of a configuration of abstract elements in a structured relationship. Kintsch (1976) suggested that the memory representation of a text is an hierarchical structure, with the main propositions at the highest level of the hierarchy. In one of his examples, the sentence "Romulus, legendary founder of Rome, took the women of the Sabines by force" is analysed into propositions corresponding to

   i   Take (Romulus, women, by force)
   ii Found (Romulus, Rome)
  iii Legendary (Romulus)
  iv Sabine (women)

(i) is the highest level proposition. Kintsch found that difficulty of recall increased with the number of constituent propositions, and that lower level propositions were more likely to be forgotten than higher level ones. Rumelhart (1975) has also proposed an hierarchical structure for memory representations of stories. His "story grammar" comprises rules for organizing the elements of a story. A story is analysed into four major elements: setting, theme, plot and resolution. Setting includes the characters, location and time. Theme consists of an event and a goal. Plot consists of episodes and outcomes. The resolution is a state resulting from an event, which is evaluated in relation to the goal. This grammar provides a sort of general schema, an all-purpose script, which serves as a framework for organizing the information in any given story.

The re-structuring that stories undergo when they are stored in memory also appears to involve transforming information from a verbal code to a more abstract code. Sachs (1967) showed that after listening to a story, people retain the meaning fairly well, but their memory for the actual words used is much more ephemeral. She gave subjects a recognition test, and asked them to judge whether a sentence extracted from the story and re-presented after an interval, was identical with the original version, or whether it had been changed. Changes of wording which left the meaning intact (formal changes) were difficult to detect, but changes of meaning were detected much better. So changing the original sentence "He sent Galileo, the great Italian scientist, a letter about it" to "A letter about it was sent to Galileo, the great Italian scientist", is a formal change of a kind that is quite difficult to detect. Changing the original to "Galileo, the great Italian scientist, sent him a letter about it" is a semantic change, and is detected more easily. The memory representation encodes the meaning of the story, but does not retain the original wording or syntactic forms.

Just as context can affect the way a particular concept is categorized, context also operates to influence the interpretation, and the subsequent recall of larger units of information like stories and texts. The context in which the new information is presented enables the listener or reader to preselect the correct script or schema to guide interpretation. The difficulty that is caused when contextual cues are withheld is strikingly illustrated by the following passage (Bransford and Johnson, 1973).

> The procedure is actually quite simple. First you arrange things into different groups. Of course, one pile may be sufficient depending on how much there is to do. If you have to go somewhere else due to lack of facilities, that is the next step, otherwise you are pretty well set. It is important not to overdo things. That is, it is better to do too few things at once, than too many . . .

The passage continues in this vein, giving little clue to the topic. Not surprisingly, subjects scored poorly on tests of comprehension and recall. However, if the title "Washing Clothes" was supplied at the outset, scores were much higher. Supplying the title after the passage had been heard was not helpful. It appears that contextual information is needed at the beginning, so that the relevant conceptual framework can be selected, and the incoming information mapped onto it as it is perceived. Context serves to enhance, or to bias, the comprehension and recall of information. Lack of context makes information difficult to understand and retain. It is reported that one subject who found the untitled version perfectly comprehensible turned out to be a Washington politician who took it to be a description of office routine.

The role of inferences in comprehension

Another group of experiments has demonstrated that subjects not only re-structure the text, but that they also make inferences from it and store this derived information additionally. Bransford *et al.* (1972) and Bransford and Johnson (1973) have extensively used a false recognition paradigm to reveal the constructive and elaborative processes that occur when mental representations of sentences are stored. Subjects who have heard the sentence "Three turtles rested on a floating log and a fish swam beneath them" tend falsely to recognize the sentence "Three turtles rested on a floating log and a fish swam beneath it" because they have derived this inference from the original. Similarly, subjects who are presented with the anomalous sentence "The floor was dirty because Sally used the mop" may make an anomaly-reducing assumption like "The mop was dirty". Frederiksen (1975) has found that repeated presentations of input sentences increase the amount of derived or inferred information, so that this process of inferring and elaborating appears to take place at the input stage rather than at the stage of recall. The nature of this interpretive elaboration can be controlled by the context. Anderson and Ortony (1975) manipulated intra-sentence context, and showed that while "fist" might serve as an effective cue for the recall of the sentence "The accountant pounded the desk", the cue "hammer" would be more effective as a cue for recalling "The accountant pounded the stake". Different assumptions about the instrument used in the pounding have been made in each case.

Clark and Clark (1977) have emphasized the role of inferential procedures in sentence comprehension. They describe the speaker–hearer as operating with a "given-new" strategy. "Given" information is either already shared by the speaker and hearer, or is presented initially. New information is then slotted into the framework provided by the given. To achieve this, the listener may need to make an inference, or, in Clark and Clark's terminology, to construct a "bridging assumption". Some examples of this sequence are as follows.

Given: Mary got some picnic supplies out of the car.
New: The beer was warm.
Bridging assumption: The picnic supplies included some beer.

Given: John was murdered.
New: The knife was found nearby.
Bridging assumption: John had been murdered with a knife.

Experiments by Clark and his colleagues showed that subjects required extra time to comprehend sequences of sentences when the bridging assumptions had to be constructed, because some of the information was not explicitly stated, but only implied.

The results of experimental studies of semantic memory indicate some of the properties that should be instantiated in a model. The mechanism of semantic memory is active and dynamic; it re-structures new information to conform to prior knowledge; it interprets and organizes. Interpretation is biased by context, and organization is predominantly categorical. Irrelevant or inconsistent details are deleted or altered; new details are added by inferential procedures to fill gaps, and build links so as to produce a coherent body of knowledge. Verbal inputs are converted to an abstract propositional form for storage. The interaction of prior knowledge, scripts, or schemata with novel information underlines the importance of the interface between semantic and episodic knowledge. One way of evaluating the models of semantic memory outlined in the next section is to consider how far they are successful in incorporating these characteristics.

Models of Semantic Memory

The models described here are of two kinds. One group can be classed as network models, and the other as set-theoretic, or attribute models. Although it is possible to point out some of the merits and failings of each, it is scarcely possible to evaluate them comparatively because they are not always very clearly distinct from each other, and because some are more detailed and specific than others.

Network models

Network models of memory consist of nodes and links. The nodes are units representing concepts, and the links represent labelled relations between concepts.

The Teachable Language Comprehender (TLC). The TLC is a network model developed by Quillian (1968), and Collins and Quillian (1969). In this model, the network is arranged in an hierarchical tree structure of sets and supersets (see Fig. 3), the organization being similar to that revealed by the recall experiments which showed category clustering. In the model concepts are defined by class membership and a property list, and the storage system generates quite specific predictions about sentence comprehension. A process of intersection search occurs whereby search originates at each of the nodes corresponding to the concepts mentioned in an input sentence. If the sentence conforms to pre-existing knowledge, the search paths will intersect. "A spaniel is a dog" maps onto the existing structure, with search from "spaniel" and "dog" nodes intersecting along the link labelled "isa".

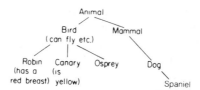

FIG. 3. *An hierarchical network model (adapted from Collins and Quillian 1969).*

The model assumes that in understanding sentences, or judging them to be true or false, the time taken is determined by the distance between the relevant nodes, so that it should be faster to verify the truth of a sentence like "A canary is a bird" in which only one link separates the nodes, than "A canary is an animal" in which two links must be traversed.

In this version of the model, properties specific to an exemplar are stored with that exemplar, and properties common to the class are stored only at the class node. This arrangement means that "A robin has a red breast" should be verified faster than "A robin can fly". The property of being red-breasted is stored at the "robin" node; but the class property of being able to fly is only stored at the "bird" node so that a rather cumbersome two-stage inferential process is necessary. (You have to check that a robin is a bird, and that birds can fly in order to verify that robins can fly.) This makes the model economical in storage space, since class properties are only represented once, instead of redundantly with every class member. However, it is clearly uneconomical in retrieval time. While economy in storage may be the most important constraint in computer simulation, speed of access may be more important in humans. Different computer models vary in the amount and type of information that is prestored. In the TLC specific facts are prestored, but more general facts have to be computed by inferential processes.

Collins and Quillian's model was designed for computer simulation, so that it is necessarily on a small scale, and incorporates only a small subset of possible relations. The major links consist of "isa" "hasa" and "can" relations, as in "A robin *is* a bird" or "A robin *has* a red breast" or "a bird *can* fly". Other links consist of conjunctive relations, disjunctive relations and a residual class of other relations which are not specified.

Many other relations such as spatial, temporal, causal, possessive and comparative relations which play an important semantic role, are not represented. It is arguable that the hierarchical structure works best for biological examples, but that much everyday factual information is not so hierarchically organized, because lateral relationships greatly outnumber vertical relationships. It is easy, of course, to point out what is missing in small-scale models, but if the original model could be extended without radically changing its character, then incompleteness is not a serious defect. An hierarchical tree structure could be viewed as one part of a more complex multidimensional network. An extended version of the model could be devised to provide a mechanism for the acquisition of new knowledge, for the modification or correction of existing knowledge, and for more types of relations.

How well is the network model supported by experimental results? Collins and Quillian's prediction that reaction times to judge sentences true or false would be a function of semantic distance is usually borne out. Sentences like "A canary is a bird" can be judged true faster than sentences like "A canary is an animal", in which the terms span a greater semantic distance, but this result is also predicted by the conjoint frequency principle, which states that the more frequently we have experienced the two elements of the sentence occurring together, the faster we respond. If subjects are asked to rate sentences for conjoint frequency, these ratings will predict the obtained reaction times (Conrad, 1972; Wilkins, 1971). Usually frequency is confounded with semantic distance, but not always. By the semantic distance principle (see Fig. 3) "A dog is a mammal" should be faster than "A dog is an animal", but the frequency principle predicts the opposite, since we more often think of dogs as animals. The results favour the frequency principle. Rips *et al.* (1973) suggest that frequency ratings are measuring subjective semantic distance which, in some cases, differs from, and overrides the objective semantic distance represented in the model.

A further problem for the Collins and Quillian model is the typicality effect. It is difficult for them to account for the fact that reaction times to judge sentences of the form "An S (subject) is a P (predicate)" vary for different instances of S when the objective semantic distance is equal. Why is it easier to agree that a robin is a bird, than that a flycatcher or an osprey is a bird? Unfamiliar or atypical examples are more difficult, so either the frequency principle or a typicality principle must be invoked to explain these findings; semantic distance on the network is not the only determinant of retrieval time.

The Spreading Activation model. Collins and Loftus (1975) put forward a revised version of the TLC, designed to overcome some of the inadequacies of the earlier model. In the TLC, the assumption was that the time to move between any two nodes should be equal, constant and additive, but a model in which the activation of associative paths is all-or-none is counter-intuitive. The Spreading Activation model modified this assumption and allowed that links might have different strengths and different travel times. More frequently-used links would have faster travel times, so this amended version of the Collins and Quillian model is able to account for the effects of typicality and conjoint frequency. We commonly feel differing degrss of confidence in our responses, as if links are more or less strongly activated. Subjectively there is a continuous dimension of truth value rather than an absolute dichotomy between truth and falsity. The modification which allows links to have differential strengths solves the problem of typicality, and opens the way for intermediate truth values.

Collins and Loftus also concede that class properties may often be stored with the specific exemplars. When, for instance, an individual learns that robins lay eggs before he learns that egg-laying is a general property of birds, then egg-laying will be initially stored at the robin node, and later re-duplicated at the bird node. It is not necessarily assumed that the earlier specific entry must be erased when the class entry is made later. As a result, more information is prestored in this model, and look-up is less dependent on inference making.

The intersection search mechanism also provides an explanation for context effects. Words which have several meanings can be interpreted by means of sentence context. Such words would have different represent-ations for each meaning, so that, for example, "plant" would appear both as a superset of "flower", and a subset of "industrial buildings". An input sentence like "A daisy is a plant" would initiate activation spreading outwards from the "daisy" node and from both "plant" nodes, but the only intersection found would be daisy–flower–plant. According to the model, this interpretation of the sentence can be checked afterwards by reference to the contextual environment or syntactic rules. A mechanism is also proposed whereby particular paths can be primed, or preactivated by foregoing context or recent use. Experiments by Mackay (1973) have shown that alternative meanings of ambiguous words may not be consciously considered when the context indicates which is most probable. Reading a paragraph about factories, or standing on the site, we can understand a sentence like "The plant is near the road" without botanical speculation.

The intersection search mechanism therefore has to include some device whereby the search is biased, and certain paths are preprimed to activate more readily or strongly.

Another problem for the original model is posed by the fact that people can respond very rapidly in rejecting false sentences like "a daisy is a fish". If responses of "false" can only be made after exhaustive search has failed to find an intersection, then it should always take longer to respond "false" than to respond "true". Why does the intersection search terminate so rapidly? As Collins and Loftus have pointed out, the model needs to incorporate a decision mechanism so that the number and type of links activated during the intersection search can be evaluated as positive or negative evidence. Different links would then contribute different amounts of evidence. Once the links are allowed to have different evidence value as well as different strengths it is easier to account for the fast negative response times. A sentence like "A fire-engine is a cherry" can be rejected as false although both concepts are linked by the common property of redness, since the "redness" link is judged to contribute only a small amount of positive evidence. In this later version of the model, some links are labelled as mutually exclusive, so that "A duck is an eagle" is judged false in spite of both being linked to the superordinate "bird". The two routes to the superordinate are mutually exclusive. Yet another modification of the model is proposed by Collins and Loftus to account for the finding that the time taken by subjects to produce an instance when given a category (saying "apple" when given "fruit", for example) may differ from the time taken to produce the category when given an instance (saying "fruit" when given "apple"). This finding necessitates the further assumption that the strength of activation of a link may vary asymmetrically with the direction of search.

Supporting evidence for an hierarchical organization of semantic memory comes from some clinical case studies reported by Warrington (1975). Three patients with some cerebral atrophy showed selective impairment of semantic memory. Although they had no deficits of perception, short-term memory span, or intellectual function as measured by IQ tests, they had difficulty in recognizing the names or pictorial representations of objects. The most interesting feature of these cases was that the broadest super-ordinate categories were spared while subordinate category names, and lower order attributes were not available. Patients identified a hammer as "some kind of tool" but could not be more precise. Shown a picture of a duck, they could answer the question "Is it an animal?" but not "Is it a duck?" or "Is it dangerous?" They also showed some dissociation of pictorial and verbal information since they were not equally impaired in the recognition of words and pictures. These cases seem to exhibit a semantic memory organization similar to the Collins and Quillian model, but with only the higher nodes still intact. How much significance can be attached to so small a number of case studies is difficult to judge. More extensive investigation might throw up different patterns of selective impairment in semantic memory. As yet these findings are only straws in the wind. It is interesting to note the way in which the earlier and simpler version of the Collins and Quillian network model has been extended and amplified to accommodate experimental findings and to counter the logical objections which exposed its inadequacy. The later version is much more complex, but has greater explanatory power and a wider scope of application. The original model was a competence model, but the modifications have incorporated performance factors.

Network models represent semantic rather than episodic information, and offer no means of interfacing the two. Collins and Loftus propose that a separate lexicon is linked to the conceptual system, but is organized differently, in terms of orthographic and phonemic properties. The Spreading Activation model is essentially a "humanized" version of Collins and Quillian's computer model. In this version strict logic gives way to a system structured by use and by salience, with fuzzy values and indeterminate propositions.

The Marker–Search model. This model (Glass and Holyoak, 1975) is also a network model. In the Marker–Search model, concepts are arranged in a network, and each concept is associated with a defining marker, or markers, representing properties. Relations of entailment hold between the markers so that the defining marker for "bird" (avian) dominates or entails the markers (feathered) and (animate). Following the convention adopted by Glass and Holyoak the markers are represented in brackets. Relationships between markers may express a contradiction so that, although the markers (avian) and (canine) are both related to the common marker (animate), the intersection is labelled as a contradiction, to express the knowledge that a dog cannot be a bird and vice versa. An anomaly in the model is that false statements where "An S is a P" relationship is asserted between two very disparate concepts (like "A chair is a fish") should take longer to reject because the contradiction only occurs at a high level where living and nonliving things intersect. In fact, reaction times to reject these very disparate false statements are substantially faster than responses to less disparate statements like "A dog is a bird".

Category relationships like "All S are P", and "Some S are P" are defined by the marker relations. "All" statements are directly linked in an entailment relation. "Some" statements are only indirectly linked. So "All birds are animals" is true because the S marker (avian) directly entails the P marker (animate), and "Some animals are feathered" is true because the S marker (animate) and the P marker (feathered) are both indirectly linked by a common marker (avian). The Marker–Search model makes the useful distinction between two kinds of falsification—falsification by contradiction and falsification by counter-example. Both "All" and "Some" statements like "All/Some birds are dogs" may be falsified by contradiction, and in addition "All" statements like "All birds are canaries" may be falsified by a counter-example such as "robins".

The variability of response times is accounted for by the frequency principle. Search through the marker system does not necessarily proceed through logically ordered hierarchical levels as in Collins and Quillian's original model. The probability of accessing a given search path is determined by frequency, so response time does not depend on semantic distance. Search terminates as soon as an entailment relation, contradiction or counter-example is encountered. The Marker–Search model handles the problem of typicality by invoking the frequency principle. "A robin is a bird" is verified faster than "A chicken is a bird" because the (robin) to (avian) link is a high-frequency path and would be accessed early in search. For the atypical instance "chicken", the (chicken) to (animate) path would more frequently be searched before the (chicken) to (avian) connection was found. Besides invoking order of search as a factor to explain differences in verification times, Glass and Holyoak also postulate redundant links forming short-cut paths for concepts that co-occur frequently.

Human Associative Memory (HAM). The HAM model developed by Anderson and Bower (1973) is also a network model, but it has a greater scope than those considered so far. The unit of representation in HAM is the propositional structure linking concepts rather than the individual concepts themselves. The system models the interface between episodic and semantic information whereby novel episodic inputs are mapped onto pre-existing long-term semantic structures. The input is analysed by a parser into an hierarchical tree structure. Figure 4 shows the principal constituents that emerge when the sentence "The car hit a lamppost on the turnpike" is analysed. The major distinction is between *context* and *fact*. Context subdivides into *location* and *time*. Fact can be decomposed into *subject* and *predicate*; and the predicate is further decomposed into *relation* and *object*. At each of the concept nodes all the knowledge associated with that concept is stored, and the node is further linked to the *tokens* and to lexical labels. The propositional representation itself is nonlinguistic, and can be constructed on the basis of visual information as well as verbal inputs. Propositional representations can be embedded within each other so as to represent larger units of information. The structure derived from parsing the input is held in working memory while it is matched serially against structures already stored in long-term memory. If the new input is not already represented there, it can be entered into the long-term store, or added on to the existing structures. Once entered, the representation can serve for recall, recognition, question answering or statement verification. Unlike the other models reviewed here, the system models the relationship between episodic information, semantic information and dictionary information. The sentence about the car accident is a lexical representation of an episode. It is transformed into an abstract propositional form and mapped onto concept modes where all the stored information about cars, accidents, etc. can be assessed.

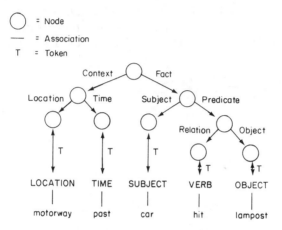

FIG. 4. *Representation of a proposition in HAM (adapted from Anderson and Bower, 1973).*

Several aspects of the HAM model have been criticized. In particular, the all-or-none serial nature of the search process that is postulated makes it difficult to explain effects of familiarity, and graded truth values. These problems have already been noted in the TLC model, and led to revisions in the Spreading Activation version where a search process proceeding in parallel along different paths with varying degrees of strength, was substituted.

ELINOR. Another model capable of representing larger units of discourse is ELINOR. Norman and Rumelhart (1975) describe their model as an active structural network, because it represents procedural knowledge (like how to cook an omelette) as well as declarative or propositional knowledge like "John ate the omelette". Like other network models the basic structure consists of nodes (corresponding to ideas) and labelled relations. Each node is linked to its natural language name where spelling and sound are presented. The relations have directionality, so that for example, the "isa" link expresses a superset relation in one direction and a subset relation in the inverse direction. The system is supposedly capable of indefinite elaboration by means of a multiplicity of links. The basic unit represented is typically an *event*. The event consists of an action which is the predicate, and elements such as agent, object, recipient, which are the arguments taken by the predicate. In the example (a) represented in Fig. 5, the predicate "give" takes "John" as agent, "Mary" as recipient, and "Fido" as object. *Time* and *location* are optional elements. While a single event centres around a single action, several events can be linked to form an *episode*, with temporal relations specifying the sequence of constituent events. As shown in Fig. 5 a sentence can undergo successive transformations from a surface level (a), through to deeper level representations (b) and (c). The representations

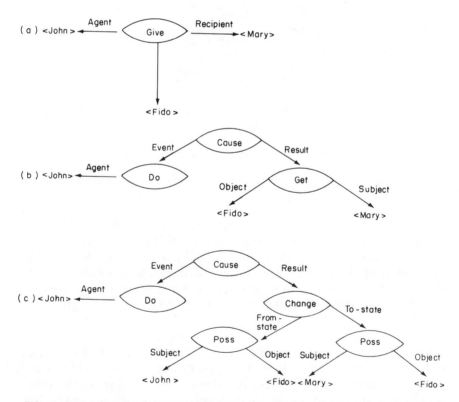

FIG. 5. *ELINOR's analysis of the sentence "John gave Mary Fido" into various levels of representation (Norman and Rumelhart, 1975).*

become progressively more abstract at the deeper levels, and are expressed in terms of semantic primitives like *cause* and *change*. The representation also becomes progressively more complex, as an event is analysed into a change from one *state* to another state, and causal relations between events are inferred and represented. The model is difficult to evaluate since Norman and Rumelhart have not made predictions about behavioural consequences, and it is not clear how these would differ, if at all, from those derived from other models.

Set-theoretic models

While network models are mainly concerned with representing the storage of information, set-theoretic models of semantic representation or attribute models, as they are sometimes called (Meyer, 1970; Schaeffer and Wallace, 1970; Smith *et al.*, 1974), have been designed to explain how we comprehend quantified statements like 'All robins are birds" (All S are P) and "Some birds are robins" (Some S are P). In these models, each concept is represented by a set of elements including its descriptive features and properties, and the names of its supersets and subsets (see Fig. 6). Concepts which share any of these elements form intersecting sets, or one set may be included within another as in Venn diagrams (see Fig. 7). The model makes some of the same predictions as the Collins and Quillian hierarchical model, though for different reasons.

Verification of input sentences proceeds by searching through sets, not traversing links, and differences in response time are attributed to category size, and not to semantic distance. It takes longer to verify that robins are animals than that robins are birds, because the animal category is larger and so takes longer to search through. In many examples the three factors of semantic distance, category size and conjoint frequency are all confounded; the higher the node, the larger the category, and the less familiar is the relationship, so the experimental results are mostly equivocal. Further experiments (Landauer and Meyer, 1972; Smith *et al.*, 1974) have confirmed

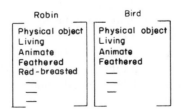

FIG. 6. *A set-theoretic or attribute model (Smith, 1978).*

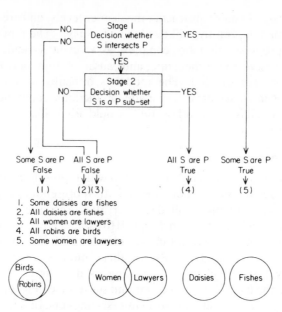

FIG. 7 *Meyer's (1970) model for the retrieval of information about the relation of S and P (adapted). 1, 2 and 5 are judged faster than 3 and 4.*

that judgements do reflect a category-size effect, but this interacts with conjoint frequency, with degree of relatedness or similarity between the instance and the category, and with whether the proposition is true or false.

In set-theoretic models, category relations have to be computed by set comparisons, whereas in network models they are sometimes prestored. In general, set-theoretic models operate by comparison processes which are classed as computational, and network models by search processes which presuppose prestorage.

The Predicate Intersection model (PIM). The PIM proposed by Meyer (1970) is a two-stage process for retrieving information from a set-theoretic model designed to explain the differences in response time to judge true and false statements with different quantifiers (the all–some difference). Figure 7 shows how Stage 1 consists of checking for an intersection between the sets, S and P. Stage 2 consists of searching through the intersection. False statements of both the "All" and the "Some" type (All daisies are fishes, Some daisies are fishes) can both be rejected equally fast at Stage 1 without needing to proceed to Stage 2 since there is no intersection. The model thus succeeds in explaining the fast negative responses which were difficult for the Collins and Quillian model to accommodate. Meyer's PIM also explains why his subjects found it easier to judge true "Some" statements than true "All" statements ("Some women are lawyers" is easier than "All robins are birds"). "Some S are P" is confirmed as Stage 1 by the existence of an intersection, but the second stage, searching through the elements of the two overlapping sets, is necessary to establish whether "All S are P". In fact, this finding may depend on the particular examples selected. Familiar generalizations, clichés and tautologies like "All ravens are black" or "All heroes are brave" may be accepted more readily than the less often asserted. "Some ravens are black" and "Some heroes are brave". A serious problem for Meyer's PIM is his assumption that there are some completely nonintersecting sets. Are any pairs of sets totally unrelated? Daisies and fishes are both members of the class of living things, and may share some features (like being sometimes found in parks). The model does not tell us how distant the relationship must be to constitute a non-intersection, but the existence of nonintersecting sets is crucial to the hypothesized two-stage retrieval process.

Another difficulty with the PIM is that the relative speed of responses to "All" and "Some" statements ceases to conform to the predictions from the model when the different kinds of statement are presented to subjects in mixed sequences instead of pure blocks of one type only. Discrepancies also arise when "Some" is interpreted to mean "Some, but not all". It looks as if the results Meyer describes may be reflecting particular strategies of knowledge retrieval, rather than fixed structures in semantic memory.

The Feature Comparison model (FCM). Smith *et al.* (1974) and Rips (1975) claim that their FCM fits the obtained data better than Meyer's model. The FCM is able to handle the problem of typicality, and explain why it is faster to judge that typical examples like robins and sparrows are members of the "bird" category, but takes longer to decide that atypical examples like ospreys, geese and penguins are birds. This model is also a two-stage one. At Stage 1 a global comparison of all features is carried out. As in signal detection theory, the decision is based on the degree of similarity between S features and P features relative to two criteria. For very typical members of the set, a criterion of high similarity is exceeded, and a fast positive response is made. If similarity falls below a low criterion, the S is rejected as nonexemplar. If the similarity index falls in the intermediate region, as when the S is an atypical member of the set, comparison must proceed to Stage 2, where a further check for the presence of critical defining features is necessary before the S can be accepted as a P (see Fig. 8). An atypical S therefore takes longer to verify than a highly representative S. The FCM predicts that the degree of semantic relatedness will affect response time for both true and false statements at Stage 1. It should take longer to reject "A daisy is a fish" than "A daisy is a stone" because daisies and fishes are more related categories by way of both being members of the set "living things". Meyer's PIM predicts no affect of relatedness on judgements of false statements, since in his model the sets do not intersect and so their features are not compared. The degree of relatedness should only affect the time for true judgements. Experiments by Rips (1975) confirmed the FCM prediction that the degree of semantic relatedness does affect both true and false judgements. The FCM also predicts that category size should influence judgement time, with the effect of category size being located at the second stage of checking the critical defining features. Since large categories logically have fewer defining features than small categories, it should take fewer comparisons, and less time, to decide if an instance is a member of a large category, but the experimental results do not confirm this prediction—the larger the category, the longer it takes to judge membership.

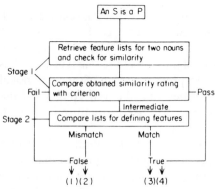

1. A daisy is a bird (False and not similar)
2. A duck-billed platypus is a bird (False but similar)
3. A penguin is a bird (True but atypical)
4. A robin is a bird (True and typical)

FIG. 8. *A two-stage Feature Comparison Model (Smith et al., 1974) for testing the relation of S and P. Typical instances are judged faster (4 is faster than 3), and dissimilar instances are judged faster (1 is faster than 2).*

One of the chief merits of the FCM is the way it allows for category membership to be a matter of degree, rather than an all-or-none affair. Category members can be graded from good examplars to poor exemplars, and this aspect of the model brings it much closer to the experimental evidence, which strongly confirms the psychological reality of graded category membership. (This question is discussed further in Chapter 4, with reference to Rosch's ideas about prototypes.)

A more general objection to the FCM is that it is hard to believe that feature comparisons are always and necessarily involved in accepting or rejecting all kinds of statement. Subjectively, we seem to know that dogs are animals, and that roses are flowers, and chairs are furniture without resort to comparison of features. On the other hand, the class membership of novel or atypical instances is something we often have to take on trust from our informants. I would agree that a cassowary is a bird because I have been told so, but I have only a hazy idea of its features. Indeed it is doubtful if defining feature lists can be supplied for many concepts. What are the defining features of a chair, for example? This problem is also discussed in more detail in Chapter 4. The verification task used in experimental testing of these models is itself rather artificial, and it is quite possible that responses of this kind can sometimes be made on the basis of information stored in the lexicon, without interrogating semantic memory at all.

In evaluating the relative advantages and disadvantages of the network models as compared with set-theoretic models, Glass and Holyoak point out that feature comparison models are more closely related to the world of perceptual experience, while the network models lack a real world interface. However, any network model has the advantage that the links can represent a variety of relationships, so that network models can be extended. It is not easy to see how a set-theoretic model could represent any relationships besides class membership and properties. In Chapter 4 it is argued that many concepts cannot be defined adequately by a set of features, but depend on the relationships between the features. For example a botanical species may be defined by being smaller than another species, flowering later, and being found further south. The need to incorporate relations between features constitutes a serious limitation for set-theoretic models.

None of the models provides a fully comprehensive account of semantic structure and semantic processing. They suggest only ways in which limited parts of the system might handle a limited selection of types of material. Because they are essentially competence models, they cannot be falsified by negative experimental evidence. Discrepancies between the ideal predictions of the model and the actual performance of the human subject are to be expected. Nor is it easy to compare the weight of evidential support for different models, because the experimental results are often consistent with more than one hypothesized mechanism. There is no logical reason why all the processes of storage and retrieval of knowledge in the human brain should conform to any single model. A composite or hybrid model comprising a combination of different mechanisms may be required to accommodate all the experimental data and observations. A theory of episodic memory need not necessarily conform to the same principles as semantic memory. It is clear that some factors which are powerful in affecting performance are lacking, or inadequately represented, in the models. Everyday knowledge is untidy, as well as amorphous, changeable, inaccessible, sketchy and idiosyncratic. Familiarity and frequency play a critical but ill-defined role in acquisition, storage and retrieval. Material may be classified in many different ways, depending on contextual cues which often cannot be clearly identified. Different strategies are employed in processing new knowledge depending on existing background knowledge, motivation, intentions and other factors which are difficult to specify and control. The comprehension of a single simple sentence involves the construction and storage of inferences and elaborated interpretations, and re-shuffling or modification of information already in store. Permanent knowledge in the semantic memory store must interact with episodic knowledge. In psychology the study of the much more complex logical and semantic structure of knowledge acquired from larger units of discourse, rather than single propositions, is only just beginning but the more we extend the scope of experimental investigations, the more difficult it becomes to construct a theory comprehensive enough to encompass all the findings.

Recommended reading

Two very comprehensive and thoughtful reviews are provided by Smith, in the *Handbook of Learning and Cognitive Processes*, edited by W. K. Estes, 1978; and by J. L. Lachman and R. Lachman in Puff's *Memory Organization and Structure*, 1979. Both of these compare and criticize various theories of semantic memory. F. C. Bartlett's classical study, *Remembering*, published in 1932, is well worth reading as an early forerunner of recent approaches. For detailed accounts of the HAM model read Anderson and Bower's *Human Associative Memory*, 1973. They provide an extremely thorough comparison of the performance of the model with the data from verbal learning experiments. ELINOR is described in greater detail in Norman and Rumelhart's *Explorations in Cognition*, 1975, and in Anderson's *Language, Memory and Thought*, 1976.

3 VISUAL IMAGERY *in* THOUGHT

The Imagery Debate

How is visual information represented in memory? This question has generated one of the most interesting and controversial debates in the cognitive psychology of recent years. The debate has centred on the nature and function of visual imagery. Most people have the subjective experience of mentally surveying picture-like images of scenes or objects while remembering, planning, day-dreaming or reviewing possible solutions to a problem. The argument is not so much about the existence of these images, but about their nature and their operational status. Do images have a functional role in thinking, or are they merely epiphenomenal? According to the epiphenomenal view, images are nonfunctional in the same way as the lights that flash up on the outside of a computer while it is working, or the noise emitted by factory machinery. The lights are systematically related to the operations going on inside the computer, just as the noise is related to the operation of machines in the factory, but neither is productive. In the same way, it is argued, visual images may accompany, but do not mediate thought processes.

The Imagist position claiming a functional role for quasi-pictorial mental representations is defended by Kosslyn and his colleagues (Kosslyn *et al.*, 1979; Kosslyn, 1981). The opposing Propositionalist point of view is argued by Pylyshyn (1973, 1981), and maintains that visual information is represented internally by means of abstract propositions. He contends that cognitive operations consist in the activation and manipulation of these propositions, and visual images have no independent functional role, and no status as an explanatory construct. This issue has been subjected to intensive experimental investigation, to introspective and philosophical analysis, and to computer simulation, but at present both sides are still deadlocked. Because the issue has proved so resistant to experimental investigation, some psychologists (e.g. Anderson, 1978) have declared that it is impossible to resolve it experimentally. Anderson argued that propositional representations and pictorial representations do not have distinct properties from which distinct behavioural consequences can be predicted. So any experimental findings can be explained equally well as arising from either type of representation. Anderson concluded that unless some decisive physiological findings emerged, the rival theories could only be evaluated by reference to criteria of parsimony and coherence. This pessimistic assessment of the power of experimental methodology has been contested by Hayes-Roth (1979) and Pylyshyn (1979), and attempts to find a solution still continue.

In order to establish that images make an independent and distinctive contribution to cognition, it is necessary to show that images and propositions represent information in different ways, which have different functional consequences. Many researchers have focussed on the nature of visual imagery, and attempted to specify its properties, and deduce its functional role from these properties. Others take the opposite route, and try to deduce nature from function. The characteristics of performance in visual information processing tasks can give clues to the nature of the underlying representation. Form and function are inter-related.

The Nature of Imagery

Although most Imagists have explicitly disavowed the "picture metaphor" (e.g. Kosslyn and Pomerantz, 1977), whereby images are likened to "pictures in the head", they nevertheless continue to endow images with many pictorial qualities. According to Kosslyn *et al.* (1979), images are quasi-pictorial: they *depict* information in a spatial medium, and resemble a display on a cathode-ray tube (CRT). Objects imaged have size, orientation and position, and these properties are instantiated in the image, not represented symbolically.

Propositions, in contrast, are defined as abstract structures that express relationships, and have truth values. A set of propositions may represent regional features of a compound array, and several sets of propositions may be inter-related to constitute a structural description of the whole. An abstract propositional representation is related to a verbal description, but is closer to the deep structure of a sentence than to its surface structure. Abstract propositional representations of visual information can be attributed to nonlinguistic organisms like animals or young children. Figure 9 shows how, given the matrix (A), the same information may be represented as a spatial image (B); as a set of abstract propositions (C); or as a verbal description (D). The question we have to try to answer is whether it is possible to infer which type of representation is utilized by looking at the input–output relations in visual information processing tasks.

Mental scanning experiments

Kosslyn and his colleagues have conducted a large number of experiments

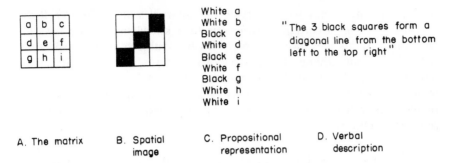

FIG. 9. *Different ways of representing the same information (adapted from Palmer, 1978).*

on mental scanning (see Kosslyn, 1980 for a full account), and their results show a close correspondence between processes of perceiving, and reports based on inspecting or scanning visual images. In these experiments, subjects are asked to construct and inspect a visual image and to verify the presence of properties or objects in the image. The dependent measure is the time the subject takes between initiating the image scan, and pressing a button to signify a decision. The results have shown a systematic relation between reaction time and the distance, size and complexity of the objects imaged.

The distance effect. In one of these experiments, subjects first studied a pictorial map of an island with objects such as a tree, hut, and rock at different locations. After memorizing the map, they were told to image it and focus on a named location. When presented with a word naming an object at a different location on the map subjects were instructed to scan towards this location, and press a button when the scan reached destination. Reaction times increased linearly with distance. It took longer for the scan to "arrive" at an object far from the starting point. Propositionalists can account for this finding by suggesting that subjects are consulting not a spatial image, but a network of propositions with distance represented in terms of degree of relatedness, rather like the network representations described in Chapter 2. Kosslyn has countered this interpretation by repeating the experiment without instructions to use imagery. When subjects were simply asked "Is there a hut on the island?" decision time was not related to spatial distance. It is only when subjects are specifically told to construct and scan an image that information processing shows corres- pondences with visual perception. Pylyshyn (1981) maintains that Kosslyn's subjects are simply responding to the demand characteristics of the task. That is, since they are told to inspect visual images they obey the instruction by behaving *as if* they were carrying out internal scans, adjusting their reaction times in accordance with their tacit knowledge of the laws of perception. If this allegation is correct, Kosslyn's subjects are not inspecting their images, but rather pretending to look at pictures, and the results tell us not about the characteristics of images, but about how well people can mimic perceptual behaviour. This is a damaging criticism which is difficult to rebut, and which underlines the weakness of experimental techniques relying on self report.

The size effect. Reaction times to report on the presence of a named property also vary inversely with size. So, for example, it takes longer to verify whether a rabbit has whiskers if the subject has been instructed to image a small rabbit. Kosslyn argues that there is a "grain" limitation, such that it is difficult to represent details on a small image. Again, a propositional interpretation of this finding can be given. Anderson (1978) suggested that people activate fewer propositions when asked to construct small images, so that detail information is not readily available. However, Kosslyn was able to show that when subjects were not instructed to consult visual images, verification times were governed by conjoint frequency, and not by size. So the question "Does a cat have claws?" was answered faster than "Does a cat have a head?". With imagery instructions, verification times were affected by size and "head" was verified faster than "claws". Imagery representations and propositional representations do appear to have different behavioural consequences in this case. Kosslyn's results are still vulnerable to the criticism that they are the product of the demand characteristics of the task. Maybe subjects are not taking longer to inspect small images, but are just behaving as if they were peering at small pictures.

The complexity effect. Experiments such as those by Beech and Allport (1978) have shown that the time required to visualize a compound scene from a visual description increases linearly with the number of objects that have to be incorporated. Again this result could stem either from a propositional representation, or from tacit knowledge about compound scenes.

Mental rotation experiments

Shepard and his co-workers have carried out several ingenious series of experiments which demonstrate how mental imagery can be generated and manipulated. Shepard (1975) wrote

> there are significant senses in which it can be said that mental images do have a
> formal or structural relation to their corresponding external objects, and that

mental images can be transformed in ways that are parallel or analogous to the kinds of transformations that occur in the corresponding external objects.

His experiments reveal an isomorphism, or functional equivalence, between mental images and perceptions of objects. For example, Shepard and Chipman (1970), using the shapes of the states of the USA as stimulus material, found that judgements of similarity made over the perceived shapes were highly correlated with judgements of similarity made when the shapes were imaged from memory. In another experiment, Shepard *et al.* (1975) asked subjects to rate the similarity of pairs of numbers presented, or imaged, in a variety of forms such as arabic numerals, roman numerals, dot patterns, written names etc. In some conditions, the numbers were presented in one form, but the subjects were asked to image them in a different form and rate their similarity in the imaged representation. The judgements of similarity were found to depend on the form in which the numbers were mentally represented, not the form in which they were perceived. If 3 and 8 were presented as arabic numerals, and judged in that form, they were rated highly similar; but if they were mentally transformed to their dot pattern versions they were judged dissimilar.

Another series of experiments measured reaction times in matching tasks. Shepard and Metzler (1971) found that the time to judge whether two objects, seen at different orientations, were identical, was linearly related to the angular distance between them (see Fig. 10). It seems that one object has to be mentally rotated until it is in a corresponding orientation to the other. The operation of mental rotation appeared to take about one second for 50°. Cooper and Shepard (1973) studied mental rotation using alphanumeric characters which were either normal ("F"), or reversed, mirror-image forms ("ꓱ"). The characters were presented at various degrees of rotation, and the subject's task was to judge whether the character was "normal" or "reversed". Reaction times increased linearly with the degree of rotation, being longest for the 180° inverted presentation, ("ꓱ" or "Ⅎ"). The reaction time reflects the time taken to rotate the character back to the upright before making the judgement. When subjects were given advance information, so that they knew beforehand which character would be presented, and at what degree of rotation, they were able to prepare a mental image of the expected character at the expected orientation, and make the normal/reversed judgement at a speed which was uniformly rapid, and did not vary with rotation (see Fig. 11). With no advance information an "F" at 180° has to be rotated back to the upright before it can be judged normal or reversed, and the time for rotation depends on the angular distance. When advance information is given, the subject can image a normal "F" at the 180° rotation

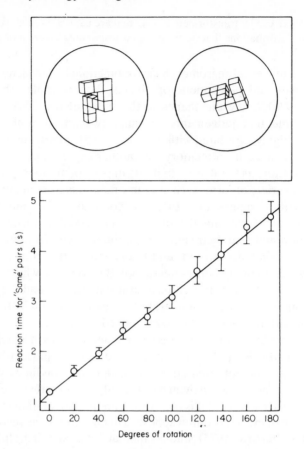

FIG. 10 *Reaction times to judge whether two shapes presented at different orientations are identical (from Shepard and Metzler, 1971).*

before the stimulus appears, and then make a rapid, direct comparison between the image and the stimulus. In the no-information condition, the mental rotation has to be performed on the perceived stimulus, and inflates the reaction time; in the advance information condition, the mental rotation is performed beforehand on the image and is not included in the reaction time.

The internal representations Shepard has studied are not just passively experienced. They are constructed, modified and manipulated to meet the demands of the task. The same kind of process occurs in everyday life when, searching for a mislaid book, we visualize it lying in various places and positions. But whether these internal representations should be classed as

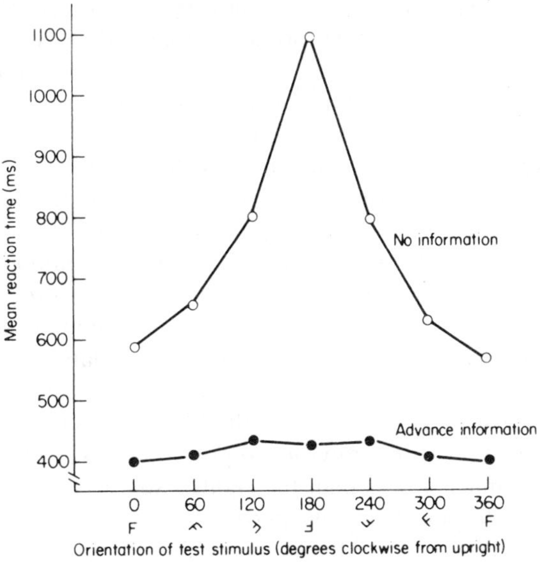

FIG. 11. *Reaction times to judge an alphanumeric character normal or reversed as a function of degrees of rotation (redrawn from Cooper and Shepard 1973).*

visual images is arguable. Shepard himself suggests that they may be abstract, schematic and amodal. His principle of isomorphism does not claim that internal representations are neural copies of external objects, but only that they have a second-order isomorphism, preserving the spatial relations of objects in a more abstract form, and that we operate on these mental constructs in ways that are analogous to the ways in which we operate on direct perceptions of external objects.

So again the interpretation of these experiments is not at all clear-cut. According to the imagery account, the linear relationship that holds between decision time and angular displacement results from continuous mental rotation of the image; according to a propositional account (Anderson, 1978), systematic alteration of the relations that hold between propositions could produce the same results. The propositional account runs into difficulties since it is hard to see why it should necessarily involve more changes to convert Ⅎ to F than to convert ㅠ to F. In order to explain why the 180° figure takes longer to transform, propositionalists have to make the arbitrary and *ad hoc* assumption that a series of stepwise transformations are carried out, converting the propositional representation successively to each intermediate state until it reaches the upright form. This assumption seems implausible.

However, the imagery account is not immune to criticism either. Kosslyn's current model (1981) proposes that spatial images may be transformed in two different ways. The shift transform operates by incremental stages on the existing display; the blink transform erases the display and regenerates a new one. To explain why subjects in the Cooper and Shepard type of experiment appear to use the incremental shift strategy rather than the blink transform, Kosslyn makes the assumption that it is less effortful to use shift transforms unless a large change is required. Blink transforms are reserved for large changes. These assumptions seem just as arbitrary and *ad hoc* as the propositional explanation. Moreover, Marmor and Zaback (1976) gave a mental rotation task to congenitally blind subjects who are assumed to lack visual imagery. The linear relationship of reaction time to angular displacement was still evident. This finding appears to support the propositional model, since the blind subjects must have been systematically manipulating nonvisual representations. Nevertheless, the blind were very much slower than the sighted subjects at performing the transformations (59° per second as opposed to 233° per second), so it does not necessarily follow that sighted subjects also employ the same kind of nonvisual representation. Most probably, normal subjects have more than one strategy available for use in mental rotation tasks.

Is an image like a percept?

Subjective reports typically describe imagery in terms of perceptual qualities such as clarity, blurring and vividness, but some kinds of image may be more closely related to percepts than others. It is possible to distinguish different kinds of visual image. Some are direct memory images of recently experienced objects; others are images generated or reconstructed after a lapse of time. It is also possible to distinguish another type of image which is completely novel and does not correspond to any previous experience, but is "imagined" and is perhaps built up from elements that have been experienced at different times. Novel images can be constructed from verbal descriptions. Much of the craft of the creative writer consists in his ability to use verbal descriptions so as to transfer to the mind of his reader the images he has constructed within his own mind. Types of imagery can be ordered along a kind of continuum according to whether they are more or less closely related to perception. After-images and eidetic imagery are like a prolongation of perception. Memory images may be of a recent perception that has never left consciousness, or may be reconstructed images of a long-past experience. The images of the artist may be created, not remembered, or may consist of a novel recombination of memory fragments. The hallucinatory images of mental illness or delirium are even further removed from the perceptions, past or present, of the individual. In asking whether visual images are pictorial, or whether they resemble percepts, it is important to remember that these various kinds of image may be qualitively different. It could be argued that the term "mental picture" might be more appropriate for some types of image than for others. Eidetic images of the kind described by Haber (1979) are sometimes called photographic because of the detail and complexity they exhibit, but this kind of imagery is a rarity, experienced by only a few individuals. It might also apply to images based on very recent perceptions, but not to reconstructed or novel images. The mental scanning and mental rotation experiments, although clearly open to more than one interpretation, can be taken as giving some support to the idea that images are similar in some ways to percepts. Yet it is obvious that there are important differences. Images are transient and unstable, and the amount of information that can be simultaneously displayed in an image appears to be sharply limited. Information that is readily available in a percept may not be recoverable in an image.

Podgorny and Shepard (1978) asked subjects to report whether a dot in one square of a 5 × 5 matrix lay in a filled or empty square. Prior to the dot presentation, subjects had either seen the matrix with designated squares filled, or imagined it from a description. Latencies were unaffected by whether the matrix pattern was remembered or imagined. Podgorny and Shepard concluded that representations arising out of visual memory, and out of visual imagination were functionally equivalent. In another condition, when the matrix pattern was present all the time so that judgement about the dot position was based on a current percept, subjects performed better. Judgements based on the percept were more efficient than judgements based on either a perceptual memory image, or a generated image, so images and percepts were not equivalent.

Waltz (1979) has suggested that images are the product of the top-down processes which in normal perception operate in conjunction with the bottom-up processing of sensory data to produce the percept. This view is rather similar to Neisser's (1976) account of images as anticipations of perception produced by the activation of the appropriate schema. Both suggest that imagery is more closely related to the knowledge base that underlies perception than to sensory processes. However, some experimental results suggest that images and percepts may overlap in visual short-term memory.

Modality-specific interference experiments. Some attempts have been made to show that imaging competes with perception for the machinery of the visual system, so that the formation and retention of visual images is disrupted by a concurrent visual perception task (Atwood, 1971; den Heyer and Barrett, 1971; Salthouse, 1974). The results of these experiments have been rather inconsistent. Atwood's study appeared to show a modality-specific interference effect, whereby recall of concrete, or easily imageable, phrases was impaired by a visual distractor task (responding to a visually presented digit), and recall of abstract phrases was vulnerable to auditory verbal distraction (responding to a spoken digit). Attempts to replicate Atwood's results have not been successful, and his experimental design has been criticized. In particular, some of his so-called abstract phrases which included items such as "Greed is the nature of pigs" and "Garden vegetables earn money" do not seem intuitively difficult to image. Moreover, the distractor tasks in this experiment were very undemanding, and were unlikely to cause much interference anyway. Den Heyer and Barrett (1971) presented subjects with letters arranged in a grid. Those subjects who performed an interpolated visual task requiring dot discrimination, could recall the identity of the letters but showed loss of the spatial-position information. Brooks (1968) asked his subjects to scan an image of the letter "F" in a designated direction, and to report whether each of the corners was external or internal. Responding visually, by pointing to the words "yes" or "no" interfered with the task more than responding "yes" or "no" vocally. However, attempts to replicate this result have shown that the interference arises because the direction of the internal scan is in conflict with the eye movements required by the visually directed pointing response (Byrnne, 1970). Experiments which aim to compare the effects of visual and non-visual distractor tasks need to equate the two distractor tasks for difficulty, and for compatibility with the primary task, before differential effects can be attributed solely to modality-specific interference. The hypothesis that seeing and imaging are necessarily incompatible is not supported. It seems that visual imagery and visual perception may disrupt each other when image and percept are in conflict, but that interference does not arise when the image and percept are consonant.

The nature of this interference has been clarified in a series of experiments by Baddeley et al. (1975). They showed that the ability to visually track a moving light was impaired if Brooks' "F" test had to be performed concurrently, but was unaffected by a verbal concurrent task. Conversely, the tracking task interfered with memory for a spatial array, but did not affect memory for verbal nonsense material. Finally, Baddeley et al. combined the tracking task with a memory task involving either abstract noun–adjective pairs (like idea–original) or concrete pairs (like strawberry–ripe). If retention of concrete pairs is by imagery, these should be more impaired by the concurrent visual tracking task, but the results showed that both abstract and concrete material was equally affected by concurrent tracking. On the basis of these findings, Baddeley concludes that if imagery is an active manipulative process taking place in visual working memory then it is susceptible to disruption by concurrent visual perception, but that memory for concrete words or phrases does not necessarily involve images, and is not in conflict with visual perception.

In everyday life we may experience the imaging/perceiving conflict if we try to visualize a scene or a problem while driving a car. To some extent we do seem to need the mind's eye for seeing. Although the congenitally blind have no visual imagery, those who have lost their sight report that their imagery is undiminished. Prior visual experience is required for imaging, but not the peripheral mechanism of sight.

How do images differ from propositions?

Are there any characteristics which reliably distinguish these two kinds of internal representation? Do they encode identical information? Do images have any properties not derivable from propositions, or vice versa? It is possible to list a number of differences. Spatial images necessarily have the properties of size, orientation and shape. Objects represented in a spatial image have a definite location relative to each other. So although a proposition may encode the relation "A next to B", in an imaginal representation A must be either on the right or the left, above or below, B. Some relations such as concealment (A conceals B) can be represented propositionally, but cannot easily be represented in a spatial image. Neisser and Kerr (1973) found that subjects were able to recall objects described as being concealed as well as objects described as unconcealed, and therefore concluded that the memory representation must be a structural description rather than a spatial image. These findings have been challenged by Keenan and Moore (1979). They presented subjects with sentences and later tested recall of items mentioned in the sentence. In one example a sentence described a coin as either lying deep inside the pitch dark barrel of an old cannon (the concealed condition); or as lying on top of the barrel of the cannon (the unconcealed version). The coin was recalled less well in the concealed condition if the subjects were instructed to use imagery. Loss of the concealed item from the memory representation indicates that spatial imagery must have been employed in encoding or in storing the information.

Besides the problem of representing concealment it is also claimed that pictorial representations could not encode information like "The lieutenant forged the cheque" as distinct from "The lieutenant signed the cheque", since the pictures would be identical. If we try to encode a sentence like "The boy throws the ball" in a pictorial image, how can we know, when we come to retrieve the image, whether the original sentence had been "The boy throws the ball", "The boy catches the ball" or "The boy plays with the ball"? Other conceptual distinctions such as time sequence, negation or absence, intentions and causality, are thought to be beyond the scope of mental pictures. Intuitively it seems difficult to represent a category by a pictorial image. We can image a particular cat, but can we image a generalized cat to stand for the class of cats? The classical problem discussed by Berkeley (1710) is still relevant today. If we can only form a specific image of a specific triangle how can this serve for thinking about the general properties of triangles? This problem can be overcome if an individual can store a set of specific images representing all possible forms of triangle: or, more economically, if his image of a triangle is a prototype, which represents the central tendencies of the set of all triangles. Work by Posner and Keele (1968) has shown that it is possible to abstract a prototype from a set of patterns. The prototype incorporates the common elements, and can be used for recognition and classification of new instances. The problem does not arise if abstract propositions are substituted for pictorial images, since there is no difficulty in encoding general properties in propositions.

Anderson (1978) discusses arguments claiming that propositional representations are superior for inference making because of their abstract truth-functional character. While this claim may hold good for some kinds of logical inference, it is not necessarily true for all kinds of inference. Spatial and relational inferences may be more easily extracted from a spatial representation.

The Function of Imagery

Experiments that attempt to establish a functional role for imagery in memory and in thinking have encountered two main obstacles. Firstly, the results can often be interpreted as proving the propositional case, rather than the imagery case. And, secondly, individual differences in the use of imagery and in the efficiency of imaging are very marked. It has also proved difficult to establish reliable correlations between measures of imaging ability, and performance in cognitive tasks thought to depend on imagery (see Ernest, 1977, for a review). This may be because the measures of imaging ability are invalid. Typically, subjects are asked to rate the quality of their own images on a scale of vividness, and this kind of introspective judgement may be unreliable. Alternatively, it may indicate that the subjective experience of imagery bears no relation to cognitive functions. In any case, the existence of these individual differences suggests that the use of imagery is an optional strategy rather than an essential part of cognitive processing.

Imagery in recall

In recent years the role of imagery in recall has been intensively studied.

Most researchers have not specified whether the images they are investigating are to be considered as mental pictures, or as more abstract symbolic descriptions. Many experiments of Paivio (1969) and others appear to show that imagery enhances recall, and this claim is based mainly on comparisons of the recall of material which is rated as having low image potential, and the recall of material which has high image potential. Lists of words like "truth, importance, democracy" are harder to recall than lists of words like "cake, giraffe, flag" and sentences such as "Punctuality is essential" are more difficult than sentences like "The cat wore roller skates". Numerous criticisms have been made of this type of experiment. The two kinds of material, do not differ only in image potential. Although experimenters usually try to control other factors known to affect recall, such as word frequency, syntactic class or structure, and word length, there are many other differences that might affect memorability. Words of low image potential are usually abstract rather than concrete. The abstract–concrete dimension, which is confounded with image potential in many studies, also affects recall (Richardson, 1975). Some abstract words are more lexically complex since they are often derived forms, and Kintsch (1972) has shown that these are harder to learn. Words like "freedom" and "owner" are examples of lexically complex abstract words derived from the simpler forms "free" and "own". While concrete, low imagery nouns are usually monomorphemic; some abstract words like "advantage" or "excuse" consists of more than one morpheme, and this may also make them harder to process and store. Abstract words are acquired at a later age, and it has been suggested (Carroll and White, 1973) that the earliest learned words are the easiest to retain. Abstract sentences may also be in some way less comprehensible, or more ambiguous, and comprehensibility is known to aid recall (Johnson *et al.*, 1972). Because of these additional confounding factors it is not clear that the better recall of concrete material is due to imagery.

Similarly, giving subjects instructions to try to form images as they attempt to memorize will improve their subsequent recall, but this does not prove that the images produced the improvement. Instructions to generate related sentences or elaborated descriptions also result in improved recall, so that, as Bower and Winzenz (1970) point out, it may be the effort to re-structure the material to be remembered which is crucial, rather than the images. A list of words like "cake, giraffe, flag" may be easier to learn because these items can all be represented in a compound image, or because they can be linked in a story framework. Jonides *et al.* (1975) reported that when congenitally blind and normal sighted subjects were given a paired associate learning task, instructions to "imagine a relationship" between members of each pair improved recall of blind and sighted equally. The facilitating effect was clearly produced by relating the items together, but the relationship must have been a non-visual one.

The same point can be made against the evidence from image-based mnemonics. One of the best known and most striking of these is the method of loci, or mental walk, said to have been used by Roman orators and recently revived for laboratory experiments. Recall of a list of items in the correct order is enormously enhanced if each item is mentally placed in a room of a well-known house, or in a different building along a well-known street. A mental walk retrieves the items. The mnemonist studied by Luria (1968) in the USSR used this method with outstanding effectiveness. The pictorial nature of this device is apparent in the anecdote reporting that, on one of the rare occasions that the mnemonist forgot an item, it turned out that the item was a white egg which he had mentally placed in front of a white front door, and so failed to discern on his journey of recall. However, it can be argued that the crucial factor in this strategy is not the use of visual imagery, but the act of re-organizing the material to fit an already familiar scheme. Some non-visual mnemonics work in a similar fashion, as when we make up a sentence of words beginning with the initial letters of the colours of the spectrum or the parts of the alimentary canal. So, although subjectively and intuitively it seems quite convincing that visual imagery aids recall, the experimental evidence is not absolutely compelling.

Imagery in problem solving

When we come to consider the use of imagery in problem solving, the evidence is more anecdotal than experimental, but is impressive in quantity, if not rigour. According to Hayes (1974), most people report extensive use of imagery in mental arithmetic calculation, especially in holding substage results, and calculating geniuses seem to rely on it more than usual. Many claim to need a blank space, free from visual distraction, on which to project their imagery. Highly skilled chess players report using visual imagery in considering projected moves. They perceive the positions of the pieces on the board in terms of the overall visual pattern, and appear to possess a sort of mental library of such patterns, associated with possible moves and likely outcomes, which they can consult (Chase and Simon, 1974). But although chess masters are much better at recalling authentic board positions than novice players, their visual memory for randomly placed pieces is not superior. This suggests that their mental representations of legitimate board positions are not just pictorial images, but rule-bound descriptions of the configurational relationships. Most people who are asked to work out Baylor's (1972) cube-dicing problems feel that they rely on imagery. Those problems concern a cube which is painted with red on the sides and blue on the top and bottom, and ask, for example, how many of the sections which result from the vertical and horizontal slicing of the cube into 27 mini-cubes, have both red and blue faces. Again, however, we cannot necessarily conclude that the subjectively experienced images mediate the solution to the problems. We cannot rule out the possibility that the cognitive processes involved in solving the problems employ structural descriptions rather than pictorial images. Huttenlocher (1968) has suggested that visual imagery is used in the solution of logical problems such as linear syllogisms. Given premises such as "A is bigger than B, C is smaller than B", it is thought that these are arranged mentally into an ordered spatial array, so that inferences can be made by simple inspection of the visual image. The answer to a question such as "Is B bigger than C?" can be read off the visual image (see p. 184 for further discussion of this theory). Some corroborative evidence for the view that imagery is involved in solving this kind of problem comes from a study of brain-damaged patients (Caramazza *et al.*, 1976). The patients had sustained damage to the right hemisphere resulting in the pattern of impairment typical of right-sided injuries. No disorder of language was observable, but there were deficits in visuospatial processing. These patients were tested on two kinds of problem: congruent problems in which the same terms were used in both premiss and question, such as "John is taller than Bill. Who is taller?" and incongruent problems in which the premiss and the question had different terms, such as "John is taller than Bill. Who is shorter?" They were able to solve the congruent problems, but failed with the incongruent problems. The authors suggest that the incongruent problems could not be solved by purely linguistic reasoning, and required a visual representation, which the damaged right hemisphere was incapable of constructing. Most of us rely on imagery in giving directions how to get from one part of town to another, planning how to seat the guests at a dinner party, or working out how to assemble a piece of machinery. The difficulty is that some few people claim to use little or no imagery at all, and yet are able to perform these tasks quite efficiently. If the problems can be solved just as well without imagery there are two possible conclusions. One is that some people do make use of imagery in thinking, but others can think equally well relying only on language, or on abstract representations. The second possibility is that imagery is never the medium of thought, but that some people indulge in it as a kind of optional extra: their thinking is enlivened with illustrations that are not strictly necessary.

Those who wish to minimize or deny the function of imagery in thinking, should pause to consider the lavish use we make of visual aids in conveying information. We use pictures, diagrams, graphs and maps to present information in ways that are more readily grasped and more easily retained than verbal descriptions. We make rough jottings as we think or calculate. Visual information has one outstanding advantage over verbal information, in that many separate items or elements can be simultaneously presented to the mind. Verbal information is necessarily sequential, and items must be reviewed in succession. Because of this, some kinds of information, for example, instructions for assembling mechanical gadgets, may be quite easily expressed in diagrams, but may be almost impossible to convey by words alone. Visual aids are a kind of external imagery, just as written words are externalized verbal thoughts. The internal forms are less stable, and so less easily reconsidered and evaluated, than the external ones, but are fulfilling the same functions. When trying to assess the part played by visual imagery in thinking, it is important to remember that visual images are not just a kind of internal home movie. We can also construct and utilize second-order visual imagery: we can visualize graphs and lay-outs, maps, signs, symbols and written language, as well as scenery. Second-order visual imagery is not subject to the limitations that apply to first-order visual imagery, and can represent temporal, causal and class relationships by conventional symbolizations.

Because visual imagery has this special quality of allowing several elements to be contemplated simultaneously, of being easily manipulated, dismantled and reconstructed, it may be especially valuable in creative thinking. Although we are far from understanding the processes of creative thought, it seems to involve forming and evaluating novel combinations of elements. In the visual and decorative arts, in architecture and town-planning, sketches are tried out in the mind's eye before they emerge on to the drawing board.

Shepard (1978) examined the role of imagery in the thought processes of creative thinkers such as Einstein, James Watt, James D. Watson and Francis Crick, among others. What is common to all these thinkers is that they report visualizing structural relationships, and suddenly perceiving solutions to problems. Insights into the theory of relativity, principles of thermodynamics, and the double helical structure of DNA all appear to have originated in this way. It is noticeable that the reports are all of "seeing" a solution, not of working it out rationally. Shepard writes "It seems reasonable to suppose that the processes leading to this sudden awareness were more holistic and analogical than atomistic and logical".

In so far as the use of visual imagery is only an optional strategy in cognitive tasks, we would not expect to find the congenitally blind, who have no visual imagery, to be intellectually disadvantaged. It is likely that they would compensate for this lack by cultivating linguistic skill and haptic (touch and movement) imagery. But if there are any cognitive tasks for which visual imagery is the only, or the most effective form of represent-ation, then the differences in the performance of blind and sighted should be demonstrable. When sighted children learn a spatial layout by touch under blindfold conditions, they can visualize the layout, and can recall positions on it as well in the reverse as in the forward order. The blind children rely on haptic imagery which does not lend itself to reversal. While visual imagery allows multiple elements in a spatial array to be contemplated simult-aneously, so that they can be read off in any order, haptic imagery seems to preserve a rigid sequential order (Millar, 1975). Although blind children are probably disadvantaged because their haptic memory lacks the support of visuospatial recoding, blind adults compensate by using verbalization to support haptic imagery. While a verbal coding is still necessarily sequential, it seems to be easier to re-organize than a purely haptic coding. The blind are able to achieve high levels of skill in chess, logic and mathematics, so that, however useful visual imagery may be as an aid to thought, it is not a *sine qua non*. When haptic imagery is combined with verbal re-coding, no deficiency is apparent.

Imagery in recognition

The importance of imagery in recognition is much better established. Firstly, there is evidence that visual patterns which seem too complex, or too amorphous, to label or verbalize, such as blobs, random scatters of dots, or snowflake patterns, can be recognized even after a delay. Experiments by Phillips and Baddeley (1971) showed that subjects could judge two dot patterns as same or different with delays of up to nine seconds between the first and second pattern. This seems to show that recognition can be a process of matching a re-presented stimulus to a stored image, but Pylyshyn (1973) argues that the original patterns were stored as abstract descriptions, and the matching takes place at the level of these descriptions. Since subjects are not aware of forming and matching descriptions, these processes must be presumed to occur at an unconscious level. This argument is difficult to counter, but Standing's (1973) striking demonstration of the almost unlimited capacity of recognition memory for pictures lend support to the view that visual memory exists, and functions as a system that is separate and distinct from verbal memory. After a series of several thousand pictures has been viewed only once, they can be recognized again, and distinguished from "new" pictures that have not been seen before with a high degree of accuracy. Recognition of verbal material is much inferior. Consequently, even if visual stimuli are stored in memory as abstract descriptions rather than as pictures, these abstract representations have special characteristics which are not shared by the memory representations derived from verbal inputs.

An ingenious series of reaction time studies by Posner *et al.* (1969) has also vindicated the role of visual imagery in recognition. In these experi-ments, subjects were asked to judge two letters "same" or "different".

When two physically identical letters are presented simultaneously (e.g. AA) a fast visual match takes place. If the two letters are physically different, but have the same name (e.g. Aa) a verbal name match takes place and the reaction time is reliably longer. When the two letters of a pair are presented successively, separated by a short interval, the first must be held in memory for matching against the second. The difference between the reaction times for fast visual matching of identical pairs, and slower matching of the same-name pairs is maintained. The first letter must have been stored as an image, else the fast visual match could no longer occur. Additional experiments have shown that if the first stimulus is not shown, but only named, it is possible to generate or construct an image of it to match against a second stimulus. A similar process may occur in everyday life when we search for a friend in a crowd. We construct an image of his face and figure, and look for a match.

A study of generated imagery by Tversky (1969) used successive presentation of schematic faces and their names. Subjects first learned to name the faces correctly, and were then asked to make same/different judgements on pairs which could be name–face, face–name, face–face, or name–name. Reaction times for the different-modality pairs could be as fast as for the same-modality pairs if, and only if, the subject could correctly anticipate the modality of the second stimulus. Thus, when the first stimulus was the name, and there was a high probability that the second stimulus would be a face, the subject generated an image of the expected face, and matching was as fast as for the face–face condition. While pairs of names differed by one, two or three letters, pairs of faces differed by one, two or three features. Examination of the "different" responses confirmed that name–face pairs were matched in the visual "face" modality, because the time taken to judge such a pair "different" reflected the number of features by which the faces differed, not the number of letters by which the names differed. Shepard's mental rotation experiments described above can also be taken as illustrating the effective use of generated images in recognition.

Reed (1974) devised an experimental technique to reveal the properties of the memory representation underlying pattern recognition. Subjects viewed one complex pattern followed, after a retention interval, by a second pattern and were asked to judge whether the second pattern was a part of the first. Figure 12 shows the complex pattern (A) and some of the candidate subpatterns (B, C and D are subpatterns of A, but E is not). Reaction times to make the judgements were measured. Reed concluded from the results that the original pattern was stored as a structural description. If the second pattern matched part of the structural description of the first, reaction time was fast. Subjects usually responded fast and accurately to the triangle and the diamond (B and C), suggesting that these shapes were directly encoded in the structural description. Responses to the parallelogram (D) were slow and inaccurate, and Reed suggested that it was not part of the stored description, so that subjects were forced to generate a visual image from the structural description, and try to recover the parallelogram shape from the image. The results underline the limitations of generated visual imagery since only 11 out of 80 subjects succeeded in recognizing the parallelogram. Embedded figures that can easily be detected when a complex pattern is perceived, are difficult to recover from a memory image.

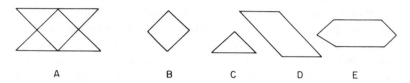

A   B   C   D   E

FIG. 12. *The complex pattern A, and subpatterns B, C and D (E is not a subpattern) (adapted from Reed, 1974).*

Imagery in the Cognitive System

Even if images are allowed to have distinctive characteristics, and to have a functional role in cognition, there is still some disagreement about the way imaginal representations are related to other forms of knowledge representation in the cognitive system.

The dual code theory

The dual coding hypothesis (Paivio, 1969) is a theory which leaves the exact nature of the image unspecified, but postulates two inter-connected memory systems, verbal and imaginal, operating in parallel. Clinical cases in which verbal memory and visual memory are damaged independently give empirical support to the theory. Patients who have sustained injuries localized to one side of the brain show this dissociation of the two memory systems. In Corsi's (1971) study, patients suffering from lesions of the left hemisphere were poor at recognizing recurring words in a series, but were able to recognize recurring abstract pictures. Patients with similar damage to the right side of the brain were impaired at picture recognition but performed normally with words. Even more strikingly, a Japanese patient with left hemisphere damage lost the ability to read Kana, the phonetic characters, but was still able to read Kanji, the ideographic characters (Sasanuma, 1974). These results indicate that verbal and visual recognition memory systems are functionally and topographically distinct, and that imagery is located primarily within the right hemisphere. The dual coding theory assumes that pictures, and concrete words that refer to easily imageable objects may be represented in both verbal and visual memory, but abstract material is represented only in the verbal system. Chances of recall are thought to be improved by the availability of two alternative traces, so that easily imageable material is better remembered. However, it is by no means clear, as we have seen, that the superior recall of concrete material can be attributed to the use of imagery. Nor is it clear how a dual coding system would function for retrieval. While the clinical evidence shows that verbal and visual memory codes can operate independently in recognition, it is not evident quite how visual images could be accessed for retrieval independently of their verbal labels. If visual information can only be recalled via the verbal system then the advantages of a dual coding are lessened. Indeed, Carmichael *et al.* (1932) showed that ambiguous visual figures, for example, one that can be seen either as spectacles or as dumb-bells, are distorted when redrawn from memory, so as to conform more closely to whichever label was adopted. This tendency for recall of visual information to be contaminated by verbal information has been strikingly demonstrated by Loftus and Palmer (1974), in their studies of eye-witness testimony. In their experiment, subjects saw a film of a traffic accident. Different groups of subjects were given different versions of subsequent questions about the film, for example "How fast were the cars going when they smashed into (hit) each other?" Later they were asked if they had seen any broken glass. Subjects who had been given the "smashed into" version of the first question were much more likely to report having seen broken glass, although in fact there was none in the film. In a similar experiment, (Loftus *et al.*, 1978) witnesses reported seeing a Give Way sign instead of the Stop sign they had actually seen, after earlier questions misleadingly suggested the sign had been Give Way. According to Loftus, the misleading verbal information is incorporated into the visual memory representation, and cannot be disentangled. Nevertheless, some kind of dual coding system does have the advantage of being able to represent some of the kinds of information that are difficult for pictorial images alone. Boys throwing balls, and lieutenants forging cheques present no problems if a combination of verbal and imaginal coding is employed. Pictorial representations can be verbally annotated.

Tricodes and multicodes

A tricode theory was foreshadowed in the model proposed by Reed in 1974. In 1978 Anderson wrote

> it seems clear that the human must process three kinds of information: visual–spatial, verbal–sequential and abstract–propositional—the kinds of information representations optimal for these three domains are different. Therefore, it

would seem that there would be a strong survival advantage pushing in the direction of three separate codes with the potential for intertranslation among them. Personally, I find this *a priori* argument quite compelling.

Figure 13 diagrams the elements of a tricode theory with multidirectional mapping relationships.

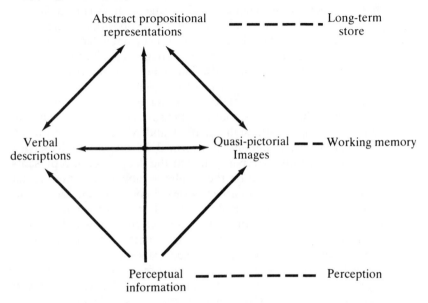

FIG. 13. *The tricode model of knowledge representation.*

A multicode model is embodied in the computer simulation described by Kosslyn and Schwartz (1977) and Kosslyn (1981). Although the model does not include the verbal component, it instantiates a tripartite relationship between abstract propositional representations, literal descriptive encodings and quasi-pictorial images in a working simulation. This is a major contribution to the study of imagery, since the representations and processes are specified in detail; predictions can be tested, and consequences examined. In the simulation, the image corresponds to a quasi-pictorial 2 D spatial array in a visual buffer store. This "surface representation" has a limited extent, and limited resolution which is highest in the centre, but falls off toward the periphery. Local regions can be selectively activated, and there is a scan process which operates by moving the image across the buffer. Other processes include adjustments of scale to dilate or contract the display, and transformations of orientation. The display is transient, starting to decay as soon as activated. So complexity is limited also, because parts of a complex image may decay before other parts have been generated. These surface images are generated from "deep representations" stored in long-term memory. Kosslyn postulates two kinds of deep representation. Literal encodings which consist of lists of co-ordinates accessed by name; and propositional encodings which consist of lists of abstract propositions. These are also accessed by names, and have pointers relating them to other lists in an hierarchical arrangement. An image display can be generated from either the literal or the propositional encoding, although well-learned facts may be retrieved direct from a deep representation without an image being constructed. Image consultation is not a mandatory operation, but is considered as being the optimal way to perform some kinds of task, especially ones involving judgements about spatial position, size, or distance, and tasks requiring mental rotation or re-arrangement. Critics have pointed out that the surface display is incapable of handling 3 D images, although Shepard and Metzler's experiments showed that people can mentally transform 3 D shapes. In Kosslyn's simulation these transforms are performed at the deep level of representation. Kosslyn's model is based on the results he obtained in the mental scanning experiments described earlier in this chapter. The model is still being tested and modified so as to conform to further experimental findings. It provides a testing-ground for theoretical predictions, but whether it can decide the issues in the imagery debate is doubtful. Kosslyn's model reconciles many conflicting experimental results, since it allows a functional role to abstract propositions as well as to quasi-pictorial images. But the model stands in direct contradiction to the views of Pylyshyn (1981) who denies that depictive representations exist as structures in the human mind, and therefore denies that any quasi-pictorial display exists to be consulted.

So is the Imagist versus Propositionalist debate to end in a drawn match? Although the opposing positions are much more clearly stated and precisely specified than they were at the outset, no solution is yet apparent. Both Imagists and Propositionalists remain mutually unconvinced by each other's arguments.

Recommended reading

For a detailed account of the Imagist view, read Kosslyn's book *Image and Mind*, or Kosslyn in *Psychological Review*, 1981. For some cut and thrust debate, see Kosslyn, Pinker, Smith and Schwartz with the comments and criticisms that follow in *The Behavioral and Brain Sciences*, 1979 (2). Palmer's chapter on cognitive representation in Rosch and Lloyd, 1978, is important and rewarding, but difficult. Cooper and Shepard, 1973, is one of the classic experimental papers. Anderson in *Psychological Review*, 1978, provides a thoughtful and readable summing-up. Loftus's work, 1974 and 1978, on eyewitness reports is an example of everyday life applications.

4 CONCEPTS *and* CONCEPT FORMATION

In Chapter 2, the models of semantic memory that were discussed focussed on the representation of facts about the elements of knowledge or concepts, and concepts like "dogs" or "canaries" were represented in the models as elements organized into sets, or as nodes linked to other nodes. The present chapter is concerned with the nature of the concepts that are the components, or building-blocks of the knowledge system; with how items in the real world are identified as being instances of a particular concept; and with how concepts are learned in the first place. Most of the semantic memory models assume that concepts consist of a list of features, properties or attributes, but the idea that a concept is mentally represented as a list of necessary or sufficient features has been challenged, and some alternative theories about the structure of concepts have been proposed. It should be clear that semantic memory and the nature of concepts are not separate and distinct topics. Although researchers have tended to concentrate on one or on the other, the issues are so closely connected that it makes little sense to consider them separately. The macrostructure of semantic memory cannot be unaffected by the microstructure of its component concepts.

Research on concepts has undergone something of a revolution during the 1970s. Earlier traditional work studied artificial concepts acquired in the laboratory by experimentally controlled procedures, and the artificial concepts consisted, for the most part, of geometrical shapes such as red circles and blue triangles. Using a range of highly simplified and standard-ized stimuli of this kind, experiments achieved considerable precision. But, arguably, the pursuit of rigour entailed the sacrifice of relevance. Finding out how subjects learn to classify circles and squares tells us very little about how people classify objects in the real world, how these natural concepts are acquired during normal life experience, and how they are represented mentally. Recent work, in harmony with the new emphasis on ecological validity, has moved away from the study of artificial concepts to concentrate more on natural concepts. Obviously it is of great practical importance to understand how best to impart concepts to other people. In education, and in any kind of information dissemination, we need to know how to structure and present a concept (1) so that it is readily and thoroughly understood; (2) so that the learner's newly acquired concept corresponds closely to the teacher's; and (3) so that the concept is well retained, is clearly and consistently related to other elements in the conceptual system, is ambiguous but modifiable, and can be utilized in thought and action. Studies of natural concepts are more relevant to education than the traditional artificial concepts. Studying natural concepts instead of artificial concepts also has the further advantage that it is more closely related to other areas of cognition such as theories of semantic memory, visual imagery, language and cognitive development.

The Nature of Concepts

Most of the definitions of a concept which are offered in the literature are very broad. According to Bourne (1966):

> a concept exists whenever two or more distinguishable objects or events have been grouped or classified together, and set apart from other objects on the basis of some common feature or property characteristic of each.

In a later version Bourne (1974) elaborates this definition to include the relationships between the critical features as integral to the concept. Thus a concept is defined by the relationship which governs the set of critical features of properties. Others define concepts in terms of their behavioural effects. For Bruner *et al.* (1956):

> to categorize is to render discriminably different things equivalent, to group objects and events and people around us into classes, and to respond to them in terms of their class membership rather than their uniqueness.

Hayes and Nissen (1971), aiming for a definition generous enough to permit animals to have concepts, formulated a rather similar version:

> a consistent response to a constant aspect of a variety of stimuli regardless of the specific context in which this aspect occurs.

Artificial concepts

Artificial concepts of the kind typically used in laboratory experiments differ from the natural concepts we acquire in everyday life in a number of important respects. Artificial concepts can be exactly specified. Red triangles and blue squares have a specifiable number of relevant dimensions (e.g. size, colour and shape), with a specified range of possible values on each of these dimensions (e.g. large/small, red/blue, triangle/ square). Irrelevant dimensions (e.g. position) are also designated and controlled.

The relationship between the relevant attributes is established by the experimenter, so that, for example, the concept is based on a conjunctive relation (red and small and triangular) or a disjunctive one (either red or triangular). The most important aspect of experimental concepts is their well-definedness, and in everyday life not many kinds of concept possess this characteristic to anything like the same extent.

Natural concepts

Natural concepts vary along a continuum ranging from concrete to abstract. It is also possible to discern similar continua ranging from simple to complex, and from nonverbal to verbal. At the concrete end of the continuum lie those concepts that are defined in terms of their physical characteristics, like a particular kind of flower or make of car. While these belong to the type of everyday concept which is most similar to the artificial concepts, they are nevertheless much less specific. The defining attributes of everyday concepts in so far as they can be identified, tend to consist of an open-ended disjunctive set of possible values. For example, a tulip may be red, pink, white, yellow or blackish. Other defining attributes may have a continuous range of possible values, so that the tulip may be between 15 and 40 centimetres in height, and flower between March and May.

Instead of a set of defining features, class membership may be determined by possession of sufficient, but not necessary features. Noncriterial, irrelevant attributes may be numerous, variable and unspecified. Consider the irrelevant attributes of a class like "flowers". These comprise characteristics which vary within the class, and include highly salient dimensions such as colour, size and shape. Moreover, as new varieties develop, the set of irrelevant attributes may change. As Smith *et al.* (1974) pointed out in their model for classification, which was outlined in Chapter 2, not all the features which define a class carry equal weight, and the features which are used for classifying instances that are typical of the class, may be different from those used when the instances are atypical. In practice, we select the features most appropriate for the context in which classification takes place. While we might use the feature "winged" to classify birds in a zoological context, we would need to choose some other features in a context which included angels and aeroplanes. The defining features of everyday concepts are not fixed, and the borderline between relevant and irrelevant dimensions is often hazy. Many of these difficulties are overcome by Rosch's account of concepts (see pp. 81–87), because, in her view, concepts are represented as prototypes, rather than as sets of discrete critical features. Hence classification of an instance need not be carried out by means of matching defining features; instead, an instance can be classified by comparison with the prototype. As was noted in Chapter 2, it seems implausible that classification should always require feature comparisons. The recognition of a rose as a flower, and an apple as a fruit seems to be instantaneous and holistic. Brooks (1978) has suggested that concept identification in everyday life is more often intuitive, implicit and nonanalytic, and that, in contrast to analytic feature-testing models, class membership of an instance is inferred from its overall similarity to another known instance of the class. If we know that one particular rose is a flower, we can infer that other similar examples are also flowers without recourse to feature comparisons. These three theories, Feature Comparison, Prototype Comparison, and Instance Comparison, provide alternative accounts of how concepts are represented, and how examples are classified. They are described and evaluated in more detail later in this chapter.

Many everyday concepts cannot be defined in terms of physical characteristics at all. Functional concepts like vehicles, tools, toys, weapons and Wittgenstein's famous "games" (Wittgenstein, 1953) are only loosely related by a common use or associated activity. A boot and a hat are both instances of the concept "clothing", but may have no physical features in common whatever. The classification of functional concepts may also depend on context, so that a dagger may be an ornament in one situation, and a weapon in a different context. When classification is dependent on context, and on the intentions, actions, and previous experience of whoever is making the classification, considerable ambiguity creeps in, and the correct classification is often doubtful. As a result, the boundaries between one natural concept and another are fuzzy rather than clear-cut. Some examples may be classified in different ways by different people at different times. Is a tomato a fruit or a vegetable? Is walking a sport or a recreation? The category of "chair" shades off into stools, benches, thrones, seats and sofas, and there is no sharp dividing line.

Abstract concepts

When we come to consider concepts that lie towards the abstract end of the concrete–abstract continuum, there may be even less consensus of opinion. There is liable to be disagreement as to the critical features of abstract concepts like "democracy" or "freedom", and disagreement about what is, or is not, an instance of such a concept. Many people have idiosyncratic or incomplete mental representations of abstract concepts. Concepts of this kind have three characteristics which contribute to the lack of uniformity. Firstly, they are higher-order concepts which rest on a substrate of underlying concepts in terms of which they are defined. So we cannot understand the concept of democracy unless we first understand something of the concepts of voting, and of the nature of government, and something of alternative systems of government with which democracy is contrasted.

Secondly, while concrete concepts can be taught either ostensively by pointing to examples, or by verbal definition, or by a mixture of both, many abstract concepts can only be acquired verbally. Since there is no object which can be pointed out as an example of "democracy", we depend on verbal descriptions, definitions and explanations. While the uniformity of human sense organs ensures that perceptually defined concepts are fairly similar for everyone, verbally defined concepts are more liable to be distorted by misunderstanding and misinterpretation. Finally, abstract concepts are also more liable to be dependent on context than physical and functional ones. Concepts like "aggression" and "freedom" are relative rather than absolute, and depend on the scale and values previously established in the experience of whoever is making the judgement, and on the current social and political context.

Table 1 shows examples of both natural and artificial concepts, together with their different characteristics. The technical or artificial concepts are distinguished by having defining features, and more clear-cut boundaries.

TABLE 1. Types of Concept.

Type of concept	Examples	Characteristics
Technical, artificial or constructed concepts	Legal (e.g. a minor, a drunk driver)	Well-defined
	Scientific (e.g. a neutron) Mathematical (prime number, isoceles triangle)	Clear boundaries
	Biological (robins, orchids)	Defining features
	Abstract (Buddhism, democracy)	Fixed criteria for classification
		All or none membership
	Formal or legal events (war, death, marriage)	Formally taught
Natural concepts	Everyday objects (Puddings, chairs, shoes, ships, toys)	Ill-defined
		Fuzzy boundaries
		No defining features
	Informal events (picnics, journeys, parties)	Gradient of typical to atypical members
	Abstract (art, freedom)	
		Variable criteria for classification
		Informally or spontaneously acquired

They are acquired by formal teaching, and membership of these categories is all-or-none. In contrast, natural concepts have no defining features, have fuzzy boundaries, are often learned spontaneously and informally, and members of these categories vary in typicality from good to poor examples.

All these considerations emphasize the extent of the gap that divides natural, everyday concepts from the red triangles and blue squares of the laboratory experiment. Although the studies of semantic memory reviewed in Chapter 2 were concerned with natural concepts, they have focussed on the structural relationships between concepts that have already been acquired, and not on the process of acquisition. We still know very little about the way people learn to categorize the real world around them.

Conceptual Behaviour

Besides employing simplified artificial concepts, traditional studies typically examine only a very restricted kind of conceptual behaviour. A typical experimental paradigm requires the subject to "learn" a concept like "a large red square". In fact the subject's task is not one of concept learning, concept formation or concept acquisition as these terms are normally used, because the subject already *has* the concept of a large red square. His task resembles problem solving more than concept formation. He has to discover which of the set of stimuli the experimenter has designated as positive instances for the purpose of the experiment. He has to identify the relevant attributes, and the relationship in which they are combined. How well does this experimental task correspond to conceptual behaviour in everyday life? The first stage in natural concept acquisition is often one of perceptual learning. Although we may be innately endowed with the perceptual capacity to discriminate between exemplars and nonexemplars of the concept, experience enhances this discriminatory power as we learn to identify, attend to and organize the relevant attributes of the stimulus. Subjectively, we have this experience when we learn to recognize the symbols of a foreign alphabet, to interpret the properties of cells seen under a microscope, or tell the difference between a genuine and a fake work of art. But when we "learn a concept" in everyday life, we usually learn a great deal more than the relevant attributes and how they are organized. We learn something about the relative importance of the defining attributes, so that we can still make a tentative classification of deviant or atypical instances. We learn how the context in which an instance is encountered may alter the weighting of defining attributes, and this will also help us to classify ambiguous or borderline cases. A pile of bricks is more likely to be considered as a work of art when encountered in a reputable gallery than on a building site. Also, instead of learning to differentiate a concept from a limited set of alternatives, we learn how it relates in terms of similarities and differences to all the other concepts we have already acquired. Everyday concepts are not learned in isolation. To learn a concept is to "place" it in our conceptual network, so that it relates, closely or distantly, to all the other concepts in the knowledge system. This is why we should hesitate to allow that someone has understood a concept like "inflation" if he could define it, and cite instances, but could not state the causes or the consequences.

Conceptual learning usually, but not necessarily, involves learning verbal labels. In the normal course of development children learn the appropriate names for the concepts they are in the process of acquiring. However, a child may acquire a concept long before he learns a name for it. The conceptual behaviour displayed in sorting tasks in Chapter 6 shows that, although grouping into functional classes, and grouping into superordinate classes tends to be associated with verbal labelling ability, grouping into concrete classes distinguished by physical features is independent of verbal ability. Both animals and language-handicapped humans can utilize simple physical concepts, and can learn conceptual relations like oddity rules, and conditional rules. In line with the assumptions made in models of semantic memory, concepts and conceptual relations are represented nonverbally, but can be mapped on to the linguistic system.

Just as there is a continuum of types of concepts, there is also a range of conceptual behaviour, which includes both nonverbal and verbal responses. When we acquire a concept we do not just learn to recognize and name instances, we may also develop emotional responses, and we learn to behave appropriately towards instances of the concept. So a cat which has the concept of "dog" can not only discriminate dogs from non-dogs, but may also experience fear, and respond with flight. The human who has learned the concept of "dog" can, in addition, make a variety of verbal responses including naming, defining and describing. The full repertoire of conceptual behaviour is not always present, so that we may sometimes be able to recognize and name an instance of a concept, but not give an adequate definition. In everyday life we have many concepts which are only partially acquired in this way, and the criteria for "having a concept" are ill defined. It is not at all clear which forms of conceptual behaviour should be taken to constitute evidence of conceptual learning. It is just this kind of confusion, which makes it difficult to decide (see pp. 154–156) when children have attained the concept of conservation. A more analytic approach to concept learning, which separates out different forms of conceptual behaviour, is likely to be helpful in dispelling some of the confusion.

Traditional Experimental Studies of Concept Formation

Because they are less relevant to cognition, traditional studies of concept formation are only briefly reviewed here. There are two serious drawbacks to the traditional experimental studies of concept formation. The first of these is the limited range of concepts and conceptual behaviour which have been examined, and the consequent limitations on the applicability of the findings to more natural situations. The second is that although experimental work has yielded lengthy lists of variables which have been shown to affect performance in concept-learning tasks, these variables are so numerous, and so interactive that, even within the highly restricted framework of the laboratory experiment, it has proved difficult to formulate law-like relations, and to predict the outcome of any given combination of variables.

Methods

Methodologically, researchers have concentrated on two experimental paradigms. In the reception paradigm, the experimenter presents a single stimulus item: the subject is asked to judge whether it is, or is not, a positive instance of the concept. Following his response, he is told whether or not he was correct. The experimenter then presents the next stimulus, and so on. Each sequence of stimulus, response and feedback constitutes a discrete trial. Trials continue until the subject is consistently responding correctly. In the selection paradigm, the entire population of stimuli is displayed simultaneously to the subject, and one item is designated as a positive instance of the concept. In order to discover how the concept is defined, the subject can select any other item in the display, and ask whether it is a positive instance of the concept or not. He continues selection until he can state the concept correctly. The main measure of performance, common to both methods, is the number of trials taken to reach solution. Solution is defined as the trial following the last error trial, or the trial preceding a correct statement of the concept. It is common practice to amalgamate the scores of groups of subjects, and plot the average number of errors made on each successive trial. Sometimes the speed of response on each trial is measured, and sometimes confidence ratings for successive trials are obtained by asking the subject to state the degree of his confidence in each response. If the researcher is interested in knowing what mental operations direct and accompany concept formation, then none of these measures gives much clue as to the subject's strategy, what hypotheses he has formed, and how he revises them in the light of the information he receives. The selection paradigm, however does allow the experimenter to form some idea of the subject's strategy by observing the pattern of his selections. Bruner *et al.*

(1956) detected four different strategies. In conservative focussing, the subject adopts an initial hypothesis that all the attributes of the positive instance are relevant, and tests it by selecting stimuli that differ in one attribute at a time. If the first positive instance is a small green square, then a large green square may be selected next, and if it also proves positive, then the subject can infer that size is not relevant. In focus gambling, instances are selected that differ in more than one attribute, e.g. a large red square may be selected. A lucky gamble results in quick accumulation of information. If the large red square is positive, then both colour and size are irrelevant, and shape emerges as the critical dimension. If the large red square proves negative, the gamble does not come off. Either size or colour must be relevant, and further tests are necessary to determine which. In scanning strategies, instead of testing for the relevance of the attributes, the subject entertains either a single hypothesis (successive scanning) or several hypotheses (simultaneous scanning) consistent with the positive instance, and revises these hypotheses in the light of information yielded by confirming or disconfirming instances. Scanning strategies impose a heavy load on memory, and require quite complex inferential reasoning. However although the selection paradigm will reveal the general pattern of the subject's choices, this is often not sufficient to allow us to infer his strategy in detail (Dominowski, 1974). Suppose, for example, that on Trial 1 the subject selects a large unfilled red circle, and is told "positive", and on Trial 2 he selects a small unfilled red circle. This response sequence is consistent with any or all of the following hypotheses: (1) size is the relevant dimension; (2) the concept is "any red circle"; and (3) the concept is "red unfilled figures". A potentially more informative technique is to ask the subject to report his current hypothesis after each trial, and do his thinking aloud, but this requirement often changes a subject's performance, forcing him to be more consistent and orderly. So we are still left with the problem of detecting what strategy the subject would employ if a vocal self-commentary was not required. To characterize performance in conceptual tasks adequately, measures of efficiency like the number of trials to solution, need to be combined with observations and inferences about the subject's hypothesis formation, so that it is clear not only what he is doing, but how and why he is doing it.

Neither the reception nor the selection paradigm bear much resemblance to the way concepts are learned in everyday life, where it is rare to encounter a series of exemplars, and contrasting nonexemplars in close succession, or in a simultaneous array. More often, exemplars are encountered at considerable intervals, and nonexemplars are classified as positive instances of different categories, rather than being simply excluded from one particular category. Learning to make classifications is, moreover, often incidental to other ongoing tasks rather than being the main focus of attention.

Experimental variables

Experiments using reception and selecting paradigms have established the importance of the characteristics of the concept, and of the way it is presented in determining ease of learning. More complex concepts are harder to learn. The complexity of a concept is defined by the number of relevant attributes; the number of irrelevant attributes; the number of possible values of each attribute; and whether the attributes are correlated, or independent of each other. Relevant attributes are more easily learned if they are salient and attention-catching, so bright colour or large size may make a concept more discriminable. Many of these stimulus factors are also likely to interact with the subject's strategy. Although this has not been systematically explored, the effect of number of dimensions, for example, would depend on whether the subject was trying to test the relevance of each dimension separately, or adopting a holistic strategy.

Another variable which is a powerful determinant of ease of learning is the type of rule, or conceptual principle, whereby the attributes are combined. If two attributes, A and B, are relevant to the concept, the rule may be conjunctive (A and B), disjunctive (A or B) or conditional (If A then B). More complex rules are relational ones (e.g. A above B, or the odd one of a set); rules containing negations (e.g. A and not B); or multiple rules [e.g. (A and B) or (A and C)]. The usual finding is that conjunctive rules are easiest to learn, and disjunctive and relational rules are about equally difficult (Bruner *et al.* 1956; Hunt and Hovland, 1960). Probabilistic concepts (sometimes but not always, A and B) are also more difficult than deterministic ones. Multiple concepts increase in difficulty with each increment in structural complexity (Neisser and Weene, 1962). Differences in rule difficulty may be partly attributable to biases established in everyday experience, which appear to favour the conjunctive principle, and these tend to lessen with practice (Haygood and Bourne, 1965). Rule difficulty also varies with the subject's strategy, and the order in which he encounters positive and negative instances.

Procedural factors, such as the sequence and timing of presentation, also affect the ease of learning. Learning is faster if positive instances are encountered early in the sequence, either close together, or alternating with contrasting negative instances, and giving subjects information about the correctness of their responses facilitates learning. Poor performance is often due to forgetting. The difficulty of concept learning is partly attributable to the memory load imposed by the task. In the reception paradigm, the subject must retain the information derived from each trial over the succeeding trials. When the method is modified to allow previous stimuli to remain on view, the memory load is lightened, and the solution is reached earlier. In the selection paradigm, although all the stimuli remain available for inspection, the subject still has to remember which have been classified as positive instances, and which as negative ones. Bruner *et al.* (1956) forced subjects to solve a selection problem in their heads, without being able to view the array. Significant changes in performance occurred. Selections were less systematic, and sometimes repetitive. The scanning strategy, which imposes a greater memory load, was, under these conditions, less efficient than the focussing strategy.

In addition to stimulus factors, and procedural factors, concept learning is also affected by the nature of the learner. Besides individual differences in strategies, which are discussed in more detail later, differences of age, sex, IQ, motivation, stress, previous experience, species and language ability are all known to influence the efficiency of concept learning. Thus even when the researcher restricts his studies to laboratory experiments in which the stimulus variables and procedural variables are controlled as carefully as possible, these individual differences contribute a further source of variability, making it difficult to discern any general laws of concept learning.

Theories of Concept Formation

While the theories of concept learning that have been proposed are in principle testable, and open to refutation, in practice it is difficult to decide which is most acceptable, because each will fit some of the data some of the time. Enough has already been said about the large number of variables that affect concept-learning tasks for it to be evident that any single theory of concept learning will be unlikely to account for all of them. The general applicability of any theory is further limited by the individual differences in concept learning which are described in more detail in the section on hypothesis-testing models. A broad distinction can be made between earlier associationist theories which view the concept learner as passively undergoing a series of experiences which bring about changes in behaviour reflecting learning, and later hypothesis-testing theories which characterize the concept learner as actively engaged in processing information, forming, testing and revising hypotheses, sifting possibilities, rejecting and deciding. While the former provide a mechanistic account of the concept-learning process in quasi-physiological terms, the latter give a mentalist description. Since the two kinds of theory are thus at different levels of description, direct comparisons between them can hardly be formulated. The passive v. active distinction is really based on a confusion of these levels. We are all "passive" at the neuronal level, and we are all "active" at the mentalist decision-making level. The choice of a particular level of description, and so the theoretical bias of a given researcher, has been largely influenced by the psychological climate of the era in which his opinions were formed. Those nurtured in the post-1950s tradition of "cognitive" psychology have tended to prefer the active hypothesis-testing models.

While earlier theories were developed to account for the performance of laboratory subjects learning artificial concepts, more recent theories are concerned with how natural concepts are learned in real world situations. The type of concept, and the type of mental representation that is postulated necessarily constrain the nature of the learning process. For artificial concept learning, feature analytic theories of one kind or another predominate; for natural concepts some alternatives to feature comparisons have been proposed.

Feature analytic models

Both the S–R associationist theories and the hypothesis testing theories outlined below assume that a concept is a set of features, and that during learning the relevant features and the rule relating them, are abstracted from the instances. The features that are abstracted may be a set of defining features, or a set of sufficient features.

S–R associationist theories According to this type of theory, concept learning is a form of discrimination learning whereby the relevant attributes of positive instances of the concept are progressively associated with a positive response, and the attributes of negative instances are associated with a negative response. The process is complicated by the presence of irrelevant attributes which may sometimes be associated with positive examples, and sometimes with negative examples. Since these attributes receive inconsistent reinforcement they are gradually neutralized (Bourne and Restle, 1959), while, because all positive instances have some degree of similarity to each other, the S–R connections generalize to novel examples of the concept. If stimulus generalization is the underlying mechanism of concept learning, then learning should occur more rapidly if the positive instances are very similar to each other, and very different from the negative instances, especially if the negative instances also form a fairly homogeneous class. Empirical findings confirm this prediction. Difficulties with the S–R account of concept learning centre around the nature of the stimulus, and the nature of the reinforcement. Many of the kinds of natural concepts discussed earlier in this chapter do not appear to possess any common attributes which could become associated to a common response.

This is true of functional, superordinate and abstract concepts, and also of the rule-based concepts like "the odd item in a set". This problem has led to a revised version of S–R associationism, which introduces an internal mediating stage intervening between the stimulus and the response. Some of the experimental findings concerning the effects of informative feedback are also difficult to accommodate within the S–R theory. If feedback functions as reinforcement, then it is surprising that delaying the feedback has little effect on rate of learning. The effects of the order of positive and negative trials are also more in keeping with an information processing account, than with an S–R model.

Mediation theory is a more complex form of associationism, designed to overcome the problem of finding a common factor to link physically disparate stimuli to the same conceptual response. A common internal mediating response is postulated to link the various instances of, say, food, to a common response. Mediators may be nonverbal, like the "fractional eating response" which, according to Osgood (1952) is elicited by any type of food, and is in turn associated with an overt behavioural response. More commonly, mediators are characterized as covert verbal labels. Fractional

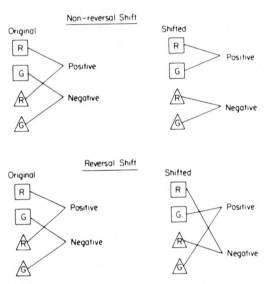

FIG. 14. *Above: the concept shifts from Red = Positive to Square = Positive (an extra-dimensional shift). Half the stimuli change from positive to negative or vice versa. Below: the concept shifts from Red = Positive to Green = Positive (an intra dimensional shift). All the stimuli change.*
   S–R theory → Reversal shift is harder, because more pairs are changed.
   Mediation theory → Non-reversal shift is harder, because the mediator (the dimension name) is changed.

responses, and other internal symbols, such as images, are less plausible as mediators for concepts such as "oddity" or "equivalence". A striking advantage of mediation theory is that the internal mediators can substitute for external stimuli, and so allow the possibility of de-contextualized conceptual behaviour in the absence of physical stimuli. We can think and talk about cabbages and kings quite as well when none are around.

Mediation theory and simple unmediated S–R theory generate different predictions about the effect of changing an experimental concept. In Fig. 14, two kinds of change, or shift, are shown for stimuli which vary in colour and shape. In the nonreversal shift, the critical attribute shifts from red to square. This is called an *extra-dimensional shift*, since the relevant dimension changes from colour to shape. In this case some, but not all, the stimuli change from positive to negative, or vice versa. The reversal shift changes the relevant value from red to green within the same dimension, and so is called an *intra-dimensional shift*. The red stimuli become negative, and the green ones positive. This produces a situation in which all the originally positive examples change to negative and vice versa. Mediation theory predicts that the extra-dimensional nonreversal shift should be more difficult, because the name of the critical dimension mediates the response, and the shift necessitates a change of mediator. In the intra-dimensional reversal shift, the same mediator, "colour", can be retained. Unmediated S–R theory predicts the opposite. The intra-dimensional shift should be more difficult, because each individual S–R connection has to be undone and re-made. The experimental results show that in most cases animals, young children and slow learners behave according to the unmediated S–R theory prediction. Adult humans and older children behave as if they use verbal mediation (Kendler and Kendler, 1962). The difference in the relative difficulty of the two kinds of shift has been attributed by the Kendlers to the development of language ability which allows verbal mediation to be used, but Slamecka (1968) has pointed out that the extra-dimensional shift may be harder for reasons not connected with the use of verbal mediation. He pointed out that when only a subset of the stimuli change from positive to negative it is harder to detect that a shift has occurred, and the post-shift pattern of reinforcement is more inconsistent. However, if extradimensional shifts are intrinsically more difficult, this is hard to reconcile with the fact that younger children find them easier than intra-dimensional shifts. It is not at all clear whether these age-related changes in conceptual behaviour are due to language development, or to some other aspect of cognitive growth.

Hypothesis-testing models These models assume that subjects form hypotheses about the concept, but in fact such hypotheses may not be very different from mediating responses, since a simple hypothesis might be "shape is the critical attribute". Since people cannot always state what hypotheses, if any, they are currently entertaining, it is further assumed that hypothesis testing may occur at an unconscious level, and this provision makes the distinction between hypothesis testing and verbal mediation somewhat hazy. However, according to H-testing models, people pursue a definite information-seeking strategy which is guided by their current hypotheses. This assumption can be partially justified because, at least some of the time, subjects can describe their strategies, and, at least some of the time, their responses show a consistent pattern, most clearly evident in the selection paradigm. H-testing may be a more difficult strategy in the reception paradigm, especially if the concept is complex, and the memory load is excessive.

Bruner *et al.* (1956) described the focussing and scanning strategies that subjects apparently were adopting in their selection task. More precise versions of these strategies have since been formulated. Restle (1962) distinguished several possibilities. A subject may select one hypothesis from the total pool of possible hypotheses, and operate on the principle of Win–Stay–Lose–Shift. That is, he retains the hypothesis if his response was correct, but discards it and selects another if his response turned out to be an error. Alternatively, he may test several hypotheses simultaneously. There are also different views as to the fate of the discarded hypotheses. A disconfirmed hypothesis may be returned to the pool of hypotheses remaining to be sampled, or it may be eliminated from the pool. Restle has shown that these two possibilities yield the same mathematical predictions as to the probable number of errors before solution.

Intuitively, a no-memory model whereby people fail to eliminate disconfirmed hypotheses is unconvincing, and evidence for the role of memory in concept learning has already been cited. Bower and Trabasso (1964) developed a no-memory model of sampling-with-replacement, the disconfirmed hypotheses being replaced in the pool, so that they are still available for re-sampling. Data from a simple concept learning task showed that the probability of error responses remained stationary up until the last error, and so appeared to reflect an abrupt transition from no-learning to learning, that is, an all-or-none type of learning, rather than a gradual incremental progress from chance responding towards complete solution. This all-or-none pattern is consistent with a total pool of alternative hypotheses remaining constant in size, because no progressive elimination occurs. The probability of selecting the correct alternative therefore remains constant, whereas if the pool steadily diminished as each disconfirmed hypothesis was eliminated from it, then the probability of sampling the correct hypothesis would steadily increase. Later experiments

(Levine, 1962; Trabasso and Bower, 1966) refuted the all-or-none sampling-with-replacement model by showing that misinformative feedback prior to solution did delay learning. If the subject had learned nothing during the pre-solution trials, random reinforcement at this stage should have no effect. This finding has necessitated modification of the original sampling-with-replacement model. In the modified version, subjects do reject disconfirmed hypotheses, but, because of the limited capacity of working memory, they fail to keep track of all the discarded alternatives, which may therefore, after an interval, creep back into the pool of hypotheses remaining to be sampled. That is, the subject forgets which hypotheses he has already tested and found to be wrong. The size of the pool may then still be fairly constant since it would consist of the number of untested hypotheses, plus the reinstated hypotheses, minus those discarded hypotheses that can be held in memory. A model which incorporates a limited and imperfect memory is much more plausible than one which permits memory to play no part at all. In general, the all-or-none model applies best to identification of very simple unidimensional concepts. When concepts are multidimensional it is possible to have a partial solution—to have learned some, but not all, of the critical attributes, and so be progressing towards the solution. When several hypotheses are tested simultaneously, it may be possible to reject several at once, so that the probability of solution is increased. Erikson *et al.* (1966) showed that response latencies decrease as the subject nears solution, and inferred that this reflected the decreasing size of the set of hypotheses remaining to be tested, selection of a new hypothesis being faster from a smaller pool. More detailed scrutiny of response patterns also has suggested that Win–Stay–Lose–Shift is too simple a way to characterize the subject's strategy. The models of Restle (1962) and of Bower and Trabasso (1964) assumed that learning occurred only on error trials, because a current hypothesis was unchanged after a correct response. Levine (1966) showed that subjects did use the information gained from positive feedback after a correct response to eliminate other hypotheses, as yet untested, that were inconsistent with this information. So what appears to be a simple example of Win–Stay can involve covert changes, with consequences on trials later in the series. Erikson *et al.* (1966) also found that response latencies continue to decrease in post-solution trials, when all the responses are necessarily correct, as the subject grows more confident.

Dominowski (1974) has pointed out that the empirical evidence is too inconsistent to give conclusive support for any one model of concept learning, and that model builders have tended to make two false assumptions. One is the assumption that the same strategy would be employed by different subjects; and the second is that the same strategy would be employed in different situations. By monitoring the performance of individual subjects, Dominowski was able to detect a striking variety of strategies between different subjects, and also strategy-shifting by individuals in the course of the task. Asking subjects to think aloud revealed that some subjects reached solution by guessing, without adequate evidence. Some tested one hypothesis at a time, and others reported they were trying to test multiple hypotheses simultaneously. Some subjects ignored negative feedback, and behaved like those in Wason's number series experiment (Chapter 7, p. 182) persisting in re-testing hypotheses that had been disconfirmed. Others tried with varying success to use both positive and negative feedback.

Commenting on the lack of uniformity exhibited by his subjects Dominowski concludes "This state of affairs not only casts doubt on any theory assuming a common strategy for all subjects, but also raises the question of whether this kind of theory is useful". As a result of his salutary observation it seems likely that future research on concept learning will abandon the attempt to produce general models, and will yield alternative models for different strategies, and different types of task.

Rosch: Prototype Theory

The idea that concepts are represented as prototypes (Rosch, 1975, 1978; Rosch and Mervis, 1975; Rosch *et al.*, 1976) has been an important influence on current thinking about concepts. Rosch has been concerned to question and revise some of the assumptions underlying the models of semantic memory and semantic processing described in Chapter 2. Although these models have mainly concentrated on describing the structural relations *between* concepts, they also make some assumptions about the internal structure of these concepts. Both the network, and the set–theoretic models, assume that concepts consist of lists or sets of features. We noted that models such as that of Smith *et al.* (1974) make the further assumption that these features can be divided into those that are criterial or defining, and those that are merely characteristic. One difficulty in applying this model to natural concepts is that the defining features of many common categories are unknown or nonexistent. We classify chairs, toys and puddings without being able to produce a list of defining features. Rosch's proposal that natural concepts are represented as prototypes, rather than as lists of features, avoids this paradox. This line of thinking owes much to a second source—the work on schema formation carried out by Posner and Keele (1968, 1970). They showed that people are able to abstract and store a schema, or prototype, representing the central tendencies of a set of patterns. Their experiments involved random forms such as dot patterns, and showed that subjects could accurately classify prototypes which they had never seen, but which exhibited the central tendencies of sets of patterns they had previously learned to classify. Moreover, subjects tended to believe that they had actually experienced the prototype patterns before, and recognized them better than the patterns they had seen. Posner and Keele also demonstrated that the nature of the stored prototype varies. When the subjects had learned a classification over a set of patterns that were highly variable (a loose concept), they were better able to recognize new deviant instances. Initial experience with a set of patterns of low variability produced a tight concept, and high rejection of deviant instances. The authors speculate that the learned memory representation involves both a central tendency or prototype, and a boundary. The concept boundaries may be more or less generous.

The novel aspect of Rosch's work is the application of Prototype Theory to natural concepts. Prototype Theory is designed to take account of several aspects of natural concepts that are difficult for conventional feature list theories to handle. These are: (1) It is difficult to list the defining features of natural concepts. (2) Natural concepts have fuzzy boundaries, rather than clear-cut divisions between them. (3) Not all members of a category are equally good examples. Instances can be ordered along a dimension of typicality ranging from good examples to poor examples, with poor examples lying in the fuzzy area at the borderline between categories.

Rosch's theory borrows from Wittgenstein's notion of Family Resemblances, whereby category members are related by a network of overlapping similarities, in which members of the same family need not necessarily have any features in common, and no set of features is common to all and only the members of that category (Wittgenstein, 1953).

What is a prototype? The prototype of a category is the central tendency of the set of instances of that category. In effect, the prototype has most of the attributes that are common to most members of the category, and fewest of the attributes of nonmembers of the category. In Rosch's terminology, the prototype has the highest cue validity. Cue validity is a measure increasing with the frequency of a given cue, or attribute, being associated with the category, and decreasing with the frequency of that cue being associated with other categories. Hence the prototype is a construct, combining the features with greatest cue validity. In addition to the prototype, a concept is mentally represented by a distance dimension along which category members are ordered by degree of typicality. Rosch explicitly states that the prototype should not be confused with any specific category member. It is not a mental object, and Rosch disclaims (1978) any intention of tying Prototype Theory to any particular form of mental representation. Prototypes could be represented as feature lists, as structural descriptions, or as images. Nor does Rosch make any claims about the nature of the matching operations for judging category membership, or about the nature of the learning processes whereby the prototype is acquired, although in fact Prototype Theory does place some constraints on the process of acquisition. Because these operational consequences of Prototype Theory are not spelled out, it is difficult to evaluate.

Experimental evidence. Prototype Theory has received some experimental confirmation. One series of experiments confirms the existence of reference points or prototypes for natural categories, with instances being arranged in order of deviation from the prototype. In one paradigm, subjects were asked to place pairs of stimuli into the empty slots of sentence frames consisting of linguistic "hedges" (see Lakoff, 1972). Examples of such hedges are "— is essentially —", "Loosely speaking, — is —". The hedges express varying degrees of relatedness between two items whereby the first is classified in terms of the second, which thus constitutes the reference point. In Rosch's experiment, stimuli were drawn from the categories of colour, line orientation and number. Placing of pairs drawn from within these categories revealed four colours as focal (e.g. the placing *"orange* is roughly *red"* shows red to be the focal reference point); horizontal, vertical and diagonal as focal orientations; and multiples of ten as focal numbers. The results were consistent across large numbers of subjects. Indeed, focal colours appear to be the same for many different cultures and languages, although the boundaries of the colour names vary. Rosch believes that basic physical categories of colour and form, which are physiologically determined, are universal and invariant for all cultures. Another experiment in which subjects placed stimuli at a physical distance from each other, so as to represent their psychological distance, revealed continua of resemblance. Rosch has also shown that the mental representations of colour categories as prototypes have psychological reality by a series of "priming" experiments. In one experiment subjects had to judge pairs of colours same or different. Colour judgements were facilitated if the name of a focal colour was given first as a prime and the colours subsequently presented for judgement were "good" examples of the category (that is, ones that closely resembled the prototype). Similar results were obtained for other semantic categories such as furniture and fruit. Prepriming the prototypes facilitated classification of "good" instances. For example, giving the category name "Birds" first, facilitated the decision that a pair like "robin–sparrow" are both members of the same category. If the items were atypical examples like "ostrich–penguin", then priming the bird prototype did not facilitate the judgement.

According to Rosch, the psychological reality of prototypes is reflected in children's concept learning. Rosch claims that good examples of categories are learned earlier, and that children have initially tight category bound-aries, being reluctant to include poor examples, but this sequence of development is inconsistent with the overgeneralization phenomenon described in the next section.

The most convincing support for Rosch's Prototype Theory comes from an experiment in which subjects were presented with a number of categories, and with a list of members of each category, and were asked to rate each example for typicality. So subjects rated items like "bed, chair, cupboard, etc." according to how typical of the "furniture" category they were judged to be. Subjects were also asked to list the attributes of each item. The results showed a striking correlation such that items rated high for typicality possessed more of those attributes most widely shared with other members of the category, and fewer attributes not shared with other members. Experiments have demonstrated that more typical examples are faster to categorize, easier to prime, more readily learned, and more likely to be produced when subjects are asked to list instances. Taken together these results provide considerable support for the psychological reality of Prototype Theory.

Levels of categorization. As a corollary of Prototype Theory, Rosch has stressed the importance of level of categorization, and asserted the predominance of what she calls the Basic Level (Rosch *et al.*, 1976). Categories are hierarchically nested with the Basic Level occupying a stratum midway between the superordinate and the subordinate levels. Basic Level categories are distinguished by their greater cue validity. At a superordinate level such as "furniture", there are relatively few attributes that are common to all members of the class. At the subordinate level, such as "Chippendale dining chair" there are many attributes shared by all members of the class, but there is also a substantial overlap with other classes, such as Sheraton or Hepplewhite chairs, so the cue validity is reduced. The intermediate Basic Level "chair" is where the within class overlap is maximized, and the between-class overlap is minimized, so cue validity is highest. Because they are more discriminable, Basic Level categories are easiest to learn, and in naming objects or pictures, people normally tend to produce Basic Level terms rather than superordinate or subordinate ones. If Rosch is correct, most of our thinking goes on at the Basic Level.

Rosch claims that Basic Level categories are learned first by young children, although Brown's observations (see p. 90) suggest that this is not always true. She also maintains that in condensed systems, such as sign languages, Basic Levels predominate, and the super- and subordinate class names are sometimes missing. Rosch believes that Basic Level categories

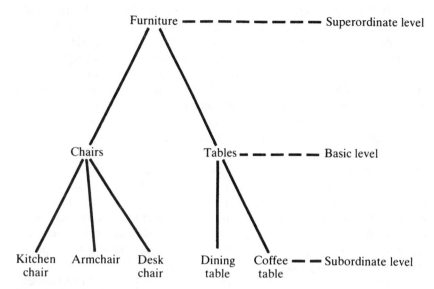

FIG. 15. *Levels of categorization.*

such as "chairs" are also distinguished behaviourally. Objects belonging to these categories invoke similar actions such as "sitting on", while higher-level categories such as "furniture" do not produce common motor responses. She asserts that visual shape similarities are greater within the Basic Level categories, all chairs being roughly similar in shape, while different pieces of furniture can be highly dissimilar. A consequence of this global similarity of shape is that Basic Level categories may be more easily represented as a visual image. However, it is not difficult to think of counter-examples. Objects from different categories like oranges, balls and globes are more similar in shape than oranges and bananas; and a motor response such as "polishing" may be common to most instances of furniture for some people. Rosch implies that the Basic Level is the product of perceptual and behavioural habits and capacities, acting in conjunction with principles of cognitive economy. Yet it is worth pointing out that the preferred level is not necessarily the same for everyone, but depends also on cognitive demands, and on expertise. For antique-dealers, and for botanists, expert knowledge and task demands probably make the sub-ordinate levels preferable.

Problems with Prototype Theory. Some objections that have been raised result from misconceptions. Weisberg (1980) criticizes the theory on the grounds that the general idea of a class such as "dogs" becomes indistinguishable from the particular when the prototypical representation may correspond to a particular exemplar of the class such as a labrador. This objection is invalid, however, since the prototype is not to be equated with any particular instance, but is simply the central tendency of the class. According to Osherson and Smith (1981) problems arise when Prototype Theory is applied to complex concepts such as "pet fish", where an exemplar like "guppy" may be highly prototypical of the combined concept, but rate low in typicality within each of the constituent concepts ("pet" and "fish"). Further problems in stating the truth conditions for inclusion or exclusion of instances prompted Osherson and Smith to suggest that judgements of category membership may be made by comparison with the prototype when only a rough and ready classification is called for, but that defining features need to be invoked for more exact and formal matching. So, for example, in an everyday social situation, a girl might be classified as a child because of resemblance to a prototypical child, but in a legal setting a more precise criterion for defining a child would be applied.

Because Prototype Theory does not specify boundary conditions dividing one conceptual classification from another, it does not provide any way to make hard and fast decisions about doubtful cases. In Rosch's model, membership of a category is determined both by similarity to the prototype, and by dissimilarity to other contrasting categories. When an item falls in the fuzzy area where category boundaries overlap, it is classified as a member of that category whose protype it most resembles. Classification will therefore be liable to vary with the context. In conformity with this model, McCloskey and Glucksberg (1978) found that subjects disagreed with each other, and were sometimes unable to decide at all, on a classification for some common objects like "pillow" or "curtain". When boundary conditions are not specified, judgements are fuzzy and fluctuating for these borderline cases.

Models that do specify defining features as the boundary conditions have the advantage, at least in principle, of providing a way to classify atypical or borderline cases clearly and unambiguously. In practice, however, as already noted, it may be difficult to identify what the defining features are, and people may be unable to decide on a classification. Prototype theory is closer to everyday usage. However, it is possible to argue that everyday judgements about everyday objects are made by reference to prototypes and these fuzzy judgements are quite adequate for fuzzy concepts. But other concepts, such as technical, biological and legal ones are not fuzzy; they do have defining features, and defining feature tests can be used to make classifications. In a computer simulation of concept learning (Winston, 1973), the concepts were well-defined arrangements of blocks such as an arch or pedestal. In this model, learning was most efficient if the boundary was defined by presenting near miss examples (see Fig. 16). The program was able to deduce essential features from the near misses. For the arch, two blocks must stand in "support" relation to a third, and the two support blocks must have a space between. Learning boundary conditions is a good way to learn concepts, but only if the boundaries are well-defined. Fuzzy concepts could not be learned in this way. To adopt this position is to argue that Prototype Theory and Feature Comparison Theory both hold good, but in different conceptual domains.

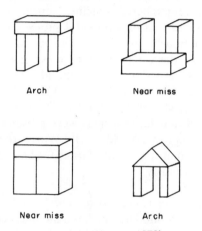

Arch   Near miss

Near miss   Arch

FIG. 16. *An arch training sequence (from Winston, 1973).*

Rosch's work has been a landmark in the study of concepts, in spite of the criticisms that have been made. However, a particular weakness of the theory is underlined by the fact that it is difficult to see how prototypes are originally acquired. Intuitively, it seems that it would be near-impossible for young children to extract central tendencies from a set of instances. The memory load would be severe, since the whole set of instances experienced would have to be held in mind and reviewed, in order to determine the feature distribution for the set.

Brooks: The Instance Comparison model

An alternative account of natural concept formation has been put forward by Brooks (1978). Instead of a complicated process of analysing instances and extracting common features, or calculating the frequency of feature representation, Brooks suggests that concepts are formed implicitly and nonanalytically without conscious hypothesizing. He believes that many natural concepts are too complex to be learned analytically, and that testing for the presence of criterial features is a cumbersome way to assess category membership. According to Brooks's model, having learned to identify one instance of a category, later instances can be identified by overall global similarity to the known instance. This Instance Comparison model has the advantage of providing an account of a way in which children could acquire concepts that would be within their cognitive capacities. By this method, instances can be recognized even if they involve concepts with very complex feature combination rules, and even if the learner has encountered only a few instances, and has an imperfect memory of them. It would be possible, for example, to recognize an orchid because it roughly resembled a vaguely remembered specimen encountered once before. Brooks has demonstrated that experimental subjects may learn concepts intuitively and unconsciously, and be able to identify instances without being able to verbalize the categorization rules, or specify the defining attributes. His subjects learned to pair structured letter strings with names of cities or animals (e.g. VVTRXRR—Paris, MRRRRRM—bison). They were unaware that these stimuli could be classified as New World or Old World items, yet when new letter strings were presented, and they were asked to classify these as New World or Old World, they performed with 60–65% accuracy. They had apparently learned the basis of the classification incidentally and unconsciously.

Modifications of the Instance Comparison model. Medin and Smith (1981) have put forward a Context model, which is a modified version of Brooks's Instance Comparison model. Just as in Brooks's model, a new instance is compared analogically with a previously encountered instance stored in memory, and the category membership of the new instance is inferred from degree of similarity. The stored representation may, in the Context model, be modified to include analytic information. So an oak may be classified as a tree by virtue of its overall similarity to a stored representation of another tree such as a beech, and analytic information about trees stored with the representation of "beech" is accessed at the same time. Medin and Smith designed experiments to test whether subjects learning a classification were performing in accordance with the Context model, or in accordance with Prototype Theory. The Context model, like Instance Comparison, predicts that ease of classification depends on the degree of similarity between novel instances and previously learned instances. Prototype Theory predicts that the distance of the novel instance from the prototype, rather than similarity to any particular known instance will determine ease of classification. In the experiments distance and similarity were separately manipulated, and, since similarity turned out to be the most important determinant of performance, the results supported the Context model.

A similar approach was adopted by Elio and Anderson (1981), who examined the effects of similarity, and order of presentation. They found that performance was facilitated by inter-item similarity indicating that subjects were using an Instance Comparison strategy; but they also found that performance benefited from a blocked order of presentation designed to make generalization easier. They concluded that subjects form general rules, and use a generalization strategy as well. According to their results, people might store known instances of dogs (e.g. Rover, Fido, etc.) together with a generalization (e.g. Dogs have four legs, are furry, can bark). Novel instances could then be identified either by application of the general rule, or by comparison with Rover or Fido. Homa *et al.* (1981) also reached the conclusion that alternative strategies are employed in concept acquisition. They confirmed the beneficial effects of item similarity, but noted that these diminished if set size increased, and if a delay was interposed between the original learning and presentation of the novel instances. Under these conditions, performance conformed to the Prototype Theory, with ease of classification being determined by distance from the central tendency.

Figure 17 shows the three main theories of concept formation that have been discussed in this section. They represent alternatives that can easily co-exist to form a battery of strategies. It appears that different strategies may be selected depending on the nature of the concept, and the degree of learning; and the existence of different strategies implies the existence of different types of mental representation. What is needed now is more detailed and precise information about the factors that govern the nature of the representation, and the processes of learning and matching.

ACQUISITION	MENTAL REPRESENTATION	CLASSIFICATION
By abstraction of features	Defining feature list ⎫ Characteristic feature ⎬ list ⎭	By feature testing
By construction	Prototype	By measuring distance from prototype
By collecting instances	A known example	By instance comparison

FIG. 17. *Theories of concept formation.*

Developmental Studies of Concept Formation

Levels of categorization

At what level of categorization does a child first classify objects? Brown (1958) in his paper *How shall a thing be called?* tackled the problem of the relationship between the child's use of names, his conceptual categories, and the objects in the world. The complexity of this relationship has also been pointed out by Olson (1970), who noted that a single word may have multiple referents (e.g. the word "eye" can be applied to visual sense organs, needles, potatoes, etc.), and that a single referent may have several possible labels (e.g. a person may be labelled as George, father, husband, lawyer, man, etc.). Brown's informal observations suggested to him that the particular labels which are learned first by the young child are selected for him by adults, and the choice is governed by a number of factors. In general, brief words that are easier for the child to reproduce are preferred to longer ones (so "dog" would be supplied in preference to "quadruped"). The brevity principle may be over-ridden by frequency. Since bananas are more often referred to as bananas than as fruit, or food, the label "bananas" is supplied. Other principles are utility and economy. The child is taught "flower" before he learns to distinguish daffodils and tulips, and "money" before he learns the names of individual coins. He does not need to make fine botanical distinctions or financial reckonings. The growth of vocabulary may therefore proceed from subordinate to superordinate class labels (bananas and apples before fruit), or from superordinate to subordinate (car before Ford and Mercedes). Labels for the highest superordinate classes like "substance" or "artefact" do not appear in the young child's vocabulary, though Brown's argument that they are ruled out on grounds of nonutility and infrequency may be only partly correct, and the major factor that dictates their late acquisition could be their complexity and abstractness. Brown's observations do undermine both the view that children's conceptual development proceeds from initially wide, undifferentiated categories by progressive differentiation and refinement towards the acquisition of narrower specific subcategories, and the opposite view that children begin with specific lower order categories, and by progressive abstraction of similarities build upwards to acquire general higher-order categories. His examples demonstrate that vocabulary growth can proceed in either direction. These observations also run counter to Rosch's claim that children learn Basic Level categories first, although a larger and more systematic corpus of first words would be required to assess the validity of Brown's arguments.

Olson (1970) lists some additional factors which govern the choice of the most suitable lexical label for making unambiguous reference. Important among these are the context of perception, and the context of communication. "Flower" is an adequate label for a given item when all the other items in the perceptual context are non-flowers, but it is not an adequate identifying label in a garden full of flowers. If the label is to serve a communicative function, the set of alternatives for the listener must be inferred by the speaker. The child who says that he lives "in the white house" may succeed in conveying his home location to a listener who lives in the neighbourhood, but not to a stranger. The child must learn to select the level of categorization required to make unambiguous reference in a given context.

Other researchers have been more concerned to discover how children learn and represent concepts than with the choice of level. Again several different theories have been proposed. There are two important aspects of children's conceptual behaviour that any theory must account for. Firstly, the suggested learning process must be one which is not impossibly difficult with the limited cognitive resources of the young child. Secondly, it must explain the phenomenon of overgeneralization whereby young children commonly overextend words so that, for example, they call all men "Daddy", or all four-legged animals "cows".

Feature abstraction theories

Several theories are based on the assumption that the child learns concepts by abstracting common features from the instances he encounters, but there is disagreement about what kind of features are abstracted first.

E. Clark (1973) proposed that children learn word meanings by observing the situations in which adults use a particular word, and abstracting the semantic features. At first, only a few of the relevant semantic features are learned, so the child's use of the word lacks some constraints, and is consequently overextended. Gradually more semantic features are accumulated and the scope of the word is progressively restricted to conform to normal usage. According to Clark, the features that are abstracted in the early stages of learning are predominantly perceptual.

Nelson (1974) emphasizes the fact that the child begins to acquire concepts before words, having a good deal of information about actions and functions before he has learned to talk. In Nelson's view, functional features predominate in early conceptual learning, and perceptual features are added later. Initially, the child groups objects according to the common actions that are associated with them. So objects that can be rolled or bounced like balls, oranges, and beads are classed together, and the words are extended (or overextended) to objects with similar functions.

Anglin (1976) is ranged on the side of those who believe that perceptual features are abstracted first. When he asked children to describe concepts, he found that the type of information they produced appeared in the order of (1) what it looks like; (2) what it does; (3) how it is used; and (4) where it is found. Experimental tests and observations to determine whether perceptual features or functional features have priority have mostly supported the "perceptual features first" hypothesis, although sorting tasks have yielded mixed results. Nelson found that children aged 19–22 months sorted objects into groups according to function. The fact that these children could

TABLE 2. Overextensions taken from Diary Studies by E. Clark (1973).

Source	Item	First referent	Extensions and overextensions in order of occurrence
Kenyeres (1926)	titi	animals	> (pictures of animals)>(things that move)
Leopold (1949)	sch	sound of train	> (all moving machines)
Pavlovitch (1920)	dzin-dzin	moving train	> (train itself)>(journey by train)
Pavlovitch (1920)	tutu	train	> (engines)>(moving train)>(journey)
Schulte (cited in Prayer, 1889)	ass	goat with rough hide on wheels	> (things that move, e.g., animals, sister, wagon)>(all moving things)> (all things with a rough surface)
Chamberlain and Chamberlain (1904)	mooi	moon	> (cakes)>(round marks on window) >(writing on window and in books) >(round shapes in books)>(tooling on leather book covers)>(round postmark)>(letter O)
Guillaume (1927)	nenin (breast)	breast, food	> (button on garment)>(point of bare elbow)>(eye in portrait)>(face of person in photograph)
Idelberger (1903)	bow-wow	dog	> (fur piece with glass eyes)>(father's cuff links)>(pearl buttons on dress) >(bath thermometer)
Leopold (1949)	tick-tock	watch	> (clocks)>(all clocks and watches)> (gas-meter)>(fire hose wound on spool)>(bath scale with round dial)
Pavlovitch (1920)	bébé	reflection of child (self) in mirror	> (photograph of self)>(all photographs)>(all pictures)>(all books with pictures)>(all books)
Rasmussen (1922)	vov-vov	dog	> (kitten)>(hens)>(all animals at zoo) >(picture of pigs dancing)
Kenyeres (1926)	baba	baby	> (adults in pictures)>(pictures in books)
Moore (1896)	fly	fly	> (specks of dirt)>(dust)>(all small insects)>(his own toes)>(crumbs of bread)>(a toad)

form groups for which they had no verbal labels also supported her contention that concept learning is initially nonlinguistic. With even younger infants, Starkey (1981) was able to infer their principles of classification by observing sequential touching of objects. Children of 6, 9 and 12 months were given sets of objects such as four yellow cubes and four blue balls; or four red squares and four red balls. The 9- and 12-month-olds showed sequential touching of same-coloured objects, or same-shaped objects, while in the 6-month-olds, the order of touching was random. Starkey concluded that the capacity for perceptual classification was evident at 9 months.

Overgeneralizations. Bowerman (1975) studied the nature of over-extensions in order to infer the basis of classification. She found that overextensions were mostly based on shared perceptual attributes, especially shape. Words like "moon" were extended to a whole range of crescent shaped objects including grapefruit segments, the letter D, pieces of paper, etc. Overextensions based on shared functions seem to be much more rare, although admittedly it is sometimes difficult to tell whether overextensions like ball–orange–bead, or stick–umbrella–ruler are based on shape or function. Table 2 shows a sample of overgeneralizations.

The idea that the child learns concepts by gradually accumulating semantic features has difficulty in accounting for the fact that over a period of time the pattern of overextensions sometimes reflects a change in the shared semantic features rather than an addition of more constraints. "Dog" may be initially used to refer to any animal, and later be used to refer to a book containing a picture of a dog. In any case, as has been pointed out by Huttenlocher (1974), and by Thompson and Chapman (1977), it can be misleading to infer the nature of a child's concepts from the overextensions that occur in his speech. When word comprehension and word production are studied separately, it is clear that overgeneralization is more prevalent in production. The child understands the difference between Daddy and other men, and knows that cows are not the same as dogs, but cannot always retrieve the appropriate label. His small vocabulary of words masks the greater richness of his underlying conceptual system. In effect the child is behaving much like an adult trying to communicate in a foreign language with a restricted vocabulary. Other considerations also suggest that it is too simplistic to view overgeneralizations as nothing more than conceptual mistakes.

Overgeneralization is not simply a reflection of imperfect concept learning, but a reflection of a very well adapted strategy. By overgeneralizing, wrong responses get corrected, and the information from errors characterizes the negative instances, so that critical differences become apparent, and the overgeneralized concept can be cut back to the positive instances. The child as concept learner is seldom operating in the reception paradigm. He is not presented with a sequence of positive and negative instances of a single concept. Nor does his learning situation resemble the selection paradigm very closely, since he will be trying to master many concepts contemporaneously over quite a long period of time, and the set of alternatives from which he can select items to test his hypothesis is constantly shifting as the perceptual scene around him changes. Overgeneralization is not wholly unrestricted, but occurs only within a limited range of semantic distance. "Daddy" is overgeneralized to "man" but not to "people". Not all features are valid cues for generalization. No instances have been recorded of children overgeneralizing on the basis of colour, for example. They do not assume that fire-engines and cherries belong to the same class because both are red. If the child failed to generalize, or generalized only to examples very similar to the first positive instance, rather like a conservative focusser, acquisition of concepts would be very slow. Because everyday concepts have very many irrelevant features, which vary independently, it would be difficult to extract the defining features by this method. An overgeneralizing response invites correction, so the child acquires a set of near-misses, and can operate like Winston's programme extracting defining features by comparison of good examples and near-misses.

It is interesting to note that overgeneralization is shown by young animals as well as young children. In a study of the alarm calls used by vervet monkeys, Seyfarth *et al.* (1980) identified three different calls to signal differentially the approach of eagles, leopards, or snakes. Infant monkeys were observed to overextend these calls, applying the leopard call to other mammals; the eagle call to other birds and to falling leaves; and the snake call to sticks lying in the grass. Obviously, overgeneralization of this kind would have considerable survival value. Infant monkeys who undergeneralized would not last long. It is quite plausible to suppose that overgeneralization in the human infant has a similar survival value.

Finally, according to Anglin (1977) the importance of overgeneralization may be exaggerated, because underextensions, which also occur, go unrecognized. Bloom (1973) recorded her child's use of the word "car" to refer only to moving cars, but Anglin surmises that many less obvious underextensions are not detected.

Developmental applications of Prototype Theory

Rosch's colleagues, Mervis and Pani (1980) have attempted to apply Prototype Theory to children's concept acquisition and to test its predictions.

As already noted above, prototype construction involves a complex process of feature abstraction and measurement of feature distribution, and may be overly demanding for the infant learner. However, Mervis and Pani tested the prediction that it would be easier to learn categories if initially exposed to good examples close to central tendency of the category. Both 5-year-olds and adults learned to group 24 objects into six artificial categories, and in accordance with the prediction, performance of both groups showed that categorization was facilitated by learning the good examples first. It is not clear, however, whether inter-item similarity was controlled. If other members of the categories were more similar to the good examples than to the poor examples, the results could have been due to instance comparison rather than to prototype construction. The finding that encountering good examples facilitates concept learning is difficult to reconcile with a Feature Abstraction theory of learning. In conformity with Winston's computer model, encounters with near-miss examples would be most helpful if defining features were being abstracted.

Developmental applications of the Instance Comparison model

Kossan (1981) looked at developmental differences in strategies of concept acquisition, and found that, at least for some types of concept, younger children were more likely to use an instance comparison strategy. Kossan constructed three types of concept out of drawings of fictitious animals. One had defining features; one had a set of sufficient features; and one had a single distinctive feature. For concepts with defining features, both second and fifth grade (7 and 10-year-old) children abstracted the criterial features. For the concepts with a set of sufficient features the younger children classified by similarity to a previous instance, while the older children learned the set of relevant features. With a single distinctive feature both age groups used instance comparison. Kossan also pointed out that children's use of this strategy is explicit in the way that they tend to cite instances when asked for definitions. Asked to define "dog", a young child will often respond "It's like Rover". She believes that feature abstraction is too difficult for the younger children, especially if concepts are complicated, and that analogical instance comparison provides an easier alternative. Her experiment underlines the way that both the nature of the concept, and the capacity of the learner determine how the concept is learned. It is increasingly apparent that it is misconceived to attempt to formulate a single theory of concept learning with universal applicability.

Keil's predicate tree structure

Keil's approach stresses the fact that learning individual concepts involves learning about the relationships between concepts. The child who is learning about the class of dogs is also learning how dogs differ from, and relate to cats, and cows and teddy bears. Keil is also concerned to emphasize that, even in the very early stages, conceptual learning is constrained. The child is not confronted with a world in which absolutely anything might be true. Many things are already ruled out as impossible, and this helps to make the task of concept learning more manageable. Keil's theory postulates an hierarchical tree structure of predicate relations. Figure 18 shows how the terms (shown in lower case) are related to the predicates (in upper case). A predicate like IS DEAD spans all the terms related to the predicates below it on the tree. That is to say, terms such as man, girl, pig, rabbit, flower, etc. can all take the predicate IS DEAD. A predicate cannot take a term related to a higher branch on the tree, so that statements like "The milk is asleep" are ruled out. In Keil's developmental studies, children were presented with sentences that either conformed to the constraints of the predicate tree (the dog is hungry), or violated them (the chair is hungry). The children were asked to judge whether the sentences were "OK" or "silly". The results showed that children do understand the constraints on predication. As age increased, violations were fewer. The scope of predicates became increasingly restricted as the predicate tree became increasingly differentiated. Even the youngest children tested (aged 3–4 years) observed the distinction between living and nonliving things. Keil's theory and findings are in conflict with other researchers, such as Nelson (1977) who believe that young children do not understand the inter-relationships between concepts until after the age of seven. It is also difficult to reconcile with the animistic remarks that are quite characteristic of young children; and given that children's books are full of constraint-violating characters like rabbits in aprons, and cartoon films and advertisements feature animated artefacts like talking tea-bags, it is remarkable if predicate restrictions are well understood by young children.

Many of the discrepancies between developmental theories may arise because researchers are examining different aspects of conceptual knowledge. It is extremely difficult to say at what stage a child has acquired a concept. When a concept is fully acquired, the child should be able to recognize instances and reject nonexemplars without error; to apply verbal labels appropriately; to act appropriately toward instances of the concept; to describe and define it; to relate it to other concepts; to order examples by degree of typicality; to list attributes and know whether they are defining, typical, or relevant. Considered in this way, it is clear that acquisition is a complex process, probably spread over a long period of time, and possibly stopping short of completion. It is hardly surprising if many different kinds of learning process are employed at different times, for different aspects of the task.

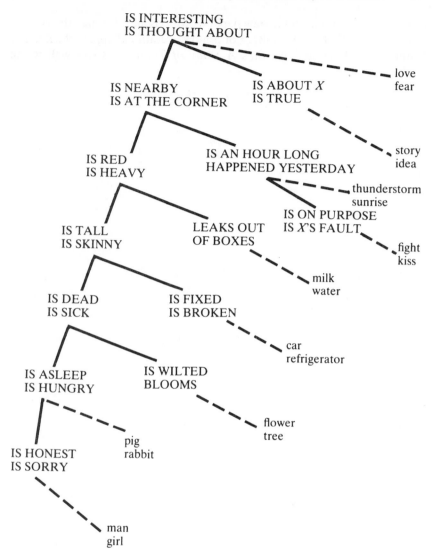

FIG. 18. *Predictability tree (from Keil, 1979).*

Recommended reading

Rosch and Lloyd's edited volume *Cognition and Categorization* (Lawrence Erlbaum, 1978) provides a good selection of different points of view. Keil's book, *Semantic and Conceptual Development* is based on a philosophical analysis. There is a useful review paper by Mervis and Rosch in the *Annual Review of Psychology* **32**, 1981. For a more traditional approach, Bruner, Bruner, Goodnow and Austin's *A Study of Thinking* is still well worth reading.

5 LANGUAGE *and* THOUGHT: WHAT *is* LANGUAGE?

While it is not surprising that a relationship as complex as that between language and thought should have generated some controversial views, it is curious that they should have polarized to such an extent. According to one view, language is necessary for thought, and determines it; according to the opposite point of view, the development of thought is prior to, and necessary for, the development of language. An intermediate position, adopted by Vygotsky (1962), is that thought and language originate independently in the young child and combine in an interactive relationship at a later stage of development. Much of this disagreement arises because there has been little consensus as to what constitutes thinking, and what is to count as a language. Without some analysis of the nature of language, and of the nature of thought, we cannot decide what evidence is admissible to the argument. Trying to decide the direction of influence between language and thought is like asking whether the chicken or the egg came first, and one way to break out of this circle is to seek for limiting cases of eggs that exist without chickens, or chickens without eggs. In the case of language and thought, this means that instead of asking whether language determines thought or vice versa, we can also ask how complex and effective thought can be when language is absent, disordered, deviant or impoverished, or how well language can be mastered by the disabled thinker. By comparing the cognitive capacities of those who are normal language users with those who are alinguistic, or language-handicapped, we can make some inferences about the role of language in thought. We should recognize that these inferences are, at best, quite crude and speculative because the comparisons are not clean. Differences between animals and humans, child and adult, the deaf and the hearing, and between members of one social or cultural group and another, are not confined to language use, and many other factors are reflected in the comparisons.

This chapter begins by considering some of the criteria for "language", and how far these are fulfilled by signalling systems other than ordinary human spoken language. The final section examines some of the differences between various human languages, and discusses how far these might reflect or produce cognitive differences.

TABLE 3. The Comparison of Vocal Communication in Animals and Man Based on Hockett's Design Features (From W. H. Thorpe, 1972).

Design features (all of which are found in verbal human language)	1 Human paralinguistics	2 Crickets, grasshoppers	3 Honey bee dancing	4 Doves
1. Vocal-auditory channel	Yes (in part)	Auditory but nonvocal	No	Yes
2. Broadcast transmission and directional reception	Yes	Yes	Yes	Yes
3. Rapid fading	Yes	Yes	?	Yes
4. Interchangeability (adults can be both transmitters and receivers)	Largely yes	Partial	Partial	Yes
5. Complete feedback "speaker" able to perceive everything relevant to his signal production)	Partial	Yes	No?	Yes
6. Specialization (energy unimportant, trigger effect important)	Yes?	Yes?	?	Yes
7. Semanticity (association ties between signals and features in the world)	Yes?	No?	Yes	Yes (in part)
8. Arbitrariness (symbols abstract)	In part	?	No	Yes
9. Discreteness (repertoire discrete not continuous)	Largely no	Yes	No	Yes
10. Displacement (can refer to things remote in time and space)	In part		Yes	No
11. Openness (new messages easily coined)	Yes	No	Yes	No
12. Tradition (conventions passed on by teaching and learning)	Yes	Yes?	No?	No
13. Duality of patterning (signal elements meaningless, pattern combinations meaningful)	No	?	No	No
14. Prevarication (ability to lie or talk nonsense)	Yes	No	No	No
15. Reflectiveness (ability to communicate about the system itself)	No	No	No	No
16. Learnability (speaker of one language learns another)	Yes	No(?)	No(?)	No

5 Buntings, finches, thrushes, crows etc.	6 Mynah	7 Colony nesting sea birds	8 Primates (vocal)	9 Canidae non-vocal communication	10 Primates—chimps, e.g. Washoe
Yes	Yes	Yes	Yes	No	No
Yes	Yes	Yes	Yes	Partly yes	Partly yes
Yes	Yes	Yes	Yes	No	No
Partial (Yes if same sex)	Yes	Partial	Yes	Yes	Yes
Yes	Yes	Yes	Yes	No	Yes
Yes	Yes	Yes	Yes	Yes	Yes
Yes	Yes	Yes	Yes	Yes	Yes
Yes	Yes	Yes	Yes	No	Yes
Yes	Yes	Yes	Partial	Partial	Partial
Time No Space Yes	Time No Space Yes	No	Yes	No	Yes
Yes	Yes	No?	Partial	No?	Yes?
Yes	Yes	In part?	No?	?	Yes
Yes	Yes	No?	Yes	Yes	Yes
No	No(?)	No	No	Yes	Yes
No	No	No	No	No	No
Yes (in part)	Yes	No	No?	No	Yes

The Nature of Language

Attempts to define the nature of language have characteristically displayed a marked degree of chauvinism. A typical procedure is to select what are thought to be the most important and fundamental attributes of human language, and to construct a list of these defining attributes. An example is Hockett's list of design features (Hockett, 1960) which are shown in Table 3. It is apparent that all animal communication systems lack some of these features. However, to conclude that "no animal other than man communicates with language-like expressions" (Marshall, 1970) is trivially self-fulfilling if "language" is defined in terms of human language. From the fact that some features of human language are lacking, it does not necessarily follow that animal communications systems are "not language". Indeed, the stringent application of Hockett's criteria would rule out written human language (by 1, 2 and 3 in Table 3); the speech of very young children (by 10 and 15); the sign language of the deaf, which is not wholly arbitrary; and the speech of aphasic and schizophrenic patients, which might fail the semanticity requirement. Yet the status of these as "languages" is not usually questioned. Instead of listing defining features, and trying to determine a dividing line which separates "language" from "nonlanguage", it is probably more interesting and fruitful to consider what are the similarities and dissimilarities of various systems of symbolization, and what are their advantages and disadvantages as media for communication, and media for thought.

Communication and representation

These two functions of language, communication and mental representation, need to be distinguished and considered separately, since it is possible to have a symbol system that is adequate for one, but ill-adapted for the other. Analyses of the defining characteristics of language such as Hockett's have tended to concentrate on its overt communicative aspects, and to ignore the characteristics required for effective mental representation. The divergence of criteria is apparent if we consider the differences between spoken language and written language. As a communication system, writing has several striking advantages. Messages can be transmitted over wide ranges of space and time to reach unlimited numbers of receivers, who can share the thoughts of those who are long dead or far distant. Because the message is encoded in a stable form, decoding can be self-paced to suit the capacity of the listener, who can also backtrack to re-inspect earlier parts of the message. Spoken language, in contrast, is ephemeral. Transmission is sharply limited in space and time, and makes heavy demands on the memory and processing capacity of the listener. In other ways, spoken language may be superior to writing for communication. Speaker and hearer are usually in an interactive relationship which permits interruptions, questions, requests for clarification and repetition, so the speaker can adjust his output to suit the personal requirements of the listener. While writing is decontextualized, speaker and hearer share the same situational context so that utterances are easier to interpret. Whatever their respective merits for communication, it is clear that written language is not well adapted for internal representation. Our power to visualize written words is too limited. So, although we may occasionally visualize words if we are deciding how they should be spelled, or trying to recall some written information, we do not "think in writing". We may use writing to externalize our thoughts, but writing cannot be internalized with the same ease and fluency as speech.

The suitability of a language system for internalization depends on the nature of the organism or mechanism employing it, as well as the characteristics of the language itself. The nature of human working memory, and its limitations in the visual modality, makes written language difficult to internalize. This aspect of the relationship between language and thought is particularly apparent in the case of computer languages. Computer languages are especially designed for computer thinking. Just as human language has to be convertible into mental representations, and ultimately into neuronal patterns of activity, programming languages for computers have to be convertible into the machine code which elicits the mechanical operations. Some programming languages are general purpose, but others may be designed to suit particular problems; the language that is appropriate for chess playing programs is not necessarily appropriate for parsing English sentences. These computer languages are adapted for particular kinds of thinking, not just thinking in general. This fact underlines an important point often overlooked in discussing the relationship of language and thought in humans. Language that is perfectly adequate for some domains of thinking may be inadequate for others. The degree of structural complexity and richness of vocabulary that is required depends on the kind of thinking. Some languages, such as the language of science or mathematics, are designed to have universality, others are context-bound and culture specific.

Since language systems that are well adapted for communication may be poorly adapted for thought (and vice versa) studies of communicative behaviour in animals do not necessarily reveal much about animals' thinking. Even if animals can be shown to use a language-like system for communication, it does not follow that it is used for mental representation as well. Although there are differences between language-for-communication, and language-for-representation, both are important for cognition. A great deal of the knowledge which is represented in thinking is derived from communication. In considering the relationship between language and thought, therefore, both representation and communication need to be taken into account.

Animal communication

The comparison of human language and animal signalling systems has been a crucial issue for nativist theories of language such as that of Chomsky (1965). For the nativist, language is both innate and species-specific to man, hence any similarities between human and animal languages are dismissed as coincidental and trivial. Because his interest in language is primarily structural, rather than functional, he finds the differences more striking than the similarities. But if we are asking how effective a language, of whatever kind, can be for thinking and communicating, then a functional analysis is more relevant than a formal one.

The evolution of language

In the discussion which follows, the term "language" is used loosely to refer to various signalling and communicating systems, but its use is not intended to beg the question of their status. Nativists have denied that animal languages are evolutionarily more primitive stages of a development which culminates in human language, and Chomsky has dismissed any discussion of the evolution of language as "mere handwaving". Of course, it is true that the issue is extremely speculative, but it does serve to raise some interesting questions. Evolutionary theories of language are of two kinds (Sebeok, 1968). If language is considered as a unitary faculty then evolution would bring about quantitative changes, and species differences would be in degree of complexity. Alternatively, if language is considered to be a composite faculty arising from various independent roots such as the development of intelligence, memory, cerebral dominance and vocal mechanisms, which are acquired evolutionarily by a process of stepwise accretion, then qualitative differences of the kind represented in Table 3 might well occur. Mattingley (1972) has argued that human language originated in the co-development of two independent mechanisms, the intellect and the speech system. There is fossil evidence (Lieberman and Crelin, 1971) that Neanderthal man had a phonetic ability intermediate between non-human primates and modern man, but there is no reliable evidence for the evolution of intelligence in man. An increase of brain size is reported to have occurred about the time that man is thought to have become a social hunter (Campbell, 1971), but there is no reliable correlation of intelligence with cranial capacity, and no compelling reason to link the development of language with social organization, since animals such as wolves hunt socially, but have not developed a communication system of comparable complexity. Intellectual development does not necessarily promote linguistic development, and there is no sign that animal communication systems increase in complexity higher up the phylogenetic scale. Moreover, non-human primates are currently demonstrating that they have the cognitive capacity for complex linguistic skills which are not developed spontaneously in the wild (see pp. 107–118). Nevertheless there is some indication that communication systems are related to ecological pressures, since the bee's dance which conveys the location of the food source to other members of the hive, varies in complexity with the foraging range of the species (von Frisch, 1967). Since non-human primates clearly have the intellectual potential to learn more complex signalling systems than the calls, gestures and facial expressions that they spontaneously employ, and also have a social way of life which would be rendered more effective, as far as we can judge, by more complex exchange of information, other factors must be implicated in the acquisition of language. On the whole, the evidence for the evolution of language, either by continuous development, or by accretion of components, is too sparse to illuminate the relationship between human and animal languages.

Essential features of human language

Hockett's list of design features (Hockett, 1960) includes some which seem incidental and unimportant, and others which are more fundamental. We can select, on *a priori* grounds, those properties that seem to be most essential if a language is to function for thinking and for communicating.

Displacement. A language with displacement can symbolize objects and events not present in time and space. De Laguna (1927) remarked that "the evolution of language is characterized by a progressive freeing of speech from dependence on the perceived condition under which it is uttered and heard, and from the behaviour which accompanies it". For all kinds of thinking and communicating which involve planning for the future, hypothesizing, evaluating possible solutions, and drawing on past experience, it is necessary to symbolize states not currently being perceived by the thinker. Displacement makes education possible, and allows information to be transmitted from one generation to another, and from one individual to another, so that the accumulation of knowledge is no longer dependent on personal sense data, and the intellectual advance of the species can progress cumulatively. Natural animal languages do not appear to have this property. One exception is the language of the bees which can, as we have already noted, communicate food location within a limited range of spatial and temporal displacement. It is possible that a language can possess the property of displacement to varying degrees, and that it is not present or absent in an all-or-none fashion. The early speech of young children exhibits only minimal displacement as in comments on disappearance like "All gone", and requests for recurrence like "More". The ability to refer to objects more remote in space and time is quite slow to develop, but it is possible that this is a cognitive problem rather than a linguistic one, and the child has difficulty in conceptualizing larger distances in space and time.

Voluntary control. This has been pinpointed as one of the most critical aspects of human language. Marshall (1970) distinguishes between informative and communicative signalling, and considers animal languages to be informative, but not communicative, because animal signalling is not "intentional". He claims that it is unintentional because it is not under voluntary control, and the signaller cannot choose to give or withhold the information. In response to external stimuli (such as food, or the presence of predators), or internal stimuli (such as fear, or sexual arousal) an animal behaves "in such a way as to" convey information to another animal. This is contrasted with intentional human signalling, in which one individual signals "in order to bring about a change" in another individual's behaviour. The operational criteria proposed for intentionality are that the signaller selects the appropriate signal from a range of alternatives, and continues to try variations until a goal is achieved. These criteria are not very satisfactory. Many animal signals such as threat gestures vary, at least in intensity, until they produce results, and not all human utterances are designed to change the hearer's behaviour. While intentionality is difficult to assess, it is obvious that a symbol system for thinking must be under voluntary control if thought is to be goal-oriented, rather than just random day-dreaming.

Prevarication is misleadingly listed by Hockett (1960) as a separate feature, but its importance does not lie simply in the ability to tell lies and jokes, but rather in the ability to symbolize what is not the case. In fact, therefore, it is an example of both displacement and voluntary control, and the same ability which allows us to deceive, and to fantasize, also allows us to think hypothetically.

Openness and semanticity. If a language is to mediate intellectual progress, it must be capable of expressing new ideas and conveying new messages. To do this economically some structural rules of patterning are required whereby existing symbols can be recombined into novel meaningful patterns. As with displacement, languages may possess this property in varying degrees, and Lyons (1972) has suggested that it is the greater complexity of the structural rules that distinguishes human language. Semanticity is commonly defined in terms of reference—the symbol system must be able to refer to objects and attributes in the real world; but this kind of reference is not enough to make a language functionally adequate. It must also be able to express relations of many kinds, and some of these were discussed in Chapter 3 when we noted that an image code might be deficient in this respect. For thinking complex thoughts and exchanging complex messages, naming is not enough; a language needs to be propositional.

Reflectiveness and internalizability. Reflectiveness is what Hockett calls "ability to communicate about the system itself", or metalinguistic ability. This is an attribute of human language which is often cited, but rarely analysed sufficiently for us to assess its importance. It is not simply the ability to reflect about the language, or to discuss it, that is crucial; nor even the ability to understand the principle of symbolization, and the representational nature of signs. What is really essential is the ability to combine linguistic information and nonlinguistic information, so that language can be interpreted on different levels, either literally, or with reference to the context and the pragmatic implications. It is this ability which allows us to interpret "It is eight o'clock" either literally as a clock reading, or pragmatically as "Hurry up, or you'll be late for work". The most sophisticated knowledge of the formal nature of language does not guarantee comprehension; we must also understand its function. We must be able to relate the purely linguistic properties of a message to our stored knowledge of the world, and our perception of the immediate situational context of the utterance.

What other characteristic does a language require if it is to serve for thinking? It is arguable whether the language needs to be internalizable. Should we deny that a man could think if he could only think out loud, or with a paper and pencil? It seems overrestrictive to insist that thinking be internal, yet subjects who are engaged in problem solving, and are asked to "think aloud" report that their overt verbalization cannot keep abreast of their inner thoughts, which are more rapid and less completely formulated. Rapidity and economy are among the advantages of internalized thought, but the thinker may also need to stabilize, manipulate, erase or modify the thinking symbols so that he can consider and evaluate a sequence, and discard, revise or accept a solution. For this kind of thinking, an externalized representation such as writing is clearly superior.

The Chimpanzee Linguists

Recent attempts to teach artificial languages to chimpanzees have raised some fascinating issues, which are very relevant to the problem of the relationship of language and thought. Do the linguistic achievements of the chimpanzees reflect a cognitive capacity which existed previously independent of language? How far are the linguistic skills which they have acquired capable of mediating thought and communication? Do they resemble human language closely enough to counter the view that language is species-specific to man? The language learning of three chimpanzees, Washoe, Sarah and Lana are reviewed in some detail in the next section, so that we can attempt to answer these questions.

Washoe

In 1966 Gardner and Gardner began training a female chimpanzee named Washoe, caught in the wild aged between 8 and 14 months. They taught Washoe to use the American sign language for the deaf (Ameslan). The gestural signs are composed of 55 basic elements or cheremes (such as position in space, moving or stationary, one hand or two, type of movement, direction of movement, configuration of the hands etc.). Washoe has learned to produce 132 of these signs, and to comprehend rather more (Gardner and Gardner, 1975). Her vocabulary includes nouns, pronouns, verbs, adjectives, possessives, locatives, negatives and imperatives. She combines these in strings of up to five signs, and is able to recombine them to produce novel strings. Her language has semanticity in so far as she correctly names objects and events, and shows semantic generalization in her application of signs to novel examples. For instance, she learned the sign for "open" with reference to a door, and generalized this to boxes, cupboards, drawers and brief-cases. Her errors show an overgeneralization similar to that observed in the language of young children. Having learned the sign for "hurt" applied to a scratch, she applied it later to a tattoo mark, and to her trainer's navel: she generalized the sign for "flower" to "smell", and her errors are sometimes within category substitution like "soap" for "toothbrush". Her communications are often requests for food, drink, cuddling and tickling. She comments on objects in the environment, and correctly answers *Wh* questions like "What is this? Where is the cup? Who is sleeping?" Interestingly, there are no reports of any ability to answer Why, How and When questions, so perhaps Washoe lacks concepts of causality and time, but children are also later in acquiring these. Her utterances are concrete, and of limited complexity.

Some critics (e.g. Savage-Rumbaugh *et al.*, 1978) have objected that Ameslan as used by chimpanzees is not genuinely symbolic, because many signs are iconic rather than arbitrary. Using the signs may be equivalent to imitating the appropriate action rather than symbolizing it. It is true that

TABLE 4. From R. Brown (1970).

	Brown's (1970) scheme for children		The scheme for Washoe	
Types	Examples	Types	Examples	
Attributive Ad + N	big train, red book	Object–Attribute Agent-Attribute	drink red, comb black Washoe sorry, Naomi good	
Possessive N + N	Adam checker, mommy lunch	Agent-Object Object-Attribute Action-Location	clothes Mrs G., you hat baby mine, clothes yours go in, look out	
N + V	walk street, go store	Action-Object Object-Location	go flower, pants tickle baby down, in hat	
Locative N + N	sweater chair, book table			
Agent-Action: N + V	Adam put, Eve read	Agent-Action	Roger tickle, you drink	
Action-Object: V + N	put book, hit ball	Action-Object	tickle Washoe, open blanket	
Agent-Object: N + N	mommy sock, mommy lunch	Appeal-Action Appeal-Object	please tickle, hug hurry gimme flower, more fruit	

some signs in ASL are iconic, but many are not. However, it is not clear whether the proportion of noniconic signs in Washoe's vocabulary is such as to justify the Rumbaugh's criticism.

Whether her language has syntactic structure is disputed. She uses some pronouns correctly, but no connectives. However, it is not clear how far her syntactic deficiencies reflect her own limitations, or the nature of the sign language itself, which is highly condensed, and omits articles, inflections, copulae and prepositions (Bellugi and Fischer, 1972). Washoe's utterances lack a stable ordering, so that subject and object are not distinguishable, and in this respect she is unlike young children, who use word order correctly and consistently. Whereas a child can reliably use the correct word order in a sentence asking an adult to tickle him (name of adult–tickle–name of self), Washoe's ordering is inconsistent and does not convey who is the intended agent, and who is the intended object of the action. However, Brown (1970) carried out a functional analysis of the speech of young children, and Table 4 shows that Washoe's utterances are functionally very similar, even if her syntax is inferior. In any case, comparisons with normal children are hardly fair to Washoe, since her language experience resembles that of a deaf child with deaf parents (Bronowski and Bellugi, 1970).

In studying Washoe and other animal linguists, the competence–performance problem arises in a special form. Whereas with adult humans it is assumed that competence exceeds performance, because much of Washoe's learning is imitative, and her use of language is context-dependent, her competence, or mental model of the language may actually be less adequate than appears from her performance. How far does Washoe's use of language reflect an internal understanding of her symbol system? No evidence is presented to show that Washoe can reject ill-formed sentences, so it is not clear that Washoe understands the rules governing sentence formation in Ameslan.

Displacement is minimal in Washoe's language, and as in early child speech, is confined to requests for recurrence ("More milk") and comments on disappearance ("Allgone cup"). Her use of language is closely tied to the immediate spatiotemporal context. Intentionality is clearly present in the utterances classified as Appeal–Action ("Please tickle") and Appeal–Object ("Gimme fruit"), since Washoe does persist with this kind of sign sequence until she gets what she is asking for. On one occasion she is reported to have forgotten the sign for "bib", and after some hesitation, invented a new one by drawing a bib shape on herself, so she fulfils Marshall's operational criteria for intentionality, persistence and variation of signal until the goal is achieved. Indeed, it is impossible to watch Washoe's language behaviour without being convinced that she not only intends, but is positively determined, to communicate.

Perhaps the most striking deficit is her failure to ask questions. In this she is quite unlike the young child whose conversation turns to an onslaught of *Wh* questions once the child catches on to the linguistic game of interrogation. Does Washoe use her language for thinking? She does not talk to herself as much as young children do, and it is only on a few occasions that she has been observed to use an isolated sign while alone. Of course, it is possible that she can internalize her signs, but there is no evidence that she does so. How far her cognitive development has been enhanced by having language does not seem to have been systematically explored. It would be interesting if it could be shown that her performance on problem solving and memory tasks had improved as a result of having a linguistic code. Currently, the Gardners have begun to train some more chimpanzees, beginning the training programme soon after birth, and they are confident that Washoe's achievements, will be surpassed, and that the upper limits of chimpanzees' linguistic skills have not yet been revealed.

Washoe herself has been taken over by Roger Fouts who reports (1978) that her vocabulary has increased to 200 signs. Attempts to breed from Washoe have not so far succeeded, although in 1976 she had an infant that died soon after birth. Washoe was observed to make the sign for "baby" as she tried to revive it, which encouraged Fouts to believe that she might communicate in sign language with her offspring if she does produce any.

Following the Gardners' pioneering work, other attempts to teach sign language to chimpanzees have followed. Fouts is studying several chimpanzees who are learning sign language, and are also allowed to interact with each other. Spontaneous communication between them has been observed, mainly consisting of commands like "You give me food" from the dominant animal. There does not seem to be free interchange of the roles of sender and receiver.

One of the most careful and thorough evaluations of use of sign language by a chimpanzee is reported by Terrace *et al.* (1979). After analysis of 19 000 multisign utterances by a chimpanzee called Nim, they concluded that there was no evidence that Nim could construct sentences, or had any understanding of the structural relations of elements in a sentence. They found that two-sign utterances did display some regularities, with the order of elements being constrained by meaning. Agent, Attribute or Recurrence usually occurred first. Place or Beneficiary were usually in second position, but these regularities were classed as "lexical habits", rather than as evidence of syntax. Longer strings were achieved by repetition of redundant signs, rather than by increasing structural complexity. Utterances like "Banana me eat banana eat" were typical of the longer strings in the corpus. This contrasts with the language of young children, for whom increasing length of utterance is closely linked with increasing structural complexity.

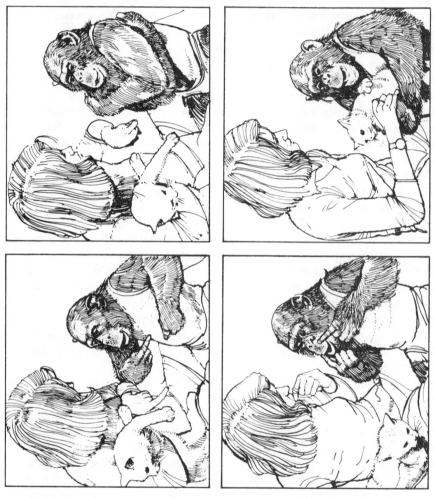

FIG. 19. *Nim signing the linear combination, me hug cat to his teacher (Susan Quinby) (redrawn from Terrace, 1979).*

Terrace *et al.* also noted that the proportion of Nim's utterances that were imitations, or partial imitations of the trainer's utterances was much higher than the proportion of imitations found in child speech. Discourse analysis revealed that 71% of Nim's utterances were prompted rather than spontaneous. In Figure 19, Nim is shown signing "Me hug cat". Inspection of the film showed that this was elicited by the trainer signing "You—who?". Although the issue is still being debated, these findings reinforce the view that chimpanzee sign language is not a truly generative use of language.

Sarah

Another chimpanzee, Sarah, has been taught an artifical language which is very different from Washoe's, and is in some ways more impressive. Premack (1970) deliberately set out to teach Sarah a language system, which, while being adapted to suit her capacities, would still be adequate to fulfil the more important criteria of "language", and thus convincingly demonstrate the chimpanzee's ability as a bona fide language user. On Premack's view, while phonology and the particular syntactic structure of human language are unique to man, the logical and semantic structure of language are not.

Sarah uses plastic chips of varying colour, size, shape and texture, each representing a word, which are arranged on a magnetic board in a vertical array to form sentences. This system relieves Sarah of the short-term memory load imposed by sequencing in a fade-out system, and there is no time pressure on comprehension since she can study an array as long as she likes. The vocabulary consists of items like the names of fruits; the names of her trainers, who figure in sentences as donors and recipients of objects; verbs like giving, cutting, inserting; and attributes like colours and shapes. Teaching is by operant conditioning. Correct responses are elicited and rewarded. The difficulty of a task can be controlled by varying the number and type of chips available to Sarah when she is constructing her sentences. Only a subset of the total vocabulary is available at any one time. Sarah has learned to understand and respond appropriately to sentences presented to her, and to construct her own sentences. Some of the aspects of sentence structure which Premack claims that Sarah has mastered are discussed below.

Sarah appears to understand the significance of word order in simple two-term relations like "green on red" as opposed to "red on green", when these are used to describe the relative positions of coloured cards. Sarah can correctly construct a sentence to describe how the cards are placed, or arrange the cards to correspond to a sentence. Even so, her ability to represent a spatial ordering correctly is not comparable with the ability to use ordering of symbols to represent more abstract relations like Agent–

Action–Object, and it is doubtful whether Sarah's ordering is more than a kind of cross-modal matching.

Sarah has also learned to handle compound sentences like "Sarah insert (banana pail) (apple dish)", but as Fodor *et al.* (1974) point out, this does not prove that she understands the constituent structure of such a sentence. She could assign fruit to container correctly on the basis of the proximity of the symbols in the sentence. It seems unfair, however, to complain that Sarah lacks the sophisticated understanding of structural relationships within sentences possessed by professors of linguistics, and it would be more relevant to have some child–chimpanzee comparisons for this type of sentence.

Sarah responds correctly to both affirmative and negative interrogatives. The training technique utilized the animal's natural ability to distinguish between identical and nonidentical pairs of objects. Presented with sentences of the form "A same as A?" Sarah replaces the question mark with the symbol for "Yes"; or, given "A same as B?" she responds "No". Similarly she responds "No" to the negative form "A not same as A?", and in "A is ? to B", she replaces the question symbol with the "not same as" symbol. As in other tasks, having learned the form with one set of vocabulary items, she transfers with about 80% success to sentences of the same form but with different lexical items.

Another set of tasks was designed to test Sarah's understanding of what Premack calls metalinguistics which corresponds to what, earlier in this chapter, we called reflectiveness or understanding of the principle of symbolizing. When she is shown a pairing of a plastic symbol and its referent object, Sarah can affix the symbol for "is the name of" between them; or if the plastic chip is paired with a nonreferent, she supplies "is not the name of". Asked what is the name of an object, she supplies the correct chip, and responds "Yes" or "No" correctly to questions like "A is the name of apple?" More impressively, when asked to assign attributes to the blue chip, which is the symbol for an apple, she assigns "red" and "round", the same attributes that she assigns to the fruit itself. These achievements demonstrate that Sarah has some understanding of the relationship between the symbols she uses, and the objects they represent, but this is only a small part of metalinguistic ability.

Other achievements are pluralization, and the use of quantifiers like "All", "None", "One" and "Several" to describe sets of objects. Sarah correctly formulates sentences like "All the crackers are round" or "None of the crackers is round" to describe sets of crackers. She also appears to understand the subset/superset relation in classifying colours, shapes, fruits etc.

Perhaps the most complex of Sarah's achievements is her mastery of conditional sentences of the "If . . . then" form. Given an apple and a banana within reach, Sarah learned to respond to sentences such as "If Sarah take apple then Mary give chocolate", or "If Sarah take apple then Mary not give chocolate". Again she was able to transfer successfully to novel versions of this form such as "If green is on red then Sarah take banana".

How far Sarah has any understanding of what she is doing is hard to judge. It has been suggested that animals performing tasks of this kind give evidence of "knowing how", that is, knowing what response to make, but not of "knowing that". They have learned a skill rather than acquired a set of beliefs. This objection appears to be countered by a study in which Woodruff and Premack (1979) claim to have demonstrated both intentionality and deception. Four chimpanzees were tested in a situation where they watched food being concealed in one of several containers. According to Woodruff and Premack, they revealed the locus of the food to a trainer who was generous and popular, but deliberately misinformed (by pointing to the wrong place) another trainer who was "selfish" and did not share the food with them. Thus they appear to demonstrate capacity to form a belief and a voluntary decision to share or conceal that belief.

Sarah's language is more complex and abstract than Washoe's, but less spontaneous. Fodor *et al.* (1974) have remarked that, unlike the young child, she lacks genuinely productive syntax, and never acquires a new syntactic form without special training. Her language does not have the element of invention that is characteristic of child language. Although she has clearly mastered some of the rules which underlie linguistic skill, the overall impression produced by the reports of her performance is that she is playing a complicated kind of board game, rather than using language to communicate. It is difficult, though, to justify this view by stating precisely what are the missing elements. This same difficulty is highlighted by a recent study (Hughes, 1975) of severely aphasic children who were taught "Premackese". Although the nonverbal intelligence of these children was normal, their spoken language at 8–13 years old had not advanced beyond a 2-year-old level. Nevertheless, using the plastic symbol system, they were able to master several sentence forms, the use of negation, class concepts and some kinds of questions. Hughes concludes that there is a gulf between an artificial language like Premackese and normal human language, but cannot specify the nature of the difference.

Whatever doubts may be felt about Sarah's achievements as a language-user, Premack has more recently been capitalizing on her educability to explore her cognitive limits. Some of Sarah's cognitive feats are described in the next chapter.

Lana, Sherman and Austin

A third chimpanzee, Lana, has been trained on a language system called

"Yerkish" (Rumbaugh *et al.*, 1974) which is quite similar to Premackese. Lana has access to a console with a bank of 75 key words, which they call lexigrams, each differentiated by a geometric symbol. Lana selects and presses the keys to construct sentences, and the result is transcribed on to a screen so that she can read what she has "written". The position of the keys is varied, so that her selection is not spatially determined, and she must recognize the geometric patterns. Lana can name objects or request food, drink, tickling, grooming etc. She can complete valid sentence beginnings, and can erase invalid ones, and she also deletes or erases her own errors, which indicates considerable understanding of the structural rules of the language. This is particularly impressive since children are not able or willing to make judgements about the correctness of sentences until about 7 years old (Gleitman *et al.*, 1972). Lana sometimes asks the name of a novel object, and then uses the name to request the object, and she also invents novel sentences. Her syntax is less complex than Sarah's, but her use of language is more productive, communicative and conversational. She exhibits some degree of displacement, in that she can request a trainer who is out of sight to come into her room and tickle her. She also seems to have surpassed Washoe in her understanding of the use of word order to signify agent and object in tickling and grooming activities. Both Lana and Sarah probably benefit from having their sequences "written" so that the elements can be simultaneously perceived, whereas in Washoe's system the sequential order of the signs must be retained in memory.

In spite of Lana's impressive performance, doubts have still been raised as to how far she is able to generate novel sentences. Thompson and Church (1980) believe that Lana simply learns stock or prototypical sentences, and then inserts learned associates into slots according to the context. For example, the sentence frame "Please —— (name of person) —— (activity e.g. give) —— (incentive e.g. food)" can be filled to produce a typical sentence such as "Please Bill give banana". Many of Lana's productions can be accounted for in this way, but not all her sentences conform to previously learned patterns. While there is general agreement that genuine syntax must be distinguished from sequence learning, it is not clear that Lana's sentence constructions can be dismissed altogether as mere sequence learning.

Since teaching language to Lana, the Rumbaughs have also taught the same system to two other chimpanzees, Sherman and Austin. These two have received a more pragmatic form of training with the names of objects being learned in a functional context. Savage-Rumbaugh *et al.* (1978) report evidence that Sherman and Austin can engage in co-operative communication directed toward a common goal, spontaneously exchanging mutual requests, and exchanging the roles of requester and provider. In training, both animals learned to use tools to extract food from a variety of containers, each of which required a different tool. They also learned to name the tools. Then the animals were placed in adjacent rooms separated by a window. Each room had a keyboard. In one room the animal saw food being put inside one of six different containers. In the other room, the chimpanzee had a tool kit with six different tools. The first animal was able to use the keyboard to request the appropriate tool, which his partner then passed through a hole in the partition. If the "provider" chimpanzee was inattentive, the requester repeated the message, or went to the window and pointed to the keyboard display.

Besides providing this demonstration of purposive communication, Sherman and Austin also give some evidence of using linguistic symbols for mental representation. Savage-Rumbaugh *et al.* (1980) describe a study in which Lana, Sherman and Austin were trained to sort six objects (three tools and three items of food) into categories. Next they were taught linguistic symbols for the categories, and learned to apply these category names correctly to the six objects. Finally they were asked to categorize ten novel items. Austin scored 10/10 correct, while Sherman scored 9/10. His tendency to classify a sponge as food, instead of as a tool, was very understandable since he habitually ate it. Lana was unable to do the task. Apparently her early training did not equip her to understand functional relationships. Sherman and Austin, who learned object names in a context of use, appear to have an understanding of functional categories, but Lana who learned to associate name and object by rote, does not. The two successful chimpanzees appear to be capable of relating a mental representation of the category, the linguistic symbol for the category name, and the perceived function of the individual object.

Studies of language learning by chimpanzees have shown that the full potential of non-human primates has not been realized by the demands of their natural environment, and it seems likely that further improvements in training techniques will extend their linguistic skills still further. It is difficult to reconcile the results of these studies with a unitary view of human language, since the chimpanzees give evidence of possessing specific components of language, and lacking others, rather than just operating on a more primitive level. The language systems they have learned do serve for simple communication, but do not appear to have a genuine grammatical structure. While some evidence that animals may learn to use linguistic symbols for mental representation is beginning to emerge, this does not amount to using language for thinking. As yet there is no indication that any of the chimpanzees have yet made the giant intellectual stride of using these symbols systems for thinking. Vygotsky (1962) wrote:

In their ontogenetic development thought and speech have different roots. In the speech development of the child we can with certainty establish a pre-intellectual stage, and in his thought development, a prelinguistic stage. Up to a certain point in time the two follow different lines independently of each other. At a certain point these lines meet, whereupon thought becomes verbal and speech rational.

On his view, this meeting-point marks the origin of true language. It is not yet apparent that the lines have met for any of the chimpanzee language students.

The Sign Language of the Deaf

Since it has been suggested that some of Washoe's shortcomings are imposed by the limitations of sign language, it is worth considering the nature of sign language in a little more detail. How adequately do sign languages, as used by deaf and dumb humans rather than chimpanzees, satisfy the criteria for language, and how well can sign language serve as a medium for thinking? Bellugi and Fischer (1972) noted that in speech, words can be produced at rates twice as fast as in signs. There is no one to one correspondence of signs to English words. The rate of articulation of signs is much more sharply limited, but the rate of producing propositions is the same in signs as in spoken language, because the sign language is more condensed, and omits many of the functors such as articles, copulas and prepositions. This results in a telegrammatic style of communication similar to the speech of young children who show a similar kind of reduction in reproducing adult utterances. For the child, reduction serves to bring a sentence within his memory span. In sign language, the reduction is more likely to be a device to speed up transmission rather than being due to limitations of either the language itself, or of the language user. Signs are adapted for ease of communication. Siple (1978) denies that Ameslan signs are primarily iconic. Abstract concepts can be expressed in noniconic signs, and signs that may have been iconic originally have become more arbitrary. The visual modality has the disadvantage of requiring close juxtaposition of sender and receiver, but it has the advantage of allowing more parallel transmission of information than is possible in the auditory modality. Signs are modified by concurrent additions to express number, manner, location, size and shape, rather than having inflections tacked on to the sign. Pauses are used to signal the end of sentences or questions. There are no tense inflections in Ameslan, but time is indicated lexically. Word order is fairly free, but according to Siple, the subject-verb-object order is adhered to when subject and object are reversible (e.g. in "The cat chased the dog", but

Pairs differing only in movement

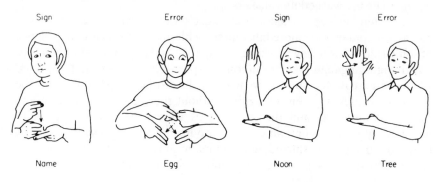

Sign   Error   Sign   Error

Name   Egg   Noon   Tree

Pairs differing only in orientation

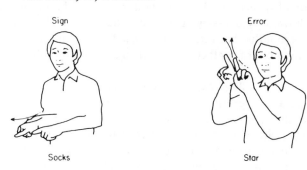

Sign   Error

Socks   Star

Pairs differing only in place of articulation

Sign   Error   Sign   Error

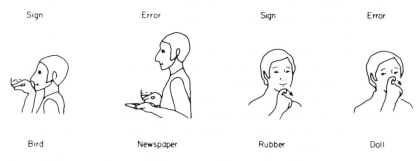

Bird   Newspaper   Rubber   Doll

FIG. 20. *From Bellugi et al. (1975).*

not in "The cat washed its whiskers").

Some sign languages such as the Paget–Gorman system are much less condensed and include more inflections. Schlesinger (1971) found evidence of some rules of ordering to distinguish subject and object in the uninflected Israeli sign language system, although typically these were not observed when contextual cues would serve to make the distinction. He noted also the spontaneous development of signing without specific training in deaf and dumb communities, and that these signs were generally intelligible to members of other communities. Sign production seems to show a certain flexibility, being more slurred, telegrammatic and unordered when there is a clear contextual background, and more careful and rule-bound when contextual cues are absent.

Acquisition of sign language by deaf children follows a pattern similar to the acquisition of speech by a hearing child. Manual babbling at around six months is followed by one-sign strings at about a year old, and two-sign strings at 18–24 months. The rate of increase in length of utterance is similar, and the development of syntactic forms such as negation follows the same progression.

A recent study by Bellugi *et al.* (1975) suggests that signs are internalized, and function as a coding system in memory. They found a memory span of four to nine signs, consistent with a rate of implicit signing roughly equivalent to the rate of overt signing. In a recall test, interesting differences were observed in the intrusion errors of deaf and hearing subjects. While the hearing tended to substitute acoustically confusable items (*house* for *horse*), the deaf substituted items represented by similar signs (*uncle* for *horse*). Fig. 20 shows how the errors preserve the basic hand arrangement of the original sign. These errors provide strong evidence that signs function as an internal symbol system in memory, but do not indicate whether they are represented as visual or as kinaesthetic images, since both aspects are confounded. Other studies (Siple, 1978) have shown that signers exhibit the same primacy and recency effects in recall of signs as hearing subjects do in recalling spoken items, which suggests that signs are rehearsed in working memory. In recall from long term memory, confusions between physically similar signs do not occur, but signs of similar meaning are clustered, reflecting a semantic organization.

However, the fact that lists of items are remembered as signs in short-term memory tasks, does not necessarily indicate that conceptual thinking and problem solving are carried on using internalized signs, although it certainly suggests the possibility.

A case study reported by Newcombe (1975) suggests that the relationship between signing and thought is a complex one. Newcombe's patient was a deaf and dumb child, Adam, who was alinguistic when he was referred to her at about 7 years old. The child was taught sign language, and learned to communicate effectively to the extent of being able to relate vivid imaginative stories to his teacher. The fascinating aspect of these stories is that they incorporate autobiographical elements and past events experienced before the child had acquired any form of language. Clearly, these experiences must have been represented in memory in a nonlinguistic form, and were translated into the newly learned sign language at a later date. The fact that the thoughts antedated the linguistic realization indicates a clear dissociation of thought and language.

Linguistic Relativity

When we come to make comparisons within the family of human languages, three questions arise:
1. Are there significant differences between languages?
2. Are there differences in thinking between members of different language communities?
3. Are the differences in thinking and in language causally related?

Relativism and universalism

For the relativist, the differences between languages are more important than the similarities. The universalist believes that the underlying structure of all languages is essentially the same. The relativist view has been expressed by Whorf (1941) following in the steps of Humboldt and Sapir. He wrote "the forms of a person's thoughts are controlled by inexorable laws of pattern of which he is unconscious. These laws are the unperceived intricate systematizations of his own language". In its strong form the Whorfian hypothesis asserts that the particular language we speak determines the way that we think. In a weaker form, the hypothesis asserts that language influences, directs or biases our thinking rather than determining it. Even in the reformulated version, the terms of this argument are too imprecise for us to be able to assess its validity. What aspects of language are supposed to influence thought? We can distinguish several possibilities here—the richness of the vocabulary, the presence or absence of particular lexical items in the language; and the structural characteristics, or the particular syntactic forms, of the language. What aspects of thought are supposed to be influenced? Most of the cross-cultural studies have sought to relate linguistic differences to differences in perception and memory, and have not attempted to examine any possible differences in more complex mental processes, such as problem solving (but see Chapter 7, p. 167). Whatever aspect of thinking is being investigated, we need to ask whether language affects *what* is thought, or only *how* it is thought. Finally, it is not clear what is meant by "influence". Influence is a relative term. If language is only one of several "influences" on thinking, we need to know how strong it is compared with cultural, educational and socio-economic influences.

Models of semantic representation such as ELINOR (described in Chapter 2) usually postulate universal elements (semantic primitives) that are common to all languages, and provide an underlying uniformity. In 1965 Chomsky wrote "The existence of deep-seated formal universals . . . implies that all languages are cut to the same pattern, but does not imply that there is any point to point correspondence between particular languages". However, the universal elements constitute only a part of the semantic system. Linguists disagree about how much of the semantic system is universal and how much is specific to particular languages. So for example, concepts like "cause", "change", "give" may be universal but it is still possible for other concepts to be represented quite differently for different languages.

There are serious difficulties in finding unambiguous experimental evidence for linguistic relativity whether it is expressed in the stronger or the weaker form. If we find cognitive differences between speakers of different languages, we cannot attribute these to the linguistic factor unless we can eliminate, or parcel out other influences on cognition. Cognitive differences between ape and man, between younger and older children, between deaf and hearing, the urban and the rural population, the professor and the miner, cannot be set down to differences in language ability when other factors such as intelligence, education, training and experience may all be confounded with linguistic skill. If we find languages which lack particular lexical items, or grammatical forms, we are not entitled to infer that users of such languages necessarily lack the related mental concepts. Nor does the presence of a particular verbal label in the vocabulary of a language user guarantee that the underlying concept is fully understood. The literature of psychology contains many examples, such as "mind", "image" or "concept" itself, which do not have precisely specified and agreed meanings. Even when there appears to be co-existent linguistic features and forms of cognition, there is usually no clear evidence to establish a causal link between them, let alone to show the direction of causation. Furthermore, any causal links that do exist between language and thought are unlikely to be simple and unidirectional ones. New lexical items may develop to express new cognitive trends, and the new term may then influence our thinking, as the new term "Ms" developed out of the need to describe a female person irrespective of marital status, and its use is supposed to change some of the ways people think about women. Here the relationship of language and thought is bidirectional.

Lexical differences

These problems are illustrated in many of the studies which have been designed to demonstrate linguistic relativity. At the lexical level, one of the ways in which languages vary is the richness of the labelling system used to mark within-category distinctions. Does this entail that the kind of semantic networks described in Chapter 2 must vary between languages? It has been noted that the Hopi Indians have a single term for flying objects encompassing insects, aeroplanes and pilots; the Eskimos have many words for different kinds of snow, and the Arabs many names for different kinds of camel. What can be concluded from these observations? There are two conditions in which a single lexical label will serve for different items. One is when the context will usually make the distinction clear; the other is when we do not need to make the distinction. In English, we have only one word "bank" for the edge of a river, and a financial institution, yet nobody would argue that we cannot distinguish between them. We do not need different words because context would almost always serve to indicate the reference. On the other hand, although a teacher confronted with a new class is quite capable of distinguishing the individual members before he or she has learned their names, knowing their names does make it easier to remember and refer to individuals. A single label of "child" would not suffice because the individuals are all encountered in the same contextual setting. Within our own speech-community, the horticulturalist and the geologist can name subspecies of flower, and kinds of rock, which the rest of us do not need to distinguish, although we could learn to do so if we chose. The absence of lexical labels does not imply that conceptual distinctions cannot be made.

There is experimental evidence to show that stimuli which have un-ambiguous and economical verbal labels are more easily remembered. "Codability" improves recognition of nonsense shapes (Clark, 1965) and of colour chips (Brown and Lenneberg, 1954). In a study of Wolof children, Greenfield *et al.* (1966) showed that the acquisition of superordinate words like "colour" and "shape", which are lacking in the Wolof language, but are learned in French at school, improved the children's ability to group objects according to these attributes. However, language learning was confounded with general education and with city-dwelling, both of which could contribute to cognitive changes. Carroll and Casagrande (1958) investigated object grouping in Navaho children. In Navaho, verbs of handling have different stems depending on the shape of the object being handled, and Navaho-speaking children appeared to be more sensitive to shape properties at an earlier age than the average English-speaking child, whose perceptual grouping is dominated by colour. However children with early experience of constructional toys performed like the Navahos, showing that shape awareness could be either language-induced or culture-induced. The most reasonable conclusion is that verbal labels come into existence in response to the needs of a particular way of life, and act to draw attention to significant perceptual distinctions and groupings, and to maintain them in memory.

Habits or capacities?

In studying linguistic relativity it seems particularly easy to fall into the "Can/Do" confusion which is prevalent in much of cognitive psychology. It may seem unnecessary to stress the obvious fact that while "do" implies "can do", and "can't" implies "don't", the reverse does not hold "Can do" does not imply "do" and "don't" does not imply "can't". In many areas of research psychologists fail to make clear whether they are investigating norms or limits, habits or capacities. Because users of a particular language "don't" habitually express certain ideas, it does not follow that they "can't". Whorf produces no real evidence to support his contention that the Hopi Indians lack an objective sense of time because they express time in terms of subjective duration. In English we can conceptualize three weeks as well as a fortnight, and we can think of an event recurring every six years as easily as one recurring quinquennially. The absence of a term does not preclude the concept. When Whorf writes:

> Hopi "preparing" activities again show a result of their linguistic thought background in an emphasis on persistence and constant insistent repetition. A sense of the cumulative value of innumerable small momenta is dulled by an objectified spatialized view of time like ours, enhanced by a way of thinking close to the subjective awareness of duration of the ceaseless "latering" of events (Whorf, 1941).

This is a splendid imaginative piece of writing, but it is not psychology.

An experimental investigation by Ervin-Tripp (1964) of Japanese–American bilinguals provides more convincing evidence of the influence of language on the content of thought. She found that when a Japanese–American bilingual performed word-association or sentence-completion tests in Japanese, the responses were typical of Japanese monolinguals; when the same speaker performed the tests in English, the responses were typical of American monolinguals. For example, when asked to say what qualities they looked for in a husband, a female subject, when speaking Japanese, would stipulate that he should be pleasing to her family; and when speaking English, that she should be in love with him. The language being used clearly influenced the nature of the thought processes being tapped. Even so, the nationality of the *listener*, and the topic being discussed were also found to influence the kind of ideas expressed in conversation, independently of the language being used.

When lexical terms are not present in a language, but are needed to express new ideas, they are invented or borrowed from another language. Languages such as Modern Hebrew or Welsh have updated their vocabularies to meet the cognitive demands of the twentieth century in this way. Young children commonly invent words, and there are instances of similar productive inventions in the sign language of both chimpanzee and the deaf and dumb. Washoe combined the signs for "water–fruit" to refer to a melon, and in Newcombe's case-study, the child used the signs "sleep–think" to refer to a dream. In Chinese there are no words for "and" and "or", but conjunction and disjunction can be adequately expressed by other means. "A and B" is rendered as "There is A, there is B"; "A or B" as "If not A, then B". There is little reason to suppose that language acts as a cognitive strait-jacket. To the extent that languages are inter-translatable, the ideas that are expressed in one language can still be rendered, however clumsily, in other languages that lack the appropriate terms or structures.

Cognitive development and linguistic structure

It may sometimes be possible to trace the influence of language on thought through cross-cultural studies of young children by looking for differences in the pattern of cognitive abilities, and relating these to the structural characteristics of the language being learned. In a study of this kind Foorman and Kinoshita (1982) compared Japanese children with British and American English speaking children in a referential communication task. The children were carefully matched for memory span and perceptual ability. The task was designed to reveal the effects of differences in the rules for adjectival ordering in Japanese and English. In English, the rule ordains a fixed order of size, colour, pattern, shape (e.g. a little yellow spotted dog). In Japanese the order is more flexible. In perceptual matching tasks, Foorman and Kinoshita established that for all the children shape was the most salient characteristic. They therefore hypothesized that it might be more difficult for English speaking children to encode a string of attributes because, for them, the linguistic order does not correspond to the order of perceptual salience. The test used an array of wooden animals including two values of each attribute (camel/dog; yellow/brown; large/small; striped/spotted). The children were required to choose an item, conceal it, and then describe it so that the experimenter could identify the chosen item. In accordance with the prediction, Japanese children benefitted from the more flexible linguistic order, and performed better than the English speaking children, although the influence of cultural factors could not be wholly excluded.

The evidence for linguistic relativity is largely anecdotal and speculative.

Where experiments have been carried out, it has not proved possible to disentangle the language component from other influences on cognition. Such as it is, the evidence suggests that a given language can influence habits of thought, semantic organization, and the ease and economy with which ideas can be expressed, but does not impose stringent limitations on cognitive functioning. In Chapter 6, when we come to examine the language–thought relationship by comparing thinking in animals, young children or those with language impairment, and normal language users, we should expect to find greater cognitive differences than when we make comparisons across different languages. We must also expect to find that such comparisons are even more contaminated by the other variables which affect cognition and that the influence of the language factor is consequently even harder to assess.

Recommended reading

Vygotsky's *Language and Thought* is a classic book and a pleasure to read. It is both useful and fascinating to read a detailed account of how a chimpanzee learns language, as in the book by Rumbaugh on the Lana Project (1977). Arguments concerning the evolution of language can be found in Morton's *Biological and Social Factors in Psycholinguistics*. For critical evaluations of chimpanzee language learning, read the paper by Terrace *et al.* (1979), and the debate following the Rumbaugh paper in *The Behavioural and Brain Sciences*, 1978.

6 LANGUAGE *and* THOUGHT: WHAT *is* THINKING?

The Nature of Thought

Different kinds of thinking

Compared with the rich and detailed analyses of thinking presented by philosophers such as Gilbert Ryle in *The Concept of Mind* (1949), psychologists have tended to adopt a narrower interpretation. If thinking is to be amenable to experimental investigation, thought processes must start from a situation which is observable, specifiable and controllable, and must issue in some behavioural response which is also observable and measurable. This means that, for the psychologist, studies of thinking tend to be restricted to goal-directed reasoning, problem solving and categorization processes, and many kinds of mental activity which take place without identifiable input and output, such as believing, reflecting, considering, musing and imagining, have received less attention.

Writing about the essential nature of thought, Craik (1943) asserted that "one of the most fundamental properties of thought is its power of predicting events". He considered that the function of thought is to create a model of reality by means of internal symbolism, and he isolated three essential stages in this process: the translation of external objects or events into symbols; the production of further symbols by inferential reasoning, hypothesizing or calculation; and the re-translation of these new symbols into external processes. Different stages of thinking, and different kinds of thinking may depend on language to differing extents. Questions about the relationship of language and thought centre on the first two of Craik's three stages, the representation of information by internal symbols, and the manipulation of the symbols. Posner and Snyder (1975) have distinguished between automatic and attentional mental processes. While automatic processes occur without conscious monitoring or effort, and can be combined with other concurrent mental operations without loss of efficiency, attentional processes are under voluntary control, are consciously monitored, are often effortful, and suffer from interference when combined with other processes. Applied to kinds of thinking, the distinction between automatic and attentional processes is similar to the distinction between intuitive thinking, and logical or rational thinking. While logical thought is conscious, analytical, sequential and orderly, intuitive thought is much more mysterious. Bruner (1960) writes "Intuitive thinking character-istically does not advance in careful well-planned steps . . . the thinker arrives at an answer, which may be right or wrong, with little, if any, awareness of the process by which he reached it". The product is a guess, a hunch, a flash of insight; the process is not conscious, not available to introspection, and not under voluntary control. We use some rather quaint analogies in trying to describe intuition, of which one of the most popular is the chicken farm analogy. Following a period of preparation (or egg collection?), a period of incubation is assumed to occur, after which ideas hatch out. Alternatively, intuition involves "mulling" ideas like claret. Both analogies suggest a spontaneous change occurring passively over time. This incubation or mulling stage is usually envisaged as being sandwiched between preparatory and judgemental stages which are rational and conscious. There does not, however, seem to be any compelling reason to suppose that intuitive thinking and rational, conscious thinking must be separate stages of a sequential process. Neisser (1963) suggests that the two kinds of thinking co-occur simultaneously:

> human thinking is a multiple activity . . . a number of more or less independent trains of thought usually co-exist. Obviously, however, there is a "main sequence" in progress dealing with some particular material in a step-by-step fashion. The main sequence corresponds to the ordinary course of conscious-ness. It may or may not be directly influenced by the other processes going on simultaneously. The concurrent operations are not conscious, because con-sciousness is intrinsically single.

If Neisser's view is correct, then attempts to characterize the thinking involved in a particular task as logical or as intuitive, are misconceived, since a combination of both may be operating simultaneously. The automatic intuitive processes may co-occur with attentional logical thinking.

The role of subvocal speech in thought

In considering how language is related to different kinds of thinking, both the extremist positions, that language is always necessarily involved in thinking, and that language is never involved in thinking, can be rejected. Watson's (1930) claim that thinking can be *equated* with subvocal speech was conclusively disproved by the heroic experiment of Smith *et al.* (1947). Smith volunteered to take curare, and reported subsequently that he was able to think coherently during a period of curare-induced paralysis which suppressed any movement of the speech musculature. While this demon-strated that thought can occur without involving the articulatory system, it is still possible that higher level linguistic representations were being acti-vated. And in more normal circumstances thought may be accompanied by subvocal speech.

Experiments involving electromyographic recording (Garrity, 1977) confirm that spontaneously occurring subvocal speech is related to thinking. The amount of activity in the speech musculature appears to vary with the nature of the task. Language based tasks like reading and writing show higher levels of activity than nonverbal tasks like drawing. Subvocal speech also increased with task difficulty, and with auditory interference. The use of inner speech appears to help the thinker to block out background noise. There is also some evidence that the amount of subvocalization that occurs while memorizing visual information such as pictures, correlates with subsequent recall. The use of verbal coding to maintain information in working memory (e.g. Conrad, 1964), and to label items in longer term memory (e.g. Melton and Martin, 1972), has received ample experimental support. None of this evidence of co-occurrence, however, establishes a necessary relationship between language and any stage of thinking. Alternative systems of internal representation may mediate thinking instead of, or as well as, language. Previous chapters have reviewed evidence for visual coding in working memory, and for an abstract propositional or conceptual code to represent knowledge in long-term memory. It is possible that language is simply one of several optional forms of internal represent-ation that happens to be especially appropriate for some kinds of infor-mation. It is also possible that language is the input–output code that is in use at the working memory stage, but is not operating at the deeper level stages of thought which are inaccessible to consciousness. The fact that, in problem solving, subjects often find it difficult to generate a verbal protocol by thinking aloud, and claim that not all of their thinking can be verbalized, reinforces the conclusion that some mental operations are independent of language. Inner speech appears to serve as a code in working memory; as a device to hold attention and mask interference; and sometimes as a means of self-direction whereby the thinker guides and instructs himself. While attentional thought processes do often appear to involve inner speech, there is no evidence that mental operations of the kind that are automatic and unconscious are mediated by language.

On the whole efforts to classify and define different kinds of thinking have not been very successful. The haziness which attends the concept of intuitive thought is made particularly obvious in the field of computer simulation (Chapter 8) where it becomes apparent that we cannot simulate intuitive thought processes because they are insufficiently understood. As will be shown in Chapter 9 a similar obscurity surrounds the intuitive thought processes which are supposed to be a speciality of the right cerebral hemisphere.

The remainder of this chapter examines the cognitive capacities and limitations of thinkers who differ in language ability, and the kinds of thinking that can be carried on without verbalization.

Individual Differences in Language Ability

Psycholinguists are increasingly coming to recognize the importance of individual differences in language ability (Fillmore *et al.*, 1979). While the universalist viewpoint dominated research, individual differences were dismissed as minor irrelevancies, affecting performance but not competence. Current opinions give more weight to these differences, and to their relation to cognition.

The relationship of verbal and nonverbal intelligence

One index of language ability in the individual is provided by traditional psychometric tests. Carroll (1979) re-analysed the intercorrelations between Thurstone's (1938) tests of mental abilities. Several interesting points emerged. Scores on the language ability tests (vocabulary, reading, comprehension and prose writing), showed large individual differences. Although these tests correlated with each other, they did not correlate with scores on tests of spatial ability, number ability, associative memory and recognition accuracy. The correlation of the language ability tests with reasoning ability was also low. Ability in inductive and deductive reasoning, qualitative reasoning and classification showed little dependence on language ability. These results indicate one of two conclusions. Either language and thought can show a considerable measure of dissociation in the individual, or, the kind of language ability required in reasoning is different from the kind tested in conventional language ability tests.

Genie: a case of language deprivation

A recent case history illustrates an extreme example of imbalance between language and cognition in the individual. Curtiss (1977) described the case of Genie "a modern day wild-child", who was discovered at the age of 13 years, having been incarcerated in a small room in appalling conditions all her life until then. Cognitive and linguistic deprivation was almost complete. Since being rescued from these conditions, Genie has received intensive language training. Her progress has been slow and rather uneven. Genie's language production is difficult to compare with that of a normal child, but is roughly around the level of a 3-year-old. Her sentences show extreme and persistent reduction to a telegraphic form (for example, "[If] Neal [does] not come [I will be] sad") whereas in the utterances of normal children the amount of reduction steadily decreases. Although Genie's sentences are genuinely creative, her application of syntactic rules is variable. Some rules have not been learned at all, and others are used inconsistently. Comprehension is much better than production, although some constructions like the active–passive distinction are not understood. In spite of this fairly low level of language attainment, in some tests of cognitive ability Genie does well. In tests of visual ability like face recognition, spatial orientation and picture completion she is at the level of a normal adult, although her auditory memory span is only equivalent to that of a 3½-year-old child. On other tasks involving memory for nonverbal sequences her performance is also poor. Curtiss has characterized Genie as a holistic right hemisphere thinker, claiming that her deficits in language and in sequential tasks reflect malfunction of the left hemisphere. Although it is doubtful whether the allocation of cognitive abilities to left and right hemispheres is as clear-cut as Curtiss is assuming (see Chapter 9 for a discussion of this issue), the study of Genie provides striking evidence that at least some kinds of cognitive ability do not require the support of a highly developed language system. Like Adam, the boy described on p. 120, Genie has been able to use her newly acquired language to tell of her experiences and emotions in the period when she was alinguistic. So events can be represented internally in memory without language.

Referential and expressive children

More subtle individual differences in language development can be observed in normal children. Nelson (1981) distinguishes what she calls Referential language users from Expressives, and suggests that these two kinds of language development reflect differences in cognitive style. The early language of the Referential child shows a preponderance of nouns that are names of objects, and, at the two-word stage, combinations of substantives. Sentence construction is based on analysis and productive recombination of elements. Speech is used primarily in the context of cognitive experiences. Expressive children appear to use language quite differently. Their speech is predominantly social or pragmatic. It contains many imitative utterances of the kind sometimes called formulaic. These phrases (for example "I-don't-know-where-it-is") are run off rapidly and holistically, without pauses between the words. The child is not, at the time, capable of segmenting the utterances and recombining the elements. Referential speech has been tentatively linked to the left hemisphere, and expressive speech to the right. The two different forms of language might, it is suggested, originate from neurological factors that govern the pattern of the child's cognitive abilities, as well as the form of language that is developed. Alternatively, the type of language the child uses may be determined by the nature of his interactions with his mother, Referential children being produced by mothers who spend a lot of time explaining the nature of objects and events to their children, while mothers whose speech to their children is mainly social and pragmatic produce Expressive children. So, while differences in linguistic style are plausibly related to cognitive differences, it is not clear whether they are causally determined by neurological or experiential factors. The interpretation of individual differences in child language in terms of experience is closely related to the interpretation of sociolinguistic differences in language ability.

Sociolinguistic differences

A form of language handicap with cognitive consequences is alleged to exist in lower social classes (Bernstein, 1971). He noted that the verbal IQ of working-class boys was lower than would be expected on the basis of their nonverbal IQ scores, and distinguished between what he calls the "restricted code", predominant in the speech of the working class, and the "elaborated code", typical of the middle class. The restricted speech code is characterized by short sentences, little use of subordinate clauses, frequent shifts of topic and requests for reinforcement (You know?, You see?, OK?). The restricted code is very context-bound, draws on a limited number of alternatives, and is highly predictable. The elaborated code is much less predictable. The speaker selects from an extensive range of possible structures, the sentence structure is syntactically more complex, and speech is context-independent, so that information can successfully be communicated to others who do not share the knowledge and immediate percepts of the speaker. Bernstein considers that restricted-code users are severely handicapped educationally, because formal schooling requires the use of an elaborated code. The restricted code is unsuited for the exchange of information, and for the expression of abstract ideas, and results in a kind of learning which, according to Bernstein (1972), "never really gets inside to become integrated into pre-existing schemata", and "orients its speakers to a less complex conceptual hierarchy, and so to a low order of causality". These views have been strongly criticized by other linguists, who believe it is easy to underestimate the richness and versatility of working-class language, especially when data samples are collected by researchers who are not themselves members of the speech community being studied (Labov, 1966). Even if we accept that linguistic skill is impoverished in the lower social class, the educational consequences cited by Bernstein are entirely hypothetical. There is no empirical evidence that working-class boys are oriented to a low order of causality, whatever that may mean. The distinction between restricted and elaborated codes is in any case a performance distinction, and difference between the users of the two codes may be much less marked at the level of competence. Nevertheless, the fact that nonverbal IQ scores and verbal IQ scores diverge, with the nonverbal scores being less depressed, again suggests some degree of independence in the relation of language and thought.

It is interesting that Bernstein's distinction between Restricted and Elaborated language is similar in many ways to Nelson's distinction between Expressive and Referential speech, but how far cognition is actually constrained by these different forms of language is not well established.

The Deaf

The cognitive limitations of the deaf ought, in theory, to define a borderline between alinguistic thought, and thinking that can only be accomplished by means of verbal language, but many factors prevent such a neat demarcation from emerging. The deaf are not a very homogeneous group, because they have differing degrees of hearing loss, incurred at different ages, and have been exposed to different methods of education designed to inculcate some facility in oral language, or in manual language, with variable success. Because it is difficult to judge how far the deaf lack language, it is not possible to conclude that tasks which can be performed successfully by the deaf are tasks that do not require the use of language. Where cognitive limitations are apparent, they cannot necessarily be attributed to language handicap. By comparison with normals, deaf subjects may be less well educated, more emotionally disturbed, poorly motivated in test situations, distractable, and unable to understand the test requirements. All these factors, in addition to language deficiencies, may depress cognitive performance. Further problems arise in selecting suitable control groups with which to compare deaf subjects. If deaf children are matched with normal controls on chronological age, the deaf almost inevitably are disadvantaged by their educational retardation. If, instead, the deaf subjects are equated with normals on selected intelligence tests, this procedure may have the effect of ironing-out real differences between the deaf and hearing populations.

Oléron (1953) accepts the view that the deaf are "inferior to those with normal hearing, particularly in the domain of abstract mental activities". The findings he cites in support of this statement are mainly drawn from the results of sorting tasks. Although there is surprisingly widespread acceptance of performance on sorting tasks as a reflection of conceptual thinking, and an index of intellectual ability and capacity for abstract thought, some doubts may be felt about the validity of this test, and the criteria for "abstraction" are confused. When a subject is asked to arrange a set of objects into groups, groupings may reflect preferences, rather than the presence or absence of concepts. We cannot always infer what categories are being used in group formation, so that a given group may reflect either several small categories (e.g. toys and utensils) or a single large category (e.g. inanimate objects). The criteria for "abstraction" as used by different researchers may include any of the following.

1. The extraction of salient features (e.g. shape).
2. The use of superordinate classes (e.g. animals).
3. The use of classes which do not have common perceptual features (e.g. tools).
4. The ability to re-classify items into different groupings by new criteria.
5. The ability to explain the principles of classification that were used.

Oléron reports that the deaf have difficulty in shifting from one sorting principle to another, although they are able to make the shift if given hints from the experimenter. He also noted that when required to explain their sorting principles in writing, they used specific, concrete labels (like "blue") rather than conceptual class labels (like "colour"), and he regards this as a failure of abstraction. It seems doubtful, though, whether Oléron is justified in regarding the explanatory powers of his deaf subjects as evidence of conceptual limitations, rather than as linguistic limitations. It is difficult to interpret his results, since his deaf subject must have had some linguistic proficiency if they were able to supply written explanations of their responses. The conclusion that their abstract thinking is defective does not, in any case, seem compelling.

Furth (1966) has maintained that the intellectual functioning of the deaf is only inferior in certain specific tasks, which are normally mediated by language, but that basic intellectual capacities such as conceptual thinking, abstraction and generalization do not depend on language, and so are not impaired by deafness. He goes so far as to assert "logical intelligent thinking does not need the support of a symbol system". This assertion is surprising in view of the facts that his deaf subjects do fail some logical tests, and that they are not wholly without a symbolic system. The poor performances of deaf subjects on a "Pick the opposite" task, and the difficulty they experience in remembering temporal sequences, are ascribed to lack of language, since Furth considers that these tasks require verbal mediation. The failure of deaf children to understand the conservation of quantity and liquids until about five years later than normal children is attributed to intellectual retardation and cultural deprivation, rather than to language handicap, since the older deaf children perform correctly without any appreciable improvement in linguistic skill. In fact, Furth's claim that the deaf are not intellectually handicapped becomes virtually self-validating if any observed deficits can be attributed either to lack of verbal mediation, or to cognitive retardation. Furth's interpretation of the results of tests of logical reasoning is also questionable. His tests explored the ability to understand and use logical symbols. One of these tests is strikingly similar to the task carried out by Premack's chimpanzee, Sarah, described in Chapter 5. Symbols for conjunction, disjunction and negation are combined with the symbols "B" for blue, and "R" for red, and applied appropriately to presentations of blue and red cards. (For example, B . R symbolizes "the blue card and the red card". B . R̄ symbolizes "the blue card and not the red card"). After learning these combinations, a transfer task was introduced, in which the logical connectives were combined with the symbols "C" (circular) and "D" (dark). On this transfer task only 11% of normal young children, and 64% of normal older children performed above chance level. All the deaf children failed. Clearly, the logical rule had not been understood, since it could not be applied to a new situation. This result is especially odd in view of Sarah's record of 80% success on similar transfer tests. However, Furth tested a group of adult deaf subjects on the task shown in Fig. 21 and they learned to respond correctly, but the ability of the subjects to transfer these rules to

Operation	Symbol	Instance	Response
Negation	$\bar{O}$	■●	−
Conjunction	O·△	▲	−
Simplification	△	■▲	+
Disjunction "Simple"	O/△	▲	+
Disjunction "Exclusive"	O/△	▲●	−
Disjunction "Addition"	O/△	▲■	+
Conjunction (1 negation)	$\bar{O}$·△	▲	+
Conjunction (2 negations)	$\bar{△}$·$\bar{O}$	●	−
Negated conjunction	$\bar{△}$·O	▲	+
Negated disjunction	O/$\bar{△}$	■	+

FIG. 21. *Sample of symbol, instance and response for ten types of logical operation.*

novel stimuli was apparently not tested. Furth considers that this success is more significant than the failure of the deaf children on the transfer task, and still claims that no purely intellectual impairment is associated with deafness. His argument that logical thinking is independent of symbolization can hardly rest on these results, since the task did employ symbols. Perhaps Furth meant that logical reasoning can be mediated by visual symbols and does not depend on verbal ones. Even so, his deaf subjects do seem to have experienced more difficulty than normals, and to gloss over this difference is doctrinaire.

The gap between the performance of deaf and normal subjects tends to widen as tasks increase in difficulty. It is still not easy to judge whether the deaf suffer from a general cognitive deficit, or whether it is their lack of language which penalizes the harder tasks more severely. The fact that the performance of the deaf continues to improve into adulthood, and responds to training, without a corresponding improvement in language, suggests that cognitive development is delayed, rather than blocked by deafness and is not wholly dependent on linguistic skill.

Bilingualism

Compound and co-ordinate bilinguals. The study of bilingualism provides some interesting insights into possible relationships between language and thought. According to one theory, both languages are mapped on to a common, higher-order conceptual system. Operations of thinking take place within this abstract system, and are not identified with either language.

Although in Chapter 5 we noted some evidence that the content and organization of thought is influenced by the particular language being spoken by a bilingual, other studies of bilingual subjects have lent support to the view that thinking is essentially independent of language. Schank (1972) presents a model of natural language processing in which he postulates

> there exists a conceptual base that is interlingual, onto which linguistic structures in a given language map . . . People fluent in many languages can pass freely from one to another . . . what they are doing is invoking a package of mapping rules for a given language from the conceptual base. The conceptual base has in it the content of the thought that is being expressed.

Schank's conceptual base is very similar to the conceptual–propositional base of Anderson and Bower (1973) which stores knowledge received via all modalities, including images and any languages, and generates output in any form. The claim that each separate language of the bilingual speaker maps on to a common conceptual base needs some modification in the light of a distinction between two kinds of bilinguals, compound and co-ordinate. Lambert and Preston (1967) define compound bilinguals as those who learned both languages simultaneously, in the same contextual setting, and for whom the symbols of Language A and Language B map on to a single meaning, having exact equivalence. Co-ordinate bilinguals learn their two languages in separate contexts, and the symbols do not have exact semantic equivalence. While compound bilinguals conform to Schank's model in that both their languages have a common conceptual base, this is not true for co-ordinate bilinguals. In practice the compound/co-ordinate distinction is difficult to make. The nature of language development in the bilingual child provides some clues. When progress in one language facilitates progress in the other, as when new syntactic forms appear in both languages in close succession, a unified compound system is involved. When development in the two languages is very uneven, the child is more likely to be a co-ordinate bilingual. Precise details of the early language learning of bilinguals are not always available. It seems very unlikely that a compound bilingual could acquire all the lexical items of his two languages pairwise, in circumstances of complete parity. Moreover, the distinction hinges on two of the knottiest problems in cognitive psychology—the definition of meaning, and the identification of the relevant elements of context. Nevertheless, it may still be possible for some bilinguals to approximate more closely to the compound type, and others to the co-ordinate type. The distinction generates various predictions, and some of these are borne out by experimental findings. In case of traumatic aphasia, patients classified as compound bilinguals are more likely to have both languages impaired. Co-ordinate bilinguals, whose two languages are less closely related, are more likely to exhibit specific impairment of a single language. Albert and Osler (1978) reported cases where the degree of language disruption was different in the two languages, and recovery was not parallel. They also found that the degree of cerebral lateralization could be different for each language, indicating some separation at a neurological level.

Experimental studies of bilingualism. Psycholinguistic experiments reveal that some stages of processing are language specific, while others may be common to both languages. The output stage is obviously specific, but at the input stage phonological analysis is unified. How far the two languages are unified at the semantic level is much harder to determine. The more unified the two language systems are, the easier it should be to switch from one to the other but the prediction that compound bilinguals should have greater facility in switching between languages has not been confirmed, and no differences in ease of switching have been detected. In a study which examined only compound bilinguals, Taylor (1971) analysed the responses in a free association test. Responses were predominantly in unilingual clusters, and the probability of switching was lower than for not switching, so that intra-language links were clearly stronger than cross-language links. However, when cross-language switches occurred these reflected semantic associations, which supports the view that cross-language linkage is at a semantic level. Further experiments have tested free recall of mixed-language word lists as compared with unilingual lists. The results are contradictory, and difficult to interpret. Predictions about the performance of bilinguals depend on theoretical assumptions about the mechanisms of storage and retrieval. Glanzer and Duarte (1971) found that lists of words with items repeated in a different language were recalled as well, or better, than lists with items repeated in the same language. A list containing, for example, "horse, neige, cheval, snow" is as easy to remember as "horse, snow, horse, snow". They concluded that in mixed-language lists, both versions of the repeated item were stored as a single meaning. Kolers (1965) reported that mixed-language lists were better recalled, but Tulving and Colotla (1970) found that, although bi- and trilingual lists were recalled as well as unilingual lists from primary (short-term) memory, recall from secondary (long-term) memory was inferior. They concluded that the semantic organization which is typical of secondary memory is harder to establish for multilingual lists because inter-item links are weaker across language boundaries.

Goggin and Wickens (1971) showed that when subjects learned successive lists of words, the build-up of pro-active inhibition (PI) was dissipated by presenting a new list in a different language. This "release from PI" effect is generally taken as evidence of independent coding. A similar conclusion was reached by Kirsner et al. (1980). In a lexical decision task the subject must judge whether a string of letters constitutes a word or not. If the letter string is a word it matches a representation of that word in the internal lexicon. Nonword strings fail to match any internal representation. Kirsner et al. mixed English and Hindi words with nonwords, and used English/ Hindi bilinguals as subjects. They found that judgements were facilitated by repetition of words in the same language, but not by repetition of words in the other 'anguage, suggesting separate lexicons for each language. On the other hand, it has been found that semantic satiation effects, whereby constant repetition of a word makes it seem temporarily meaningless, will spread to affect translation equivalents.

One reason for discrepancies between these studies is that subjects may have differed along the compound-co-ordinate dimension. Another is that the different tasks involve different components of the language system which may be interconnected or unified to different extents.

Lambert and Preston (1967) used the Stroop test to find out how far the two languages of bilinguals are separated, and whether one can be "switched off" while the other is in operation. In the Stroop test, the subject's task is to name the colour of the ink in which a word is printed. When the word is itself the name of a different colour (e.g. the word "blue" written in red ink) the correct response of "red" is delayed by the interference generated by the conflicting word meaning. Lambert and Preston compared the performance of bilinguals naming the ink colour in Language A when the conflicting word was in Language B (saying "red" when the word was "*jaune*") and naming the ink colour in Language A when the word was in the same language (saying "red" when the word was "yellow"). If the two languages are stored separately, then the interference caused by conflicting information should be less if the conflicting inputs are in different languages, than when they are in the same language. The results showed that interference was reduced when the competing responses were in different languages, which implies a degree of separation, but the fact that some interference did occur in the mixed-language condition indicates that separation is not complete, and subjects could not switch off one language absolutely. To sum up, the experiments with bilinguals suggest that within-language links are stronger than across-language links, but that cross-language links exist, and are mainly at the semantic or conceptual level, although there is clearly considerable variation between individuals in

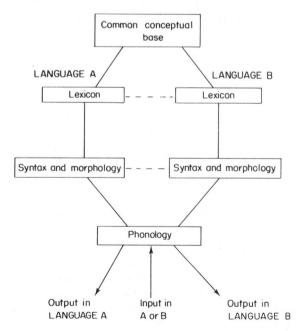

FIG. 22. A model of language organization for a compound bilingual with a unified conceptual system.

the way their languages are organized. The existence of high-level semantic links between languages does not necessarily confirm the existence of an alinguistic conceptual base on to which the different languages are mapped. These results are quite consistent with a system whereby the lexical items of the two languages are mapped directly on to each other. The experiments where mixed language inputs and single language inputs produce no differences in performance give stronger evidence of a common conceptual system. Figure 22 shows a model of language organization for a compound bilingual with a unified conceptual system.

Thinking Without Language

Cognitive abilities of nonhuman primates

Studies of animal learning help to define the upper limits of cognitive processes in animals, and the extent of the gap between animal and human cognitive ability. Language is, of course, only one of many factors which contribute to the existence of this gap. Many of the tests employ tasks which penalize animals because they fall outside the naturally occurring repertoire of the animal's behaviour. Physical limitations may be compounded with intellectual ones if the perceptual and motor demands of the task are difficult for the animal to meet. Animals are especially disadvantaged in that the nature of the task cannot be directly communicated to them, and their previous experience may give little clue as to what is required. Because of these problems, we are not entitled to argue that deficits in animal cognition result from the absence of language, but we can point to the achievements of animal cognition as an indication of how effective non-linguistic thought can be. In this section a few studies of non-human primate learning are selected in which the animals solve quite complex problems with a surprising degree of success.

Viki. An excellent example of primate cognitive ability is provided by the studies of Viki, a chimpanzee home-reared as described by Hayes (1951). From shortly after birth, Viki's environment and experience were exactly the same as for a pre-school child. Viki did not succeed in learning language, so that her success with nonverbal tasks gives quite a clear indication of how far mental development can proceed independently of language, and how this compares with the performance of a young child. In a series of tests described by Hayes and Nissen (1971), Viki was presented with instrumentation and manipulation problems. Viki showed ability to adapt previous knowledge to new situations, and to utilize objects in the environment in new ways. She up-ended a rectangular box to raise a box-stack to the height needed to reach a suspended lure. She spontaneously replaced a defective hook on the rope of her swing by tying a knot, and profited from slight gestural "hints" indicating that box-opening problems could be solved, in one case by using scissors to cut a string, and in another, by inserting a crank into a hole and turning it. Her performance on these tasks was very similar to her child co-subjects, except that Viki did not benefit from seeing pictorial representations of the required responses, but only from the experimenter touching or pointing to the critical elements in the situation. Hayes and Nissen point out that the pictures may not have been meaningful for Viki. In a series of increasingly complex latch-box problems which required two-handed manipulation to depress springs, turn keys etc. her performance was as good as, or better than, the children, and showed rapid improvement through successive problems.

On some well controlled number perception tasks, Viki at the age of 3½ years performed at the same level as a 3½-year-old child. On a number-matching task, in which the card bearing the same number of spots as a target card had to be selected, her accuracy deteriorated as the number of spots increased, especially if the difference between alternative cards was only one spot. In a discrimination task requiring her to remember an absolute number of spots over a series of trials, and respond positively to corresponding cards, she broke down on the four spots v. five spots discrimination. She also failed at a task requiring reproduction of a given number of temporally presented taps. In these tests, Viki's ability is equivalent to that of a child who has not yet learned to count. Children who can count verbally, and, oddly enough, birds, do better.

In concept-discrimination problems Viki showed ability to discriminate between pictures of animate v. inanimate items, male v. female people, large v. small objects, red v. green, circles v. crosses, and complete v. incomplete pictures (e.g. a dog without legs). The accuracy of Viki's discrimination was within 5% of her child fellow subjects. In sorting tasks, an ingenious method was used to reveal the principles of classification Viki was employing by introducing ambiguous objects. When she was apparently sorting objects into eating tools and writing tools, Viki assigned wooden chopsticks with the writing set and a metal pen with the eating set. She was sorting by material, and not by function. Viki was also tested for "abstraction" as defined by the ability to re-classify the same objects in different ways. A set of buttons could be divided into 40 white and 40 black, or 40 large and 40 small, or 40 square and 40 round. Viki sorted the button collection first by colour, then by shape, and then by size. With other sets, Viki sometimes changed her sorting principle and re-classified spontaneously, sometimes in response to prompting. Viki does not appear to suffer from the rigidity and concreteness which some researchers have claimed to be characteristic of the deaf and aphasic, so that these defects of sorting behaviour do not necessarily stem from linguistic disabilities.

In a conditional matching task Viki achieved 88% accuracy. Pairs of objects had to be matched by colour if presented on a blue tray, and by shape if presented on a white tray. The task imposes considerable demands on memory and attention since the performer must remember the rule, and attend to two dimensions. Another task, which proved beyond Viki's powers, required her to learn arbitrary temporal sequences of string pulling. Eventually, she became distressed and attempts to teach her this task had to be abandoned. Hayes and Nissen noted that 3-year-old children succeeded by verbalizing and chanting the sequences, and speculate that "language and sequence behaviour may be intimately related in that language development is dependent upon flexible re-ordering of the same units; and the sequence experience involved in using language may transfer to other sequencing situations". In corroboration, we have already noted that deaf children have difficulty in learning temporal sequences, and that Washoe's signs lack consistently meaningful ordering and other studies of primate learning have also reported very limited memory for sequential order.

Sarah. Even more remarkable than Viki's cognitive achievements are the abilities demonstrated by Premack's language-learning chimpanzee Sarah, and other chimpanzees in his laboratory. Whether Sarah's performance in cognitive tasks is mediated by internalization of the symbolic represent-ations she has learned is quite unclear. More probably, her language training has simply made her generally receptive to higher education.

Woodruff *et al.* (1978) claimed that, at least in some conditions, Sarah showed conservation of liquid and quantity. In their tests, the liquids were displayed initially in two identical containers A and B. The liquid in B was then transferred to a differently shaped container C, and Sarah was asked to judge whether A and C were the same or different, using her plastic symbols to respond. For the quantity judgements, two quantities of modelling clay were initially identical, and then one was manipulated into a different shape. Sarah responded correctly as long as she could observe the transformation operation taking place, but not if she only saw the items *after* transfor-mation. While great caution needs to be exercised in trying to infer what an animal "understands" in such a task, Sarah apparently had some grasp of the principle of invariance under transformation, but was unable to understand the compensatory relationship of variations in height and width.

In a further experiment, Woodruff and Premack (1981) tested Sarah and four other young chimpanzees on tasks involving concepts of proportionality and numerosity, in a match-to-sample procedure. Three different types of object were used. Spherical items of food such as apples; grey wooden discs; and plastic cylinders containing tinted water. In the proportionality judgements, each kind of item could take the value of 1 (complete); ¾ (¼ segment missing, or, for the cylinder ¾ full); ½; or ¼. The animals were required to view a sample item and then choose which of two others matched the sample in terms of proportion. When all the items were of the same kind (all discs, all spheres, all cylinders) Sarah was nearly always correct, and the other chimpanzees could do the easy matches. That is, they could choose correctly between ¾ and 1, but not between ¾ and ½. When judgements had to be made across dissimilar items, for example matching ¼ grapefruit to ¼ full cylinder, only Sarah was successful. The results for matching numerosity (1, 2, 3 or 4 items) were similar. The ability to match proportions is cognitively complex, involving an inferred relation such that ¼ grapefruit is to a whole grapefruit as a ¼ full cylinder is to a full cylinder. Since Sarah has not learned labels for proportional values this type of reasoning apparently occurs without symbolization.

Controversial results were obtained by Premack and Woodruff (1978) in a series of experiments which sought to demonstrate that Sarah was able to infer the mental state of a person, and vicariously solve that person's problem. Sarah was shown film of a person in a variety of problem situations (e.g. locked in a cage unable to get out; shivering with cold and unable to light a stove; trying to wash a floor with a hose not properly fixed, etc.). Sarah was then given a choice of two pictures, one showing the appropriate solution object (key, lighted wick) and one showing a different inappropriate object. Whether Sarah's ability to choose the correct item with an above chance success rate really shows that she could understand the intentions of the actor in the film, and empathize with his problem is not at all certain. Some critics consider this interpretation of the results to be over-rich, and suggest that Sarah might have been simply matching the chosen object to an item in the film (key to door, lighted wick to stove) in an associative pairing. Another important point is that if this type of test is to give evidence of insightful understanding, as opposed to some kind of trial and error learning, it is the animal's *first* response that is crucial, not the percentage of correct choices in a series of trials.

Memory and rule learning. It is a general feature of studies of primate learning that performance tends to break down when the memory load, or information processing load, is increased beyond a certain point. Jarrard and Moise (1971) reported that primates could judge two successively presented stimuli to be the same or different when the interval between them was less than 10 s, but response accuracy declined to chance level when the second stimulus was delayed by 30 s. It is reasonable to assume that the greatly superior performance of adult humans is boosted by verbal mediation, which assists them to bridge longer delays. Weinstein (1941) compared 4-year-old rhesus monkeys, and 3-year-old children, on a delayed matching-to-sample task. A sample object was presented for matching and handling, and then removed. After a delay of 5, 10 or 15 s, choice objects were presented and the subject had to select the one which matched the sample. Both children and monkeys reached an 80% correct criterion at all delays, but showed signs of stress at the longer delay, and the monkeys required more than ten times as many training trials as the children. In classical delayed response experiments, food is placed in one of two identical containers, which are then covered, and after a delay the animal is permitted to make a choice response. Performance on these tasks declines sharply as the delay is increased, but critical delay intervals cannot be taken as an accurate reflection of the duration of the animal's memory, because of the many other variables which govern delayed responses. These include the presence of spatial cues or other perceptual cues, orienting responses made by the animal, motivation, activity and distractability during the delay. The characteristics of trial sequence are also an important factor. The animal may perform better if the location of the food can be predicted on the basis of previous trials, and find the task more difficult if location is randomly varied from trial to trial. Because there are so many determining factors, different critical delays emerge with different experimental paradigms, different species, and different individuals (Tinklepaugh, 1928). In more natural settings, animals are observed to locate buried food after intervals of days, rather than seconds, so that although experimental procedures yield estimates that compare unfavourably with human memory, they may not be a valid index of the capacity and duration of animal memory. And Tinklepaugh has shown that monkeys remember not only where food was hidden, but what food was hidden. His monkey subjects liked lettuce quite well but preferred banana. If lettuce was hidden and later found, they ate it happily, but if they saw banana being hidden and lettuce was substituted, the finder threw a tantrum and rejected the lettuce in disgust.

The ability of primates to learn rules implies that quite complex internal representations must be formed and stored, but little can be inferred about the nature of these representations. Harlow's (1949) studies of problem-to-problem transfer effects revealed that training on a set of problems of one type improved proficiency at learning new problems of the same type. The monkeys' performance over successive problems exhibited a phenomenon Harlow called "learning to learn" or the formation of a "learning set". Typically, the number of trials required to learn a discrimination response shows a dramatic and orderly decrease over successive problems, even though the specific stimuli and the critical cues are changed or reversed. The improvement is not a temporary phenomenon. Braun *et al.* (1952) found that learning sets were retained over a period as long as 8 weeks. What is the nature of cognitive change that takes place when a learning set is formed? According to Harlow, inappropriate error-producing response tendencies are being eliminated. Levine (1965) has derived a Hypothesis model from a mathematical analysis of patterns of responses. According to this model, the animal progressively adopts an hypothesis, H, which is a mediating process or rule, having general applicability to a group of problems. Examples of hypotheses include a position-alternation rule (e.g. choose the left-hand object on trial n and the right-hand object on trial $n + 1$, in a LRLRLR sequence), or a Win-Stay-Lose-Shift rule (repeat the response if it was rewarded on the previous trial, change the response if it was not rewarded). Some evidence for hypothesis learning comes from an analysis of double alternation problems, in which the correct sequence of responses is LLRRLLRR etc. Systematic patterns of responding can be observed at an early stage, before the correct sequence has been fully mastered. Some of Harlow's monkeys also succeeded in learning a generalized oddity rule, that is, they learned to choose the odd item out of three, two of which were the same and one different, and transferred the principle successfully to new groups of items.

By comparison with adult humans, primates learn very slowly, and require arduous step-by-step training programmes; not all individuals succeed, and learning is less flexible once established. By comparison with prelinguistic children their cognitive abilities are scarcely inferior. Problems in which humans normally employ verbal mediation, such as learning sequences, delayed matching and counting, appear to be especially difficult for primates. It is a reasonable conclusion that verbalization improves retention, and reduces the information load. How far the achievements of primates can be considered to exemplify "thinking" depends, of course, on how thinking is defined. Probably Viki's performance on the instrumental tasks, and Harlow's rule-learning experiments come closest to the definition of thinking discussed at the beginning of this chapter. There is plenty of evidence that primates possess many of the components of thinking such as memory, some forms of abstraction, concepts, the ability to learn and apply rules and to make judgements, but there is relatively little evidence of the prolonged goal-directed covert mental activity, or of the sequential chains of inferences, that are typical of human reasoning.

Cognitive development in children

In the course of development a child changes from being a nonlinguistic animal to being a linguistic animal, but the expectation that the acquisition of language should produce a clear transformation in cognitive development proves to be naive, and objective causal links between increasing mastery of language and enhanced cognitive ability are elusive. Both theoretical and descriptive accounts of the cognitive development of children are controversial.

Although it has been traditional to describe development in terms of stages, there is disagreement as to the nature of the successive stages, and even as to their existence. There is also disagreement on whether the sequence of stages is universal and invariant, and on the relative influence of maturation, experience and language on development. In considering the relationship of language to cognition, we are primarily interested in knowing what factors govern the course of development, what causes the transitions from one stage to the next. Does the increasing mastery of language underpin the child's cognitive development, or is increasing cognitive competence the basis for language acquisition? Such questions are, of course, much too simple.

In the normal child, cognitive development occurs in parallel with maturation, with increasing experience and education, and with improving linguistic skills, and it is impossible to determine the effect of any one of these factors in isolation. Nevertheless, some researchers have tried to show the temporal, or logical priority of either thought or language.

The primacy of cognition. Macnamara (1972) argues that some cognitive structures are a necessary pre-requisite for the acquisition of language, at least in the early stages. These arguments are mainly of an intuitive kind. For instance, it is suggested that a child could not learn to apply a name to an object, unless he already has a concept of the object. According to this view the child could not learn the correct referents of lexical labels without falling victim to the impasse described by Quine in *Word and Object* (1960). Quine argues that a linguist trying to learn a strange language could not know whether a term like "rabbit" referred to the animal, or some part or attribute of the animal, or some co-occurring feature of the scene. For the child (and, indeed, for the linguist) this problem can be resolved if he is equipped with perceptual biases and constraints similar to those of the rest of the speech community, so that what is perceptually salient for other observers will also tend to be salient for him, and, secondly, with a general inductive learning strategy which allows him to generalize across instances, and to modify or correct his hypotheses in accordance with feedback. If he initially infers that "rabbit" refers to any small furry animal, his misapplications of the term will be corrected, and his overgeneralization will eventually be cut back until his use of the label is confined to acceptable instances. In Chapter 4, evidence that just this kind of strategy does operate in children's concept learning is discussed. Whatever the cognitive basis required for learning the referents of lexical labels, it is clearly also possessed by the chimpanzee linguists. More sophisticated cognitive precursors are required, according to Macnamara, for learning syntax. For example, he states "the child must use his non-linguistic knowledge to arrive at the notions of direct and indirect object". Before he can understand the difference between "John drove the car" and "John drove home", he must understand the nature of the objects and actions mentioned. Similarly, he cannot understand tense usage until he has acquired some understanding of the concept of time. Bruner (1975) has stressed the role of early experience in nonverbal communication and signalling, whereby the child comes to understand concepts such as agent, action, object and recipient, which later emerge in language as case-forms. The intuitive appeal of these arguments receives experimental support from a study by Moeser and Bregman (1973) who found adult subjects unable to learn the syntactic rules of an artificial language, unless they were shown pictured referents for the symbols which provided a semantic basis for learning. If we accept these indications of the primacy of cognitive bases in some of the initial stages of language learning, it is not necessarily true of all the later stages, since many aspects of language which are purely formal and arbitrary, and have no semantic force (such as noun gender in some languages), are nevertheless mastered successfully.

Gopnik (1982) studied the meaning of the very earliest words to appear in the speech of 1–2-year-old children, and found that these were used primarily to express the child's cognitive discoveries. At an age when the child is experimenting with actions designed to bring about events, and studying the causal relations involved in changes, these words mark aspects of the concepts he is exploring. Gopnik found that words like "gone" and "down" marked changing spatial relations like disappearance, falling or moving downward, and were initially confined to movements caused by the child's own actions, and later extended to movements brought about by other people. "There" and "Oh dear" were used to signal success or failure, respectively, of the child's own actions in attempting to bring about a planned goal. "No" was used to oppose other people's plans, or to signal a change of the child's own plan when an action was suspended and a new one substituted. "More" was first used to mark repetition of an action, and only later for numerosity. Gopnik's detailed account of the context of utterance for these early words provides a convincing picture of what she describes as the "child-as-scientist" using language to label his discoveries. Although this account implies that language and cognition are developing in tandem, it is the child's growing awareness and understanding of the dynamics of the real world that supply the driving force, with language in a supporting roie.

Nelson (1978) and McCartney and Nelson (1981) have argued that children's ability to understand language depends on prior knowledge. The complexity of the knowledge base that is required for understanding even very simple stories has become apparent from work in artificial intelligence on language understanding programs. Computers need to be programmed with a great deal of factual knowledge in order to understand even a little language. In the same way, Nelson believes that young children need to acquire by experience the "scripts" or mental representations incorporating basic knowledge of the sequence of events, actions, actors and roles involved in episodes of daily life before they can understand stories, descriptions and anecdotes. Nelson has succeeded in eliciting such scripts from very young children for episodes like "having lunch", "going to bed" and so on, and showing that their ability to recall stories is influenced by the possession of appropriate scripts.

The current emphasis on cognitive prerequisites for language learning comes as a corrective to the imbalance created by the nativist theories of language acquisition, which have tended to treat language as a separate faculty developing independently of cognition. Both are in contrast with the views that were expressed by Vygotsky (1962), which describe the inter-active development of thought and language in a complex reciprocal relationship. Vygotsky considered that language and thought originate independently in the very young child. The earliest "thinking" (as, for example, the mental activity involved in reaching for and handling objects) is nonverbal, and the earliest speech is social or emotional, but not intellectual. At the age of about 2 years, thought and language become linked, and for the next few years this interaction is overtly demonstrated in the phenomenon of egocentric speech. Children of this age talk aloud to themselves, as well as communicating with others. The child gives himself instructions, and cautions, or acts out imagined stories. This regulative function of speech is observable in some aphasic patients as well as in young children (Luria, 1967). Vygotsky believed that, at a later stage of develop-ment, around seven years of age, this egocentric speech is internalized, and comes to resemble the inner speech of adults, overt speech being restricted to social utterances. The stages of development may not be so clear-cut as Vygotsky represented them. It is quite possible that much of the child's thinking is carried on by means of internal language at an age when egocentric speech is still occurring. The use of egocentric speech by the child may be seen as a form of language-play, rather than as being due to the inability to internalize, and the dropping of egocentric speech is perhaps due to social sanctions, and growing self-consciousness, rather than marking a new stage of cognitive development. In private, egocentric speech persists a good deal later than the age of seven, and is not so very unusual in adults.

However, Vygotsky's interpretation is consistent with the observation that egocentric speech changes in character, becoming more elliptical and idiosyncratic before it disappears, in a way that is typical of adult inner speech. Piaget's theory that egocentric speech simply atrophies, and is replaced by social speech (Flavell, 1963), is not so easily reconciled with this observation. Although Vygotsky believed that thought and language merge in inner speech, he maintained "the two processes are not identical, and there is no rigid correspondence between the units of thought and speech". He pointed out that the distinction between a thought and the language in which it is expressed is subjectively apparent when we become aware of a discrepancy, of having failed to capture a thought, and crystallize it in the right linguistic form. Thought and language are still separable in the adult, since thought can be nonverbal, and language unthinking.

Experimental efforts to reinforce the "primacy of cognition" hypothesis aim to show that children can think before they can talk; or can perform a cognitive task before they know the terms in which it would be verbally mediated, if it were verbally mediated; or before they have acquired the habit of verbal mediation; or before they can verbally explain how they do the task. One obvious weakness with this approach is that even when the relevant verbal skills are not overtly present, some rudimentary form of internal verbalization could be available. And, conversely, the presence of well developed verbal skills does not guarantee that a given task is verbally mediated. Adherents of the "primacy of language" hypothesis cite tasks which are performed poorly by children before language is well established, and performed better when language learning is more advanced. The objection to comparisons between subjects with different levels of linguistic skill is that the children who do better are not only better linguists; they are also older and more experienced, with improved memory spans, less distractability, higher motivation and better understanding of the task requirements. In practice, developmental comparisons are just as muddy as the cross-cultural comparisons discussed in the last chapter.

Transitions in cognitive development. What controls or instigates the transition from one stage of development to the next? If it can be established that stages of cognitive development conform to an invariant and universal sequence this would strongly suggest that maturational factors such as neurological and hormonal changes are responsible. According to this view, the development of language and of cognition are both controlled by maturation, rather than being causally related to each other. Brainerd (1978) has objected that what looks like an invariant sequence of cognitive stages may be only a "measurement sequence", an artefact of the methods of testing. By this he means that the behaviour patterns used as evidence of

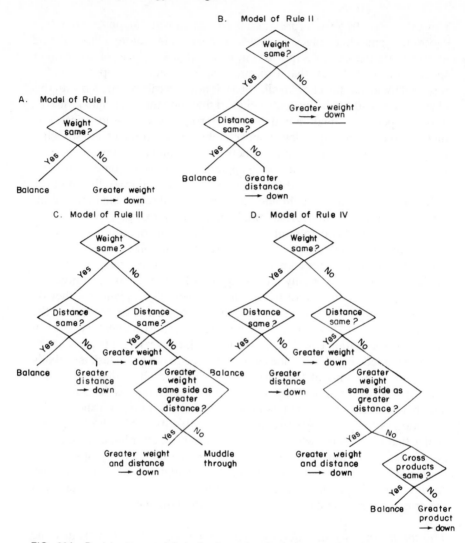

FIG. 23A. *Decision tree model of rules for performing balance scale task.*

attainment of a given stage logically presuppose and depend on the behaviour that characterized the previous stages. The appearance of an invariant ordering of stages is thus ensured by the logic of the test sequence. Clearly, the way that stages are characterized has a powerful effect on the way that transitions between them are explained.

Application of the computational metaphor to child development results

Problem-type	Rule			
	I	II	III	IV
1. Balance 	100	100	100	100
2. Weight 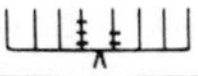	100	100	100	100
3. Distance 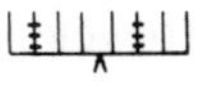	0 (Should say "Balance")	100	100	100
4. Conflict-weight 	100	100	33 (Chance responding)	100
5. Conflict-distance 	0 (Should say "Right down")	0 (Should say "Right down")	33 (Chance responding)	100
6. Conflict-balance 	0 (Should say "Right down")	0 (Should say "Right down")	33 (Chance responding)	100

1. Balance problems, with the same configuration of weights on pegs on each side of the fulcrum.

2. Weight problems, with unequal amounts of weight equidistant from the fulcrum.

3. Distance problems, with equal amounts of weight different distances from the fulcrum.

4. Conflict–weight problems, with more weight on one side and more "distance" (i.e., occupied pegs farther from the fulcrum) on the other, and the configuration arranged so that the side with more weight goes down.

5. Conflict–distance problems, similar to conflict–weight except that the side with greater distance goes down.

6. Conflict–balance problems, like other conflict problems, except that the scale remains balanced.

FIG. 23B. *Predictions for percentage of correct answers and error patterns for children using different rules.*

in describing behaviour patterns as resulting from "production systems" of computational rules for generating output from specified inputs. Transitions occur through modification of the existing system by addition, deletion or substitution of new rules (Young, 1976). As in Brainerd's measurement sequence, each successive modification is a more powerful version of the previous one, so the developmental sequence is fixed and determined by the internal logic of the production systems. This account of software development can also be combined with a maturational explanation of hardware development whereby capacities and rates of processing increase with age. An example of this kind of computational account of cognitive development is Siegler's study of rule development in children's ability to perform a Balance scale test (Siegler, 1978). The subject is required to predict which

TABLE 5. Modal Course of Development on Balance Scale Task (From Siegler, 1978).

	Aspect of development			
Age	Existing knowledge	Encoding	Response to feedback	Supplements that aid Response to feedback
3 years	No rule	Neither weight nor distance	Does not learn Rule I from weight and balance problems	50% learn Rule I if given weight-encoding training before feedback
4 years	50% Rule I 50% No Rule	Weight	Learns Rule I from weight and balance problems	—
5 years	Rule I	Weight	Does not learn Rule III or IV from conflict problems	Learns Rule III if given weight and distances encoding training before feedback
8 years	50% Rule II 50% Rule I	Weight and distance	Learns Rule III from conflict problems	—
13 years	Rule III	Weight and distance	Does not learn Rule IV from conflict problems	50% learn Rule IV if given both quantitative encoding instructions and external memory aids along with feedback
17 years	Rule III	Weight and distance	Does not learn Rule IV from conflict problems	Learns Rule IV if given either quantitative encoding instructions or external memory aids along with feedback

side of the balance would tip down if it were released, taking into account, so far as he is able, the number and distance of the weights on each side of the fulcrum. Figure 23A shows the sequence of decisions in applying Rules I-IV to this problem. Figure 23B shows how the simpler rules produce successful solutions for simpler versions of the Balance problem, but the more powerful rules are required as problem difficulty increases. Table 5 shows the stage of rule development that is typical for each age group, and the effects of attempts to produce a transition to the next stage. Siegler derived this classification from the pattern of errors made by his 5–17-year-old subjects on the task. The correspondence of the observed pattern of errors to the predictions shown in Fig. 23B allows the experimenter to infer which rule is being applied. Siegler found that before 5 years of age behaviour patterns were not rule governed. The effect of training procedures interacted with age. Older children could be taught to use more powerful rules, while younger children were less able to progress.

According to Case (1974) transition from one stage to the next requires an enlargement of working memory capacity, as well as experience of situations in which existing rules fail to solve problems. Although changes in memory capacity can be viewed as structural changes arising from neurological maturation, Case regards them as functional changes. He maintains that capacity increases because more operations become automatic, so that the number of operations requiring attentional control and monitoring decreases with age. Since automatization depends on practice, this account of transitions assigns a key role in cognitive development to practice.

Other developmental psychologists have stressed the importance of strategy development without invoking the automatic/attentional process distinction. Chi (1978) suggests that cognitive development is brought about by the interaction of three factors; an increasing stock of more highly organized knowledge; development of strategies such as verbal labelling, grouping and rehearsal of items; and increasing capacity of working memory. The three factors are interdependent and mutually facilitative. For example, the increase in capacity of working memory derives from more knowledge and better strategies. Chi has demonstrated that children who are good chess players have better recall of chess positions than adults who are novice players. This result confirms her view that knowledge and strategic factors may over-ride maturational differences. However, this particular example, where a specific and precociously acquired expertise transcends age effects, may not be representative of cognitive development in general.

Although there is a lack of consensus as to the relative influence of various causal factors in bringing about developmental transitions, there is general agreement that cognitive development is the product of an inter-related set of factors in which language is only one component. In the next section some of the tasks that have figured in controversy about the role of language in cognition are selected for discussion.

Conservation tasks. Conservation tasks provide an illustration of the way in which essentially the same empirical findings can be variously interpreted according to the particular theoretical axe which is being ground. In a typical conservation experiment, a child is shown two identical containers, A and B, filled with identical quantities of liquid. The child watches while the liquid in container B is transferred to a third container, C, which is taller and thinner. Below the age of about 8 years, children tend to judge the quantities in A and C to be unequal, and most often state that C, which has the higher level, contains more. For the purposes of the present discussion, the crucial issue is whether the incorrect response is cognitive or linguistic in origin. Piaget and his followers take the view that cognitive development unfolds as a result of the child's experience and interaction with his environment, and that increasing linguistic skill reflects, rather than promotes, cognitive growth. Although he allows that logical reasoning is facilitated by language, language itself cannot bring about understanding of logical principles. Failure in conservation tasks is attributed mainly to the child's inability to grasp the principle of invariance, and to understand that quantities remain unchanged over perceptual transformations. At this age, judgement is dominated by perception rather than by logic. Intervention studies, in which attempts are made to educate the child's judgement by various training procedures, have been used to try to reveal the key factors in the development of conservation. Empirical support for Piaget's interpretation rests on the evidence that training in the use of the relevant linguistic terms (more, same as, bigger than etc.) does not improve performance (Sinclair-de-Zwart, 1969). On the other hand, extensive practical training in variations of the task carried out by Smedslund (1961) also had little facilitating effect. Bruner *et al.* (1966) suggest that a child has three cognitive modes of representation. The earliest is the enactive mode, which codes actions; the iconic mode is based on internalized perceptions or images; and the verbal or symbolic mode is acquired last. The enactive and iconic modes predominate in the cognition of the younger child. According to their theory, erroneous judgements in conservation tasks are made because attention is focussed on perceptual aspects. In the conservation task, the symbolic system "knows" that the liquid is the same after being poured into the new container, but the iconic system insists that it is different, and the iconic system dominates the response. Bruner's group showed that if the perceptual differences were concealed from the child by a screen which allowed him to see the pouring take place, but not the resulting discrepant levels, he was shielded from misleading perceptions and was more likely to judge correctly that the quantity of liquid poured from one container to another remained the same. While Piaget maintains that the child lacks the necessary understanding, Bruner believes that the principle of conservation is understood, but is overridden by conflicting evidence, so that correct conservation responses emerge only if the perceptual evidence is weakened, or later when the verbal system becomes stronger. In spite of Sinclair-de-Zwart's results, there is some evidence that linguistic confusions are linked to nonconservation. Donaldson and Balfour (1968) studied young children who used "more" and "less" synonymously to mean "not the same as", and whose behavioural responses were similarly confused. They suggested that an underlying competence at a conceptual level is lacking, and that its absence is reflected in both language and behaviour.

Wales *et al.* (1976) carried out a cross-cultural study of English, Tamil and Polynesian children age 3–4 years, and found that "more" and "less" were not equated by any of these language-groups, but all the children were better at judgements of "more" than judgements of "less". This suggests that understanding of the concept of relative quantities can be partial and asymmetrical.

Correct nonverbal conservation responses can, however, be elicited before linguistic usage has conformed to the established norms. Cohen (1967), in a tea-table experiment found that 4½-year-old children who were asked to share out quantities "fairly" were extremely zealous and accurate in compensating for the differences in the shape of the containers provided, although a matched group of children gave the typical erroneous verbal responses in the standard Piagetian versions of the task. This experiment illustrates an important but neglected fact about the concept of invariance. In everyday life, invariance is not a golden rule of logic which, once understood, will serve in any situation. It is a convention which applies in some contexts and not in others. Some objects, conventionally retain their identity over perceptual transformations, others do not. A given object after transformation may sometimes be considered identical, and sometimes different, depending on the context, and on the linguistic description which is applied. Green and Laxon (1970), in their delightful paper, *Conservation of number, mother, water and a fried egg chez l'enfant*, point out that quite young infants are able to grasp that mothers and eggs remain invariant over changes of clothing and cooking. But a set of bricks is a tower when the child has built it up, and not when he has knocked it down again. The family puppy, under the description of Fido, retains his identity in spite of changes in size and appearance as he grows older; but when he is described as "the puppy", invariance is not preserved. Learning about invariance is not so much like learning an abstract concept, as like learning a rule of thumb. Decisions about invariance depend on knowing whether the unchanged aspects are more important than the changed aspects, and the child has to learn to extract this information from the context. The acquisition of conservation is liable to be a piecemeal affair, and to involve the gradual accretion of inductive evidence from a variety of different contexts. In Green and Laxon's view "the child learns about quantities of liquid from Baconian experiments conducted in the bath, sink or gutter", a method they described elsewhere as "suck it and see". To make correct conservation judgements, the child has to learn specific conventions of invariance, rather than an abstract principle; and in order to make correct verbal responses in conservation tasks, he has to learn to apply linguistic terms like "more" and "same" in accordance with these conventions.

Transposition tasks. Exponents of the verbal mediation hypothesis claim that age-related changes in performance on transposition tasks reflect a growing verbal skill and increasing reliance on verbal mediation. Kuenne (1946) found that 4-year-old children, who learned to respond to the larger of two stimuli, could select the larger member of a new pair only when the new stimuli were not much different in size. Older children could select the larger member of a new pair even when these were very different from the originals. She inferred that younger children could not respond in terms of the relation "larger than", and transpose this to the new stimuli, because they lacked the necessary verbal codings. Several horses and carts have since been driven through this interpretation. If younger children are given an initial training with more than one example of a stimulus pair, then they can successfully transfer a relational response to new pairs that are very different in size. Furthermore, relational responding has been elicited in nonlinguistic species such as rats, so it clearly does not depend on verbal mediation.

Problem solving. In solving more complex problems, knowing the relevant linguistic terms is by no means a sufficient condition of success. Performance on many problems improves with age without any discernibly relevant growth in vocabulary. In an extremely neat experiment, Huttenlocher (1963) confronted 6–12-year-old children with a light-switch problem and found significant age differences. The children saw two light switches, each of which had two possible positions, and a light bulb which was either on or off. From changing the position of one switch only, the children were required to decide how the light was turned on. The problem varies in difficulty through four possible sequences produced by the switch movement (see Fig. 24). Version 1 (Off–On) is easiest. Moving the top switch from A to B brings on the light. In Version 2 (On–Off), moving the top

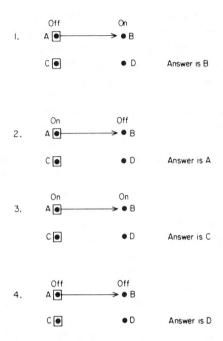

FIG. 24. *The light-switch problem. Which position of which switch brings on the light?*

switch from A to B turns off the light, so the child must infer that the initial position A turned on the light. In Version 3 (On–On), the light stays on after moving the top switch from A to B, hence the present position of the other switch must turn on the light. In Version 4 (Off–Off), the light stays off after moving the top switch from A to B, so the other switch must need to be in its other position to bring on the light. Performance varied with the number of steps of reasoning required for solution. The younger children could do the easier versions, but not the harder ones. Although all the children had adequate command of language to formulate the problem, the younger ones could not hold all the relevant information in memory. Memory capacity also emerges as the critical factor in Bryant and Trabasso's (1971) study of young children's performance on transitivity tasks. Piaget *et al.* (1960) reported that after making two length comparisons, A > B and B > C, children below 8 years were unable to infer the relationship of A and C. Bryant and Trabasso demonstrated that this failure was not due to either logical incompetence, or linguistic incompetence, but to the inability to retain the information from the original comparisons in memory. With more extensive training, so that the A > B and B > C relations were thoroughly memorized, the 4- year-olds could make the correct inference. In some tasks younger children are penalized not only by their poorer memory capacities, but also by the lack of appropriate, problem-solving heuristics. Mosher (1962) tested children's performance in a game similar to *Twenty Questions*, and concluded that younger children did not use optimal strategies for seeking and organizing information. Older children asked constraint-locating questions and accumulated information in an organized sequence. The younger children asked very specific questions such that negative answers yielded little information. They behaved like a player who instead of starting the game by asking "Is it inanimate?", starts by asking "Is it the bottom waistcoat button on the statue of Nelson in Trafalgar Square?". It is hard to judge whether this is because young children do not have their concepts arranged in hierarchies, or because they have not learned the techniques of moving through these hierarchies by successive bifurcations.

Klahr (1978) studied the ability of preschool children to solve problems requiring planning and subgoal formation. He used a version of the Tower of Hanoi problem with cans stacked on pegs. The children had to move the cans from an initial arrangement so as to produce an arrangement designated as the goal state. Problems were designed to require from 1–7 moves for solution. For a successful solution, the goal state must be decomposed mentally into a series of temporally ordered intermediate subgoals. The difficulty of a given problem is determined by the type of moves required as well as the number. A can may be moved off one peg directly onto the target peg; or it may be moved so as to get at the can beneath it; or it may be moved so as to put another can in its place. These last two types of move are harder than the direct one. Klahr found large individual differences in performance, but there was a clear trend of improvement with age. Some children were able to verbalize a planned sequence of moves before beginning, including an impressive 4-year-old who verbalized a correct six-move sequence. Other children could do the task, but could not verbalize it. Older children showed better planning, and less distractability. What developed with age was not verbal ability, but problem solving skill. Klahr notes that the kind of subgoal formation tested in this task is also observable in everyday life situations, and quotes the example of his own young daughter whose conversation revealed a chain of subgoals leading from "My socks are in the dryer" to going for a bicycle ride.

The fact that emerges most clearly from these studies of children is that cognitive development has many components: memory, attention, experience and cognitive heuristics are all implicated as well as language. Although the relationship of language and thought proves so complex and confusing, by drawing on the evidence from all the various sources reviewed in this chapter, and in the preceding one, we can advance some tentative conclusions. Language is not a sufficient condition of intellectual success, but the thinker without language is cognitively disabled. Language enables the user to formulate abstract concepts, hypotheses and inferences, rules and general principles at a level of complexity unattainable by the nonlinguistic thinker. Language allows the thinker to rehearse mentally, to direct and maintain his attention, and to arrange information in ordered sequences and nested hierarchies. The difference between thinking without language, and thinking with language is rather like the difference between doing mathematical calculations with an abacus, and with a sophisticated electronic calculator. Perhaps the most important advantage conferred by language is that it enables us to acquire information not just from our own personal experiences, but from the accumulated experience of the other past and present language users, giving us access to the entire knowledge pool of our generation.

Recommended reading

Read Curtiss's book *Genie* for a detailed blow-by-blow account of the language development and cognitive development of a "wild child". R. S. Siegler's edited volume *Children's Thinking: What Develops?* contains some very important papers. Young's book *Seriation by Children: a Production System Approach* shows how the computational metaphor provides new theoretical insights and a new methodology for developmental psychology. *The Behavioural and Brain Sciences* **1**, 1978, devotes a whole section to a debate on animal cognition.

7 PROBLEM SOLVING
and REASONING

Attempts to provide a general characterization of the process of problem solving have met with only partial success, being either too vague, or too incomplete, or both. This is hardly surprising since the kinds of task which come under the heading of problem solving are extremely diverse. Problems which have been studied include such disparate tasks as solving anagrams (Ekstrand and Dominowski, 1965), syllogistic reasoning (Henle, 1962), laying out patterns of matches (Scheerer, 1963), getting hobbits and orcs across rivers (Thomas, 1971), constructing hat-racks (Maier, 1930) and measuring required quantities of water with pitchers of specified capacities (Luchins, 1942). To construct a theory of problem solving which will encompass all these is like trying to provide a theory of art broad enough to cover everything from pottery to electronic music, in that there is not a great deal of common ground. However, a common framework for the study of problem solving is provided by the information processing approach.

The Information Processing Approach

This approach stems from the work of Newell *et al.* (1958). Information processing methods allow problem solving behaviour to be analysed and decomposed into a set of labelled stages. In its most general formulation, solving a problem involves transforming an initial state by a set of operations into a goal state. The stages whereby this is achieved can be listed as follows.

Stages of problem solving

1. Representation of the problem. At this stage the solver constructs a "problem space". This involves representing both the initial state and the goal state, understanding the instructions and constraints on the problem, retrieving relevant information from long-term memory, or gathering additional information about the task. All this knowledge constitutes the problem space. The problem space is not supplied ready made with the problem, but must be constructed by the solver. His past experience, and stored knowledge will affect his interpretation of the problem, so different solvers construct different problem spaces for the same problem. The same solver may even reconstruct the problem space

before reaching solution, if he finds it necessary to reinterpret the problem, or bring different knowledge to bear on it.

2. Selection of operators. At this stage the solver selects the operations for transforming the initial state. Sets of operators may be already associated with the problem space that has been constructed, but may have to be re-evaluated, or new ones may have to be selected. When the problem space is small and highly constrained as in Noughts and Crosses (Tic Tac Toe), it is easier to select the correct operator. When the problem space is large, as in chess, the selection of operators requires a heuristic search. A common heuristic for the selection of operators is means–end analysis. The search system finds differences between the current state and the goal state and selects the operator which will reduce these differences. Previous experience may allow the current state to be recognized as one that has appropriate operators associated with it.

3. Implementation of the selected operations. This stage results in a new current state which may or may not correspond with the goal state. In some problems, the solution is reached in a single step. In others a series of operations is required.

4. Evaluation of the current state. If this is judged to correspond to the goal, a solution is reached, and the solving process terminates. If not, further transformation operations must be selected and implemented.

These stages are not necessarily strictly sequential. The problem space evolves as the operations are carried out. The solver may decide to backtrack to a previous state; or he may decide to set up subgoals and advance toward the final goal through a planned sequence of subgoals.

The information processing approach emphasizes the dependence of problem solving behaviour on components of the cognitive system such as working memory, long-term memory and attentional mechanisms. Problem solving is treated as one of the processes that utilize the general cognitive system. Information processing provides a general framework which can be elaborated to yield a more detailed analysis of the specific processes involved in solving specific problems.

The Computational Approach

Computer modelling of problem solving has developed out of the Information Theory approach. Simon (1979) identifies several important advances in the study of problem solving which can be attributed to computer modelling.

The influence of the computational metaphor

Strategies. There is now greater awareness of the range and diversity of strategies that can be employed in solving a given problem, and some understanding of the factors that govern the choice of strategy. For example, limitations on the capacity of short-term memory, and on the rate at which information can be transferred to long-term memory, make strategies involving backtrack moves, or extended forward planning difficult to implement. The amount of information about past attempts, and about the planned path to solution, that has to be held in memory may exceed capacity, and make such strategies impractical.

The knowledge base. Computer models have also shown the importance of the knowledge base. This has been particularly evident in simulation of chess playing. The expert chess player is able to chunk the overall configuration of pieces on the board into familiar subpatterns, so that the number of chunks is within the capacity of short-term memory. Novice players can only encode piece positions individually, and so cannot hold in mind the overall configuration. Simon and Gilmartin (1973) simulated the process of learning to recognize chunks in a system called the Memory Aided Pattern Perceiver. Their program learned about 1300 familiar patterns, which is equivalent to the knowledge base of a Class A player. It is estimated that grandmasters are able to recognize many thousand patterns. Charness (1976) showed that good players are able to recognize more and larger chunks, and to encode them more rapidly, so that information can be quickly transferred to long term store where it is more resistant to interference. A more extensive knowledge base facilitates information handling at all stages.

Representation. Computer modelling has also served to underline the crucial nature of the representation stage of problem solving. Progress has been made in modelling the initial process of understanding the problem, and constructing the problem space. In computer simulations this process typically depends on isomorphs. A current problem is understood by analogy with a previously encountered one. So, for example, logical or algebraic problems may be perceived as isomorphic with similar problems that have already been solved. The various MOVE problems described on pp. 170 (Towers of Hanoi, Missionaries and Cannibals, etc.) are all isomorphs of each other. The same pattern of moves can be applied in each. However, in this case human subjects rarely perceive the analogy.

Production Systems. Computer simulation has generated the concept of Production Systems as a method of formalizing the cognitive processes in problem solving. Any model of problem solving behaviour must incorporate control systems. These are the mechanisms which control the selection and sequence of operations. Although this can be done by means of a fixed hierarchy of routines and subroutines, Production Systems provide a more flexible type of control. Production Systems are composed of a set of productions each consisting of a Condition and an Action. The Condition is the current state: identification of the current state evokes an Action. The basic rule of a production is "If state $= X$, do Y". Productions are ordered hierarchically so that if the current state corresponds to more than one condition, the production with the highest priority is implemented. Each production modifies the information state, which in turn elicits the next production, and the complete production system corresponds to a program for solving the problem. The development of skill and expertise in problem solving can be viewed as corresponding to the acquisition of more productions. The chess player or mathematician, like the child learning to solve balance problems and number seriation problems, learns to recognize more states as constituting the conditions for particular actions.

Methods of Studying Problem Solving

Computer simulation of problem solving behaviour provides a method for testing theories. A precisely specified and detailed theory can be modelled, and the computer scientist can see whether it works, how its performance compares with human performance, and how its performance varies when parameters of the model such as memory capacity, or the amount of information than can be accessed, are manipulated. It is possible to tinker about with a model and see how this affects its ability to solve problems. Besides generating and testing theoretical developments in this way, computer simulation has also stimulated the development of new methods for constructing theories, such as the use of verbal protocols.

The use of verbal protocols

In experiments on problem solving the traditional dependent measures are speed and accuracy, time to solution and number of errors. In almost every kind of task, human performance reflects a speed–accuracy trade-off. A task can be carried out rapidly and carelessly, or slowly and carefully. The two criteria of success, speed and accuracy, tend to vary inversely, and the relative weight attached to each differs according to the task, the instructions received, how they are interpreted, and according to the personal cognitive style of the individual. This trade-off relation constitutes a serious difficulty for research on human performance. If an experimenter wishes to determine whether task A is more difficult than task B, he can only conclude that the tasks differ if one is performed both faster, and with fewer errors than the other. If the speed–accuracy trade-off differs for the two tasks, so that, for example, task A is carried out faster, but with more errors than task B, no conclusion can be reached. The experimenter may try to "fix" the speed–accuracy trade-off by giving instructions such as "Respond as fast as possible, but try not to make errors", but an instruction like this will not be interpreted uniformly by all subjects. If the experimenter decides to discard from the experiment those subjects who make more than a predetermined proportion of errors, or slow responses, he can ensure standardization of performance, but the results will only be representative of a selected sample of subjects.

Another difficulty is that the problem solving process may take some considerable time, and much of it is not observable. Chains of covert mental operations take place before eventually issuing in a response. The experimenter has to try to infer the nature of the intervening mental operations by systematically varying different aspects of the problem, and observing how these variations affect the subjects' responses, but this method is often speculative. Ericsson and Simon (1980) have emphasized the need for greater temporal density of observations if we are to understand the nature of the covert cognitive processes. The use of verbal protocols supplies this need, but their validity has been questioned. Verbal protocols are obtained by asking subjects to overtly verbalize their thought processes, and to "think aloud" while solving the problem. The recorded verbalization is then encoded phrase by phrase, and formalized to create production systems. These production systems can be combined into a computer program and tested. The verbal protocols provide the information that enables the computer simulation to reproduce human internal mental operations. Nisbett and Wilson (1977) have challenged the validity of this method, claiming that verbal protocols are spurious as evidence of higher mental processes, on the grounds that people do not have introspective access to the cognitive processes involved in problem solving. They believe that protocols reflect the subject's tacit knowledge about plausible causes for his responses. He is offering a hypothesis to explain what he is doing, but because he has no access to his own thought processes, this report is no more reliable than the conjectures supplied by an observer. According to Nisbett and Wilson, the chess player cannot report why he moved his castle, but can only give some reasons that would be plausible. In support of this view, they cite a number of cases in which subjects are either unable to report their reasoning, or are obviously inaccurate in doing so. Many of these examples turn out to be concerned with perception, emotions, or motives rather than with reasoning. However, some instances of inability to verbalize do occur in problem solving tasks. These are mostly one-step problems of the kind solved by "insight", such as Maier's (1930) pendulum problem. In this task, the subject is required to fasten together two strings hanging from the ceiling, which are too far apart to be simultaneously grasped. The solution is to use another object present in the room, such as a pair of pliers, as a pendulum weight, and swing one string across to the other. Subjects who fail to see the solution may be helped if the experimenter casually sets one of the strings in motion. The fact that these subjects are not aware of having been influenced by this "hint" is cited by Nisbett and Wilson as evidence for the inaccessibility of thought. In other examples, mathematicians and inventors report problem solutions "dawning" without any consciousness of how they were reached. Ericsson and Simon have put forward a defence of verbal protocols that is both careful and convincing. They identify two crucial questions. Do verbal protocols reflect underlying thought processes accurately? And does having to produce a verbal protocol significantly change or distort normal thinking? Ericsson and Simon maintain that verbal reports are validated by their correspondence to behaviour, and by the "goodness of fit" between the performance of computer programs based on protocols, and the actual performance of the human subject. They concede that the accuracy of verbal reports varies with the nature of the task. Accuracy is highest if reporting is concurrent rather than retrospective, and if prompting by the experimenter is kept to a minimum. Verbal reports are most reliable when the subject is reporting the current contents of short-term memory. Information retrieved from long-term memory is more likely to be mixed up with other stored knowledge. Only attentional processes can be reported since, by definition, automatic processes are unconscious and not accessible to introspection. Highly practised subjects for whom some of the problem solving operations have become automatic may be less able to describe them than the unpractised novice subjects. Insight solutions can be accounted for as the outcome of automatic processes. In general, problems with multistep solutions are easier to verbalize than single-step solutions because they require continuous attentional monitoring, and successive steps have to be held in short term memory while keeping track of the overall plan. Ericsson and Simon have compared the performance of subjects with and without concurrent protocol production, and concluded that in most cases performance is not significantly changed by having to produce a verbal report. In some cases changes may occur because the thought processes are particularly difficult to encode verbally. Levelt (1981) has pointed out one kind of difficulty that arises in mapping thought onto language because of the need for linearization. In verbalizing a linear ordering has to be determined even though the underlying knowledge structure may not be linear. Levelt studied the responses of subjects who were asked to describe network patterns.

Linearization of even simple patterns like the one shown in Fig. 25 required choosing a path at the T junction and back-tracking to the choice point (3), and working memory must keep a continuous record of the output. So it is harder to describe this kind of pattern than to think about it. Although it is conceded that verbal protocols are not invariably an accurate record of the cognitive processes involved in solving all kinds of problem, they do yield valuable information about many problems. Behavioural data and verbal report data can be combined and cross-checked so as to amplify and confirm each other.

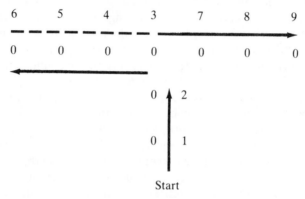

FIG. 25. *Linearization of a simple network pattern (adapted from Levelt, 1981).*

Individual Differences

Differences in ability and experience

Performance in a problem solving task is determined by the characteristics of the individual problem solver as well as the problem itself. The general intelligence and the previous experience of the individual are perhaps the most powerful variables in determining the outcome of any task. In animal experiments researchers will carefully select "naive" animals, or those whose experience from birth onwards has been strictly controlled and matched. In human experiments the background knowledge and training of individual subjects varies greatly and usually only a very crude matching based on level education is attempted. Disparities between subjects may still be enormous. The star performer on an anagram problem may be a sparetime crossword freak, and subjects with training in logic or statistics may be at an advantage in reasoning problems. Previous experience may have established highly relevant or wholly inappropriate sets before the subject comes into the experimental situation.

Just as in concept learning tasks (see p. 81) individuals have preferred strategies for problem solving, and individual differences in choice of strategy may be the result of cognitive biases. Paige and Simon (1966) noted that some subjects solved verbally presented algebra problems by constructing abstract equations, while others generated diagrammatic spatial representations of the objects named in the problem. This latter type of representation made it easier to detect contradictions or impossibilities in the solution. Individual differences in strategy have been reported also in deductive reasoning tasks (p. 189) and in three-term series problems (p. 183). The kind of individual differences described here arise at the stage of constructing the problem space because different individuals have preferred forms of representation. Some find it easier to represent information abstractly, and some prefer to use visualization.

Motivational factors

Individual differences in problem solving can also originate from differences in motivation. While the animal experimenter can exercise some control over motivation by, for example, a schedule of food deprivation, human subjects may be bored and sleepy, or alert and keen. Payment and bonuses may provide a considerable incentive for the impoverished, and none at all for the affluent. Subjects may want to impress the experimenter with their brilliance, or be quite indifferent to his opinion. Anxiety in the test situation may impair or improve performance according to the Yerkes Dodson law, which states that the optimum level of arousal varies with the difficulty of the task in such a way that high anxiety may be beneficial in simple tasks, but detrimental for very complex tasks. The level of anxiety induced by the testing situation is also liable to vary between subjects. Performance may also vary with age and sex. Older subjects tend to be more anxious than younger ones, and typically experience more difficulty with unfamiliar problems: problems which place a heavy load on memory; problems containing a high proportion of irrelevant information; and tasks which put a premium on speed.

Cross-cultural differences

Cross-cultural differences in problem solving ability have generally revealed large differences between literate and nonliterate, schooled and unschooled, traditional and modern societies. Education appears to be the most powerful factor in producing successful performance. Nevertheless, as Cole (1977) has pointed out, it is not legitimate to conclude that higher cognitive processes are defective in the uneducated, or that higher cognitive processes are reserved to literate, educated, technological societies. While successful problem solving shows what can be achieved by primitive people, failure cannot be interpreted as evidence of cognitive deficit. Cole showed that the failure of the Kpelle of Liberia to solve a puzzle-box problem was due to unfamiliarity with the materials, and a different version of the same problem could be solved successfully. As with young children, the tests may fail to reveal underlying cognitive ability. As Cole points out, aborigines fail formal tests for conservation of liquids, but they do not store their water in tall thin containers so as to have more of it. Scribner (1977) demonstrated that although performance with logical syllogisms was at chance level among uneducated people in several cultures, inferential reasoning was not necessarily defective. Conclusions were being based on empirical, practical reasoning from personal experience, and not on formal theoretical reasoning. Given the syllogism

To carry corn from his farm Jose needs a horse and cart.

He has the horse, but he does not have the cart.

Can Jose carry corn from his farm?

the illiterate Mexican replies "Yes" on the perfectly reasonable grounds that Jose will borrow a cart. The concept of a formal and purely arbitrary problem in which only the information given should be considered is something inculcated by education, and is not readily understood by the uneducated. As a result, the representation of the problem—the problem space—is different for these people, but their ability to carry out the operations required in inferential reasoning is not defective. Scribner's findings showed that when level of education was equated, differences in problem solving ability due to culture were negligible. Fourth grade (9-year-old) students in Liberia or in Mexico performed as well as fourth graders in the USA. It is interesting to note that while uneducated people sometimes give "wrong" answers because they do not confine themselves to the information presented in the problem, educated people sometimes fall into the opposite kind of trap. By confining themselves rigidly to the information supplied, they fail to take into account some general world knowledge, and produce a silly answer. An example of this kind of trap problem is—"A boat is tied up in the harbour at low tide at 10 a.m. A ladder fixed to the side of the boat has ten rungs showing above the water, and the rungs are 0·5 m apart. As the tide rises the depth of water increases at a rate of one metre per hour. How many rungs of the ladder will still be showing at 4 p.m.?"

Types of Problem

Ill-defined problems

Problems vary greatly in the extent to which they are well defined or ill defined. Lack of definition may characterize either the initial state (the problem elements), the goal state, or both. In a problem like "Find the square root of 169", both are well defined. In a problem like "Fix the electric light" or "Mend the car", the initial state is ill defined, but a problem like "Design a fine town centre" has an ill-defined goal state. Lack of definition is more characteristic of everyday problems than of those used in laboratory testing, and it is clear that the relative difficulty of the stages of problem solving must vary according to the state which is ill defined. In the car repair problem, the main difficulty is to analyse the initial state. In the town-centre example, the heart of the problem is to specify the exact nature of the goal state. With ill-defined problems, it is difficult to construct a problem space, since there is no boundary on relevant information, and there are no criteria for evaluating the legality of moves, or for deciding when the goal has been reached.

Greeno (1978) has distinguished three main types of problem. The taxonomy he constructs does make some useful distinctions, but many problems do not fall neatly into a single category, and turn out to be hybrids.

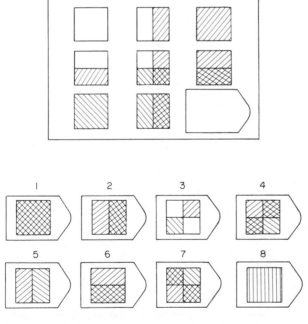

FIG. 26. *One of the Raven's matrices problems.*

Problems of inducing structure

In this type of problem some elements are given, and the subject's task is to identify the structural pattern present among these elements. Examples of this kind of problem include analogy problems (A is to B as C is to ?); series continuation problems (12834656 ?) and Raven's Matrices, where the missing element in the matrix must be inferred from the relations holding across the rows and down the columns, and the correct alternative chosen. (See Fig. 26 for an example.)

Problems of transformation: MOVE problems

Included within this category are all versions of MOVE problems. One of the earliest of these to be studied was the water-jug problem (Luchins, 1942), shown in Fig. 27. In this task, subjects are asked to solve successive problems requiring given amounts of water to be measured using a set of pitchers of different capacities. They hit on a procedure of pouring from pitcher to pitcher which successfully solves the first few problems. Later

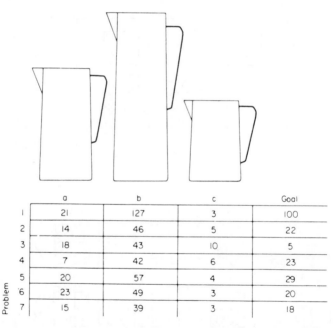

Problem	a	b	c	Goal
1	21	127	3	100
2	14	46	5	22
3	18	43	10	5
4	7	42	6	23
5	20	57	4	29
6	23	49	3	20
7	15	39	3	18

FIG. 27. *Fixation because of habit is illustrated by this series or problems. In each a quantity of water (the goal) must be measured out; there is an unlimited supply of water but the only tools available are three pitchers, a, b and c, the volumes of which are specified for each problem. Once the subject hits on a successful pattern of filling and pouring (b–a–2c) he tends to follow the pattern even when, in Problems 6 and 7, there is an easier solution.*

problems in the series could be solved much more simply, but subjects tend to persist in using the cumbersome procedure adopted earlier. It is difficult to shift from the response strategy which has been reinforced by success on the earlier problems, but not all subjects show this inflexibility to the same extent.

Another well-known problem of this type is the Towers of Hanoi shown in Fig. 28. The problem is to transfer the tower of rings from A to C so that they end up stacked in the same order, moving only one ring at a time, and without placing a larger ring on top of a smaller ring. A general strategy for this sort of task is means-end analysis with operators being selected so as to reduce the difference between the initial state shown in Fig. 28 and the goal state. Using this strategy, a computer model called the General Problem Solver, originated by Newell *et al.*, (1958), solves both the water-jug problem (Atwood and Polson, 1976), and the Towers of Hanoi. Human subjects, however, may select any one of several strategies. One way of solving the problem is to use recursive subgoals (e.g. Get the smaller rings over to B, then move the largest to C, then shift the smaller ones on top of the largest at C). Another strategy is called the perceptual strategy, and consists in identifying the largest unobstructed ring and aiming to move that one to the goal peg. This strategy places smaller demands on working memory than the recursive subgoal strategy. Finally, the problem may be solved by simply rote learning the correct pattern of moves.

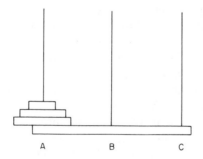

FIG. 28. *The Towers of Hanoi problem.*

Other MOVE problems include the monster problem (Simon and Hayes, 1976) in which three different sizes of monster each hold a different-sized globe, and the task is to re-allocate the globes so that the large monster holds the large globe, the medium-sized monster holds the medium globe and the small monster holds the small globe. Only one globe may be transferred at a time; if a monster is holding two globes only the larger one may be transferred; and a globe may not be transferred to a monster already holding a larger globe. The missionaries and cannibals problem (Simon and Reed, 1976) requires that five missionaries and five cannibals be moved from the left bank of the river to the right bank, with a boat that holds a maximum of three persons, and with the constraint that cannibals must never outnumber the missionaries, neither on a bank, nor in the boat. Studies comparing computer performance, and human performance on these problems have been useful in revealing the similarities and differences. Simon and Hayes computer program UNDERSTAND was tested on the monster problem. The UNDERSTAND program constructs an internal representation of the problem from the instructions, and a set of operators for selecting legal moves within that problem space. It assumes that the problem is completely understood before any solution moves begin. Human solver protocols showed that the humans engaged in preliminary efforts to understand the problem thoroughly, before attempting any moves, often requesting clarification of the instructions and querying the legality of possible moves. This stage was not represented in computer simulation. Both humans and computer were able to select the relevant information in the initial presentation of the problem, and discard the irrelevant information, such as the colour of the monsters. Human subjects appeared to use feedback from error moves to modify their interpretation of the problem, and this ability was also not represented in the computer program. Although both humans and computer showed a similar order of difficulty for various versions of the problem, the interesting feature of this study is that differences emerged from the protocol-program comparisons, even though performance, in terms of number of moves to solution, was quite similar. Clearly, equivalent results do not guarantee equivalence of procedures. Atwood and Polson's simulation of the water-jug problem (Atwood and Polson, 1976) leads to the same conclusion. Again, equivalent orders of difficulty over a series of problems were obtained, but move-by-move comparisons showed that human subjects selected their moves in accordance with a familiarity principle not represented in the computer program. Subjects preferred moves which brought about states familiar from previous experience. In their simulation of the missionaries and cannibals problem, Simon and Reed (1976) compared the frequency with which particular moves were made. Quite close agreement of human and computer data was found. Both systems employed a means–end strategy of moving the maximum number across, and the minimum number back on each trip. Task manipulations such as providing a subgoal (e.g. get three cannibals alone on the far bank at some point), produced similar shifts in the move selection strategies of both the computer and the human solvers.

Jeffries *et al.* (1977) developed a General Problem Solver type of model for the missionaries and cannibals problem, using a means–end heuristic which selected each move on the principle of reducing the initial-goal state difference; producing a new state and not returning to an old one; and evaluating the selected move for legality. This model has no look-ahead and move planning is strictly local. Human subjects behave differently in that they plan ahead for a short sequence of moves. A general characteristic of human performance in MOVE problems is an aversion to backtrack moves which involve temporarily moving further away from the goal state, and also increase the memory load because of the need to remember the sequence of moves leading back to the old position, as well as the planned onward path.

Problems of arrangement

Greeno's third category in this taxonomy of problems consists of problems of arrangement where the elements presented have to be re-arranged to meet some criterion. This category includes anagrams, and the crypt-arithmetic problems like

DONALD
GERALD
_____
ROBERT

in which the subjects must work out how to substitute numbers for each letter so that the sum adds up correctly. To reduce the number of possibilities in these tasks, the subjects must invoke constraints such as spelling rules in anagrams, or the rule that adding a number to itself must produce an even number in the cryptarithmetic problem.

Some problems straddle more than one of Greeno's categories. Chess playing involves both transformation and arrangement. The candle–box problem is, according to Greeno, a hybrid of arrangement and inducing structure. The subject in this problem (Glucksberg, 1962) is given a candle and a box of tacks and told to fix the candle to the wall of the room. To solve the problem he must perceive that the box is a potential shelf, and nail it to the wall. If the tacks and box are presented separately, subjects find the solution more readily, because the box is less liable to be classified as a container. The importance of the representation of the problem, and the nature of the problem space constructed by the solver is again underlined in this problem.

Logical Reasoning

Logical problems form another category. Recent research has focussed on the errors people make in logical reasoning tasks, and from the nature of these errors has attempted to identify systematic faults in the cognitive system. Overemphasis on faulty reasoning, and on cognitive failures has been misleading in some ways, since it is much more illuminating to try to understand how and why people reason in the way they do than simply to label their mental processes as "irrational". These issues are apparent in the discussion of the particular logical problems that are reviewed below.

Processing negative information

It is generally, though not invariably, the case that negative propositions are harder to remember and take longer to judge true or false, than affirmative propositions. This holds good whether the proposition has to be judged by reference to stored knowledge (as in "7 is not an even number"), or verified by matching against physical objects or pictures (as in "The green square is not on the left of the red circle"). A number of explanations have been advanced to account for this difficulty in handling negation, but none of them can accommodate all of the findings satisfactorily.

The linguistic explanation. The linguistic explanation assumes that negative propositions are harder to process because they require syntactic recoding. Working within the framework of generative grammar, Miller and McKean (1964) argued that negative sentences undergo syntactic transformation to the base affirmative form, and that the processing time for negatives reflects the extra time required for this transformation. In their experiment, reaction times did increase when subjects were induced to carry out the transformation, but there was no evidence that this stage necessarily occurs during the normal processing of natural language. A linguistic explanation fails to account for the fact that the difficulty with negatives diminishes or disappears entirely in some semantic contexts. There are some kinds of "natural" negatives which are handled as easily as affirmatives. An example of a natural negative is one which expresses exceptionality. Given an array of eight circles, seven blue and one red, it is more natural and more rapid, to encode a description of the odd circle negatively as "Circle 3 is not blue", than to encode it affirmatively as "Circle 3 is red" (Wason, 1965). Another kind of natural negative is one which denies a previous assertion, or presupposition. In a pair of sentences like "x exceeds y" and its denial, "x does not exceed y", the negative does not cause difficulty, but if the negative is used "unnaturally" to preserve or re-express the same meaning, instead of denying it, as in the pair "x exceeds y" and "y does not exceed x" then the negative is harder to process (Greene, 1970). Similarly in everyday speech a negative which denies a prior assertion (e.g. "The train is not late today" following "The train is always late"), or negates a presupposition (e.g. "I don't want a drink") is not difficult to process. These examples, which Wason calls "negatives in the context of plausible denial", indicate the importance of contextual and semantic factors, and show that an explanation of the negation effect in terms of syntactic processing cannot apply to all classes of negatives. In a recent study, Clark and Lucy (1975) found that sentences which are negative in their literal, surface form, but positive in their conveyed meaning, such as "Why not open the door?" yield verification times consistent with an affirmative form, and sentences which are literally affirmative but implicitly negative like "Must you open the door?" produce response times more consistent with processing negatives. This finding suggests that semantic factors are more powerful than syntactic form in determining how a sentence is processed.

The emotional explanation. Eiferman (1961) has suggested that an emotional dislike of negatives arises because they are associated with prohibition and frustration, and so arouse anxiety and inhibit responses. This explanation is consistent with theories of perceptual defence which give a similar account of delayed recognition for words with unpleasant associations, but it cannot be an adequate account of the negation data, since it must postulate that the emotional effect is strong enough to carry over to nonprohibitive uses of the negative (as in "7 is not an even number"), but somehow not strong enough to affect the natural negatives. Since there is no obvious way to resolve this discrepancy, the emotional explanation is unconvincing. The experimental results on which Eiferman based this theory are, in any case, of doubtful validity. Sentences containing prohibitive negatives took longer to process than other sentences with nonprohibitive negatives, but the difference between the two groups of sentences persisted even when both were changed to an affirmative form. So the difference in difficulty of processing did not depend on the type of negative, but on other characteristics of the sentences.

The ambiguity explanation. A possible source of difficulty with some types of negative proposition is that the exact scope of the negative is not clear, and several interpretations are possible. In a sentence like "The dog did not chase the cat" it is not clear which element in the sentence is negated. This point is well illustrated in an experiment by Engelkampf and Hörmann (1974) which demonstrated difficulty in the recall of sentences like "The policeman did not stop the truck", but showed that the difficulty disappeared when the sentence was presented together with a disambiguating pictorial representation, e.g. "The *policeman* did not stop the truck" with a picture of a hitchhiker stopping the truck, while the policeman stands by; "The policeman did not *stop* the truck" with a picture of the policeman waving the truck along; or "The policeman did not stop the *truck*" with a picture of him stopping a car while the truck goes by. In everyday speech the scope of the negation is usually made clear by intonation, or, as in the natural negatives, by the context of the utterance, whereas experimental sentences are usually presented in written form, and without context. It seems likely, therefore, that some of the negation effect is due to the artificiality of the experimental task.

The recoding explanation. The negation effect is accounted for by the assumption that negative propositions are recoded to an affirmative form for comprehension and storage. This explanation is similar to the linguistic explanation, but the hypothesized recoding is semantic rather than syntactic. Sentences like "7 is not an even number" are translated to "7 is an odd number", and the extra step of recoding is reflected in longer verification times. Although the recoding operation would be quite simple for sentences in which the affirmative and negative forms are binary alternatives, it is less easy to apply to sentences like "The dog did not chase the cat", where the correct form of affirmative recoding is not clearly indicated. The ambiguity effects discussed above need to be incorporated into the recoding explanation. Attempts at affirmative recoding can sometimes be introspectively experienced, especially when processing sentences containing more than one negative. When applying for a British driving licence we are required to answer "yes" or "no" to the question "Are you without either hand or foot?", and a recent Italian referendum asked "Are you in favour of rescinding the law permitting divorce?". In examples like these people often find themselves trying to reformulate the question in a more positive version. However, in some cases recoding may remove the semantic implications which governed the choice of the negative form in the first place. If I say "It is not unlikely that X will get the job", I do not mean to assert "It is likely that X will get the job". I only intend to exclude one end of a scale that runs from certainty to impossibility.

Experimental evidence of recoding comes from work investigating the latency of truth value decisions. Information processing models have been constructed by Trabasso *et al.* (1971) and by Clark and Chase (1972) to explain how positive and negative sentences are judged to be true or false descriptions of a pictorial representation. Trabasso's translation model is shown in Fig. 29. The model makes the assumption that subjects start with an initial bias to respond "true". In terms of the model, the response index is pre-set for "true". Consider a binary alternative situation in which the picture represents a circle which can be either blue or red. On a given trial the circle is blue. The True Affirmative (TA) sentence "The circle is blue" gives a direct match, and produces the response "true". The False Affirmative (FA) sentence "The circle is red" produces a mismatch at Step 4, and requires a shift in the response index to "false". The True Negative

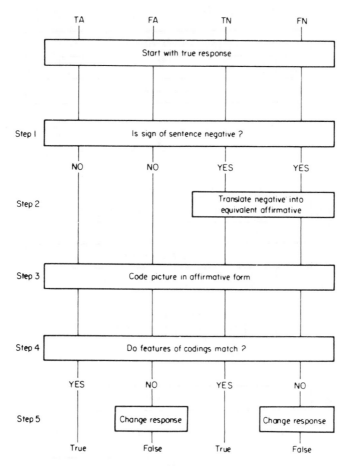

FIG. 29. *A recoding model for processing negatives in binary situations (Trabasso* et al., *1971).*

sentence (TN) "The circle is not red" requires recoding to an affirmative form at Step 2. The False Negative (FN) sentence "The circle is not blue" requires both the affirmative recoding, and the shift of the response index following a mismatch. The obtained order of latency for these four types of sentence is TA, FA, TN, FN. Responses of "false" are slower than "true", and negatives take longer than affirmatives. It is additionally assumed that the operation of recoding negatives to affirmatives takes longer than the mismatch detection and response shift (Step 2 takes longer than Step 5) to account for the finding that TN is slower than FA.

For nonbinary situations, as when the circle could be any colour, Clark

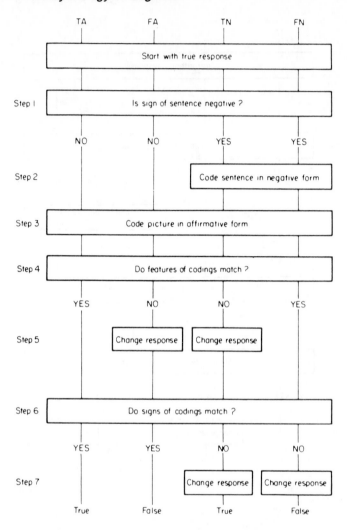

FIG. 30. *A recoding model for processing negatives in nonbinary situations (Clark and Chase, 1972).*

and Chase proposed a conversion model (Fig. 30), which can handle cases in which the negatives cannot be recoded as affirmatives because the correct affirmative form is not known. This model codes negatives by bracketing the proposition with a negative sign outside the bracket. Verification involves matching both the bracketed elements and the signs. Again suppose a picture showing a blue circle. The TA sentence "The circle is blue" is coded with a positive sign as [True (the circle is blue)]. The FA sentence "The circle is red" is also coded positively as [True (the circle is red)]. Negative sentences are coded with a negative sign, so that the TN "The circle is not red" produces [False (the circle is red)], and the FN "The circle is not blue" produces [False (the circle is blue)]. The picture is coded in Step 3 as [True (the circle is blue)]. At Step 4 the inner brackets are compared, and a mismatch shifts the response index to "false". At Step 6 the signs in the outer brackets are compared, and if these fail to match the response is changed to "true". This model fits the obtained order of response latencies, TA, FA, FN, TN. TN is slowest because it involves a double shift of the response index. FN needs only one shift because the outer signs mismatch. FA needs one shift because the inner bracket features mismatch, and TA needs no shift. To account for the finding that FN is slower than FA, the model makes the further assumption that a sign mismatch (the outer bracket) takes longer to process than a feature mismatch (the inner bracket). Figure 31 illustrates the processing of the TN sentence.

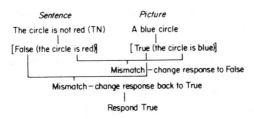

FIG. 31. *Processing a true negative sentence in a sentence-picture matching task.*

It is important to remember that these models are based on the performance of highly practised subjects working as fast as possible on a task which excludes the contextual and semantic factors which influence the processing of negatives in everyday language, so that it is difficult to know whether these processing strategies would be employed in less artificial tasks. Also, since the recoding explanation of the negation effect rests on the assumption that there is an initial bias towards affirmative coding of information, it can be criticized as begging the question of why there should be such a bias. It is possible that affirmative coding is preferred because it conveys more precise information, or because it can be more easily represented in a visual image. In the sentence–picture matching task, when the verbal description is presented *before* the picture, subjects commonly report generating a visual image and matching the image to the picture, instead of converting the picture to a verbal coding and matching this to the sentence. Since images represent what is, rather than what is not, it is plausible that the preference for affirmative coding arises because it facilitates image-mediated matching. It is still not clear, however, why verbally based comparisons need to be carried out in the affirmative form. The bias toward an affirmative or positive coding may be a feature of human cognition with considerable generality, since it extends beyond the sentence processing tasks reviewed in this section. A similar phenomenon emerges in matching tasks when the subject is presented with two stimuli such as letters or shapes, and asked to judge them "same" or "different". It is usually (although not invariably) found that "same" judgements are faster than "different" judgements. A number of explanations have been advanced to account for the superiority of "same" judgements; for example, that subjects carry out a double check before deciding "different", or have higher criterion, and require more evidence in order to make the "different" judgement. In effect, these explanations postulate a bias toward positive coding in the same way that the recoding models of negation assume an initial bias toward "true" responses and affirmative forms.

Negative inferences. The SCHOLAR program (Collins *et al.*, 1975) models negative inferences. Since facts that are not true are not stored, it requires an inference to generate a negative conclusion. To respond negatively to questions like "Is an X a Y?" SCHOLAR carries out an intersection search through a semantic network, similar to the procedures employed in the Marker–Search model (p. 33). Negative conclusions may be licensed if X and Y have no common superordinate; or if they are marked as mutually exclusive; if they have different distinguishing properties, like different spatial locations; or sometimes by default, for lack of knowledge. The complexity of the procedures for reaching negative conclusions in the model conforms to the behavioural difficulty in encoding and evaluating negative information.

Processing conditional propositions

The four-card problem. Wason and Johnson-Laird (1972) have reported results which appear to show that subjects have a built-in tendency to test the truth of conditional statements by seeking confirming instances, and fail to realize that a falsifying instance would be more conclusive. In one experiment, the subject is shown four cards displaying the symbols E K 4 7, and told that every card has a number on one side and a letter on the other. He is given the rule "if a card has a vowel on one side, then it has an even number on the other". His task is to name those cards, and only those cards, which need to be turned over to determine whether the rule is true or false. The great majority of subjects choose E and 4, when they should choose E and 7, since the rule would be proved false if 7 had a vowel on the other side. They neglect to look for falsifying evidence. Their choice of "4" is irrelevant because the rule does not necessarily imply its own converse; it is not the case that if there is an even number on one side then there must be a vowel on the other side. This failure persists through variations of the task using different symbols. When the array is a red triangle, a blue triangle, a red circle and a blue circle and the rule is "If there is a red triangle on one side there is a blue circle on the other", the subjects choose the red triangle and the blue circle, instead of the red triangle and the red circle. There are a number of possible explanations for this apparent failure to reason logically. It may reflect a bias towards seeking verification rather than falsification, as Wason suggests, but this offers us only a re-description of the subjects' behaviour, not an explanation of it. Alternatively, it could reflect a perceptual set, a bias of attention towards the items mentioned in the rule (Evans, 1972), but this perceptual matching hypothesis cannot explain why more concrete everyday versions of the rule tend to elicit correct solutions. When the cards showed a place on one side, and a means of transport on the other (Leeds, Manchester, train, car), and the rule was "If I go to Manchester, then I travel by train", a majority of the subjects reasoned correctly, and selected "Manchester" and "car". Their failure with the letter–digit and triangle–circle versions of the task must therefore be due to misinterpretation rather than to a general inability to reason logically. One possibility is that this misinterpretation originates from the difference between conditional abstract rules, and conditional everyday facts. An abstract, de-contextualized form of the problem, like the E K 4 7 example may be seen as an arbitrary rule rather like the rules of games or puzzles, which describe conventions rather than facts, like "If you throw a six, then you get two turns". Rules of this kind are prescriptive, but are neither true nor false. In everyday language, logical connectives have different connotations than they do in pure logic, and the "if . . . then" condition is commonly used to express temporal or causal connections as in "If I work too hard, then I feel tired". Whereas rules are more often bidirectional (if you throw a six, then you get two turns, and if you get two turns then you must have thrown a six), the causal types of connection expressed by the everyday conditional are more often unidirectional, so that while it may be true that working too hard results in tiredness, it is not the case that feeling tired necessarily implies having worked too hard. If a statement of the form "If P then Q" is bidirectional, then it follows that "If Q then P". The subjects who choose E and 4 in Watson's test misinterpret the rule as being bidirectional. In the Leeds, Manchester, car, train version they more readily perceive that it is unidirectional, and that even if going to Manchester implies travelling by train, travelling by train does not guarantee that the destination was Manchester.

Staudenmayer and Bourne (1978) suggested that subjects interpret the rule in terms of elements instead of classes. So "If it has a vowel on one side there is an even number on the other" is translated as "If it has an E on one side there is a 4 on the other". With this interpretation of the rule, it is correct to respond, as a substantial number of subjects do, by choosing only E. These attempts to clarify the reasoning process underlying the errors in this task all point to the conclusion that it is the representation of the problem that is faulty, not the execution of the logical operations.

The number series problem. In another of his experiments, which showed a similar reluctance to seek falsification, Wason (1960) presented subjects with the number series "2 4 6" and asked them to discover the rule governing the sequence. The subject could generate successive triplets, and the experimenter informed him whether each example did, or did not, conform to the rule. The subject was instructed to test his hypothesized rule until he was sure it was correct. In fact the rule was "Any numbers increasing in magnitude", but subjects were slow to discover it. Having formed an incorrect hypothesis, such as "Add two to each successive number" they continued to generate positive instances (10 12 14), instead of generating a negative instance which would have revealed that their hypothesis was incorrect. Even after receiving disconfirmation, subjects were reluctant to abandon their original hypotheses. Again it may be argued that this bias is acquired because it is appropriate in natural everyday situations. Everyday rules commonly have exceptions, so that negative instances may not convey much information. Generalizations like "Smokers get lung cancer" or "First-born children have greater academic success" are supported by an accumulation of positive instances, and are not invalidated by finding some instances of stupid first-born children or noncancerous smokers.

Mynett *et al.* (1977) have examined hypothesis-testing behaviour in a different task. In their experiment subjects observed a screen displaying moving particles, and objects that differed in size, shape, location and brightness. The task was to initiate particle movements, and deduce the law governing their motion. In fact, the brightest objects had invisible boundaries which blocked the movement of the particles. In attempting to discover this law, the subjects behaved like Wason's in failing to generate multiple hypotheses, but if they did obtain falsifying data then 91% of the subjects took this into account, and revised their hypothesis accordingly. Tweney *et al.* (1980) went on to dissect the strategies used in the 2-4-6 problem by requiring subjects to produce verbal protocols of their reasoning. They found that subjects could use disconfirmation strategies when instructed to do so, but this did not improve their performance. Subjects who sought disconfirmation were no better at reaching the solution than those who used a confirming strategy. When the subjects were forced to entertain two alternative hypotheses at the same time, so that feedback which disconfirmed one hypothesis supported the other (and vice versa), performance did improve dramatically. Simply seeking falsifying evidence is not necessarily the right way to solve the problem. Tweney *et al.* have argued that, contrary to the Popperian view, scientific hypotheses are best tested by seeking a body of confirmatory evidence before applying falsifying tests. Their findings also suggest that it is important to entertain and test several hypotheses, not just one. In common sense terms, it is a waste of time trying to falsify a hypothesis while it is still only a conjecture. The most effective and economical strategy is to strengthen a chosen hypothesis by gathering positive support first, before trying to see if it can be falsified.

What the laboratory experiments have shown is not so much that people reason illogically, as that habits of reasoning acquired in everyday life are not appropriate in the decontextualized test situations. It is interesting to note that although the conditional problems seem to be easier when they are expressed in a concrete, rather than an abstract form, other problems, especially mathematical ones, may be easier when they are converted to abstract symbols. Abstraction seems to be helpful when the original problem contains irrelevant and distracting information, but can be solved by the application of fixed, well-learned rules once it has been correctly formulated. Concretization may be more helpful as a checking device when it is not clear how the problem should be formulated. We can often decide whether an abstract problem has been correctly formulated by testing whether a concrete version gives a semantically acceptable answer.

Solving three-term series problems

Three-term series problems, sometimes called linear syllogisms, or relational inferences, are problems in which inferences are drawn from premises stating a transitive relation such as "A is bigger than B, B is bigger than C". They have been quite intensively studied, and have produced considerable theoretical controversy. Some of the proposed models are outlined below.

The operational model. The operational model (Hunter, 1957) maintains that a unitary internal representation of the information in the premises is formed, so that the answer to a question such as "Which is biggest?" can be directly read off from the representation. For this to be possible, the terms must be arranged in a "natural" order. In the example above, A, B and C are arranged in order of size, and because the same relation "bigger than" is used in both premises, the internal representation is such that the terms are still correctly related even if the middle term is deleted (A > B > C). This theory generates some predictions about the relative difficulty of various ways of presenting the premisses. If the initial premisses were "A is bigger than B, C is smaller than B" it would be harder to form the internal representation because both the relation and the order of the terms is different in the second premiss, so that it would be necessary to convert one of the relations and re-order the terms before a "natural" unitary representation could be formed.

The Spatial Imagery Theory. Huttenlocher's (1968) account of how three-term series problems are handled extends the operational model and specifies the nature of the unitary representation which is created. This is characterized as a spatial image in which terms are placed along a vertical or horizontal axis, and read off from left to right, or from top to bottom. Problem difficulty is alleged to depend on two factors; the order of terms within each premiss, and the order of the premisses. The easiest form of the problem is one in which an end-item is the first term to be presented, and the order of presentation of the remaining items is such as to allow them to be consecutively entered into the imaged array working in a preferred direction (rightwards or downwards). Thus, A > B, followed by B > C should be easier to process than B > C, followed by B < A. Evidence in support of this theory comes from the fact that the predicted order of difficulty is reflected in reaction times and errors in responding to questions. It has also been noted that, given a paper and pencil, subjects tend to jot down the terms along an axis in the way described, and that the same order of difficulty is found in a placement task requiring subjects actually to place coloured bricks in slots in a vertical array. It proves easier to place a blue brick following the instruction "The blue brick goes under the red brick" than the instruction "The red brick should be on top of the blue brick". Since this task involves a visually perceived array, and the results are similar to those obtained with the mental problem, it is argued that the mental representation in three-term series problems must be a visual image. However, these observations do not provide very strong grounds for inferring that the information is represented in a visual image since they are equally consistent with a verbal or conceptual re-organization of the information. The similarity between the block placement task, and the mental solution of three-term series problems could just as easily arise if the block task is verbally mediated instead of the verbal series being visually mediated.

The linguistic model. Clark (1969a, b) has proposed a linguistic model which is in conflict with both the Operational and the Spatial Imagery explanations. According to Clark's theory, the internal representation of the problem is not imaginal, and it is not unitary. His theory generates different predictions about problem difficulty. The linguistic model incorporates three principles. According to the first principle, a premiss such as "A is better than B" is transformed into two internal representations corresponding to "A is good" and "B is good". Since the comparative relation is removed by this operation, it is necessary to assume some weighting of the terms so the relation can be retrieved later by a comparison of the weights. So the "A is good" representation has a greater weighting than the "B is good" representation. According to the second principle, an unmarked comparative adjective is more easily processed than a marked one. Unmarked adjectives such as good, tall, high, deep etc. are neutral, conveying only relative position on a scale. Marked forms like bad, short etc. convey absolute information as well. The unmarked form is often the name of the dimension (e.g. height). The unmarked question "How high is X?" carries no implication as to absolute height, whereas the marked question "How low is X?" implies that X is low. We use the unmarked form with quantitative units (e.g. 5-feet tall) not the marked form (5-feet short). However, experiments by Brewer and Lichtenstein (1974) failed to show any bias towards superior retention of unmarked forms in memory. In fact, the effect of marking is variable in concrete tasks, and depends on semantic context, implications and presuppositions. Banks *et al.* (1975) showed that subjects were faster at selecting the higher one of two pictured balloons which were up in the air (since these were both perceived as high), but faster at picking out the lower one of two yo-yos hanging down on strings (since these were both perceived as low). Clark's third principle concerns the congruence of the premisses and the question. Following "A is better than B, B is better than C", the congruent question "Who is best?" is easier to handle than the incongruent question "Who is worst?", which has to be converted. The linguistic model and the imagery model make different predictions about a class of premisses called negative equatives. Of the two premisses "B is not as good as A" and "A is not as bad as B", the imagery model predicts that the first should be harder because the image would have to be constructed in the nonpreferred upward direction. The linguistic model predicts that the second should be harder because the adjective is marked. The results conform to the linguistic model, but it is quite possible that different strategies are employed in different circumstances. Wood (1969) claimed that subjects tended to shift from an image-based strategy to a verbal strategy with practice.

The image theory cannot account for the effect of congruence between question and premisses, because the same imaginal representation is constructed whatever the form of the original premisses. If the premisses "A is better than B, B is better than C" produce the imaged array

A
B
C

it should be just as easy to read off "Who is worst?" as "Who is best?". Many people are not aware of constructing imagery during this task, and even when imagery is reported, it is not clear whether it actually mediates the solution, or is simply a mnemonic aid. The linguistic theory accounts for the congruence effect, but as Potts and Scholz (1975) have pointed out, it cannot explain why the order of presentation of the premises should influence problem difficulty when the model postulates separate representations for each premiss, not a unitary array. Potts and Scholz also showed that the congruence effect is only apparent when the premises are immediately followed by the question, and not when the question is delayed. In everyday discourse, the question often precedes and elicits the relational information. If we ask "Who would be best for the job?" or "Do the Jones have a big house?" then answers like "Tom is better than Dick, but not as good as Harry" or "The Jones' house is bigger than the Smiths', but smaller than the Browns' " do not intuitively seem especially difficult to understand. Perhaps difficulties arising from the order of presentation are lessened when the context supplies a focus of attention. The models of reasoning derived from the abstract de-contextualized tests used in laboratory experiments seem very laborious and cumbersome. How far they have application to reasoning in natural context-bound situations is doubtful. Even in so far as the models are successful in representing the reasoning processes which are most typical of the subjects tested, there has been little attempt to explore individual differences in reasoning strategies.

One exception is a recent study by Shaver *et al.* (1975). They found evidence that spatial imagery is useful but not necessary for solving linear syllogisms. Problems involving those attributes for which different subjects consistently reported the same spatial arrangement were easier (above–below was easier than better–worse, and lighter–darker, which produced very inconsistent arrangements, was the hardest). Problems presented in writing were harder than when presented auditorily, perhaps because reading interferes with the construction of imagery, and subjects with higher scores for spatial ability performed better. The results suggested more use of imagery as the subjects became more practised, the opposite of Wood's finding. The authors concluded that imagery made it easier to hold the problem in short-term memory, but noted that subjects who did not give evidence of using imagery could still perform the task. Griggs (1978) claims that two types of subject can be identified. There are those who construct an internal representation of linear order as in the Operational Model, and those who store a list of adjacent pairs. The main difference between the various forms of representation (like the different models of semantic memory in Chapter 2) can be characterized as prestored (the operational and spatial imagery models) and computational (the linguistic model and the list type representation). With prestored representations the relationships can be read off directly, whereas with computational models relationships must be computed.

Syllogistic inference: reasoning with quantifiers

A problem which sometimes causes difficulty is cited by Revlin and Mayer (1978). "A man bought a horse for $60, and sold it for $70; he then bought it back again for $80 and sold it for $90. How much did he make in the horse-dealing business?" Difficulty with this problem originates from incorrect representation of the information. Conflating the two transactions may produce the wrong answer. Presenting the problem as two separate transactions with two different horses makes it easier to solve.

Similarly, errors in syllogistic reasoning, as in a number of the other logical problems that have been discussed can often be explained in terms of idiosyncratic representation of the premises, rather than invalid inferential reasoning. In Chapter 2, different models of representation in semantic memory yielded different predictions about the relative ease of verifying statements quantified by "All" and "Some". Erickson (1978) has pointed out that in formal syllogisms a premiss of the "All A are B" form is ambiguous, since it could mean A and B are identical, or that A is a subset of B. Different conclusions follow, depending on which meaning is selected. Revlin and Leirer (1978) developed a conversion model. They found that when this type of premiss is interpreted as expressing an identity relation, subjects validly convert it to "All B are A". In one of their studies, subjects were given premisses similar to those shown below, and asked to choose the correct conclusion from the alternatives 1–5.

All criminals are psychotics

Some psychotics are alcoholics

Therefore (1) All alcoholics are criminals

             (2) No alcoholics are criminals

             (3) Some alcoholics are criminals

             (4) Some alcoholics are not criminals

             (5) None of the above is proved

Subjects tended to choose (3) rather than (5) which was designated as the correct conclusion, but this response is not the result of faulty reasoning, but of treating the set of "all criminals" as identical with the set of "all psychotics". On this interpretation (3) is correct. If the premises are disambiguated, or if the identity interpretation is obviously absurd (as in "All flowers are tulips"), conversion does not occur and the formally correct response is more likely.

Some of the errors that occur in syllogistic reasoning can be explained by Johnson-Laird's theory of mental models (1980, 1981). This theory is quite similar to Huttenlocher's spatial imagery theory, but is able to handle several other aspects of comprehension in addition to syllogistic inferences. The theory postulates that comprehension of a verbal input involves two stages. At the first stage a direct linguistic representation is constructed. At the second stage a mental model of the state of affairs described is constructed. This second stage is not mandatory. A listener may not go beyond the first stage of forming a linguistic representation. The mental model is similar to perceived or imagined events, and constitutes an interface between natural language and the real world. The mental model is not equivalent to a propositional representaton. It is an analogical representation which can be scanned, manipulated or constructed in any direction. In this respect it is more similar to an image, but it is not necessarily associated with any subjective experience, and need not be pictorial in character. Construction of the mental model involves prior knowledge as well as current input.

A mental model extends comprehension in several ways. It clarifies the reference of terms that may be ambiguous in a linguistic form. In sentences like:

John arranged to meet Bill.

He was late arriving.

The reference of "he", which is ambiguous in the linguistic version, would be explicit and unambiguous in the mental model. The mental model also allows deductions to be made by inspection or search of the model without the application of formal rules of logical inference. Johnson-Laird has instantiated the theory in a computer program that builds a spatial model of relations between entities. Information such as:

The knife is in front of the spoon

The spoon is on the left of the glass

The glass is behind the dish

is entered into an array, and the spatial relationships that were not stated in the verbal input can be read off the mental model. If the relationships are indeterminate, as in:

A is to the right of B

C is to the left of A

which is compatible with either C B A or B C A, the program selects one interpretation, and may reconstruct the model later if future information proves incompatible with the selected model. In this respect the program is unlikely to resemble human performance since the recursive reconstruction strategy places a load on working memory that may exceed human capacity.

The mental model theory has also been applied to story comprehension and explains how listeners or readers are able to understand the relationships (such as the temporal sequence, the spatial and causal relationships), between events and elements in a story, and to maintain the continuity of reference.

In reasoning with quantifiers, Johnson-Laird suggests that people construct a mental model of the relevant individuals showing the identity relationships between them. The heuristic that governs this process is to try to simplify the relationships by establishing as much identity as possible. So, given the premises:

All of the singers are professors

All of the poets are professors

the mental model initially constructed would represent:

singers = professors = poets

The next step is to test the mental model by trying to break the identities without violating the premises. This procedure establishes that:

singer = professor

professor = poet

is a valid representation. That is, the premises are not violated when none of the singers are poets. The mental model theory is able to predict the kind of errors and biases that occur in reasoning with quantifiers, and the order of difficulty for different types of syllogism. Errors are due to failure to carry out all the necessary tests on the mental model; biases are due to a preferred order of testing. The procedure is essentially a semantic one, not a logical one. No rules of inference are applied. Instead the mental model is manipulated by re-assigning identity relationships and testing the resultant models against the premises. According to Johnson-Laird, the rules of formal logic are derived from experience of the outcomes of searching mental models. Because of its emphasis on semantics rather than on logic, the mental model theory has the advantage of being able to explain why problems expressed in concrete terms, and premises that conform to our experience are easier to handle.

The variety of ways in which a problem can be organized and internally represented is illustrated in a deductive reasoning task described by Polich and Schwartz (1974). The problem is a whodunnit puzzle in which subjects are presented with varying amounts of information about a number of spies (their names, hair colour, locations and special expertise (see Fig. 32)). Paper and pencil working provided direct evidence of the ways in which subjects arranged this information preparatory to deducing the identity of a particular spy from clues provided, and showed that a variety of different strategies were used. The alternative modes of representation were classified as matrix, network, grouping, re-writing in sentences and miscellaneous. The matrix mode generated more correct solutions, and was adopted more frequently as the amount of information supplied increased. This study suggests that Huttenlocher and Clark may both have over-estimated the uniformity of the internal representations constructed by subjects in solving linear syllogisms.

This is a problem about four different spies. Each of the spies has his contact located in a different location. Each spy also has a different spy speciality and a different colour of hair.

1. The spy with brown hair specializes in secret missile plans.
2. The spy whose contact is located in Peking specializes in germ warfare plans.
3. One of the spies has red hair.
4. The spy who specializes in electronic bugs has his contact located in Tokyo.
5. Paris is the contact location of one of the spies.
6. The spy who has black hair has his contact located in London.
7. The spy named Irving has grey hair.
8. One of the spies is named Boris.
9. The spy whose contact is located in London is named Edmond.
10. The spy named George specializes in germ warfare.
11. One of the spies specializes in scientific papers.

What is the name of the spy whose contact is in Tokyo?

FIG. 32. *Example of deductive reasoning problem (four dimensions, four values) (from Polich and Schwartz, 1974).*

In Chapter 2, the studies of semantic memory failed to produce compelling evidence that knowledge in the permanent memory store is uniquely represented in the structural form proposed by any one model. It also seems clear that the information supplied in problem solving tasks can be restructured in a variety of different ways.

Making predictions: reasoning about probabilities

Recent studies by Kahneman and Tversky (1973) showed that people tend to make predictions which are not in accordance with statistical proba-bilities. They ignore information about the prior probability of an event, and base their judgement primarily on two other factors which Kahneman and Tversky call representativeness and availability. For example, if asked to consider whether a certain person whose characteristics are described, is more likely to be a farmer or a scientist, people consider how far the individual possesses the characteristics they regard as typical of farmers or of scientists (representativeness), and may be influenced by how many instances of each profession are personally known to them (availability).

They ignore information which is supplied by the experimenter about the relative numbers of farmers and scientists in the population, which determines the prior probability, and should be taken into account in making the judgement. If 50% of the population are farmers, and only 10% are scientists, then there is a greater probability of a given individual being a farmer than a scientist even if the individual is described as pale, intelligent and wearing spectacles. However, the way in which people operate in this kind of task is not so inept as it may appear. Statistical probabilities are more relevant to predictions about sets than to predictions about individuals. In everyday life, the prior probabilities may not be known, or they may be fairly similar for the alternative outcomes. When the prior probability has an extreme value, it may be given greater weight. If people were asked to rate the chance of a given individual being President of the USA, it seems intuitively obvious that they would pay more attention to prior probability, and place less weight on representativeness. Also, if no descriptive information is supplied, people will take the prior probabilities into account. Although Kahneman and Tversky claim (1974) that people fail to combine information from prior probabilities with specific evidence, this may not be invariably so. In quoting terms for a life insurance policy, the insurance agent will take into account both the known probabilities of life expectation, and the specific age, health and way of life of the individual. In laying bets on a horse race, a serious betting man will take into account the number of runners (the prior probability) as well as the track records, breeding and fitness of the runners, and the weather conditions prevailing. In these examples, very strong specific evidence may outweigh prior probabilities.

Tversky and Kahneman found additional evidence that subjects flout statistical principles in making judgements about probabilities in a problem involving sample size. Subjects were given the information that

> In a large hospital 45 babies are born every day; in a small hospital 15 babies are born every day. 50% of all babies born are boys. Over one year each hospital recorded the days when more than 60% of the babies were boys. Which hospital recorded more such days?

Twenty-one of the subjects said the larger hospital; 21 said the smaller, and 53 said both the same. Clearly, many subjects failed to take account of the fact that large samples are more likely to reflect the distribution of the population as a whole. Again, however, it is possible to cite instances of everyday common sense reasoning where people do apply the principle correctly. Anyone who seeks advice and receives two conflicting opinions will tend to prefer the opinion of the adviser with the widest experience, on the grounds that the information derived from the larger sample is more likely to be reliable.

Judgements of probability, like inferential reasoning in logical problems, have been too readily dismissed as invalid. As a general rule, it can be shown that people can and do reason correctly, but that when problems are presented in ways that are ambiguous, unfamiliar, or misleading, the representation of the problem goes astray, so that even correctly applied reasoning operations yield erroneous responses. Given the range and variety of problems that have been studied, and the different kinds of strategy that can be employed in solving them, it is hardly surprising that it proves difficult to construct a universal theory of problem solving. The information processing approach does provide a method for analysing the problem solving process, and a general framework within which models for specific problems can be elaborated.

Recommended reading

Johnson-Laird and Wason's book *Thinking* provides a wide-ranging collection of papers and is well worth reading. Revlin and Mayer's *Human Reasoning* concentrates on logical problems. The debate about verbal protocols between Nisbett and Wilson, and Ericsson and Simon, is stimulating and of general importance for most areas of cognition, not just problem solving. Simon's review paper in the *Annual Review of Psychology*, 1979, provides a clear and readable introduction to computer modelling of problem solving and more detailed accounts are available in The Open University *Cognitive Psychology* text *Learning and Problem Solving* Part 3. For more about mental models see Johnson-Laird in *Cognitive Science* **4**, 1980.

8 ARTIFICIAL INTELLIGENCE
and
COMPUTER SIMULATION

The purpose of this chapter is not to attempt a comprehensive review, but rather to try to evaluate the power of machine analogies as a technique for investigating the nature of human thought, and for testing models of cognitive processes.

The AI/CS Distinction

It is useful, as a preliminary, to clarify the distinction between Artificial Intelligence (AI) and Computer Simulation (CS). This distinction is an important one for the cognitive psychologist, since the empirical data and theoretical insights furnished by each differ in status. The distinction is usually made in terms of the difference in goals or aims. The primary aim of AI is to get a machine to do a particular job, such as translating a text, diagnosing a disease, or keeping accounts, as efficiently as possible. The primary aim of CS is to instantiate and test the adequacy of a psychological theory of human performance. While CS is specifically designed to mimic or model human performance, it does not matter whether an AI model happens to resemble human performance or not. The kind of tasks tackled by CS and AI tend to differ also. It is hardly possible to attempt a simulation of human performance unless there is already a fairly well developed psychological theory, so in some areas a CS approach is ruled out because there is no adequate theory to simulate. AI systems are not restricted in the same way, and may tackle tasks where clear and detailed knowledge about human performance is lacking. AI is constrained by the task demands, not by psychological theories. It may be more efficient for a machine to recognize a letter by counting corners, or in chess playing to evaluate several hundred continuation board states. Such strategies need bear no relation to the way humans do these tasks. Differences between AI and human performance are virtually ensured by the fact that the human and the computer are not subject to the same constraints. Anderson (1977) warns we should be extremely careful of computer based models of cognition, since the capacities of the mammalian brain and the computer are very different, the divergence in abilities occurring by deliberate and conscious design. The talents of the brain and the computer complement each other, rather than mimic each other, and we should be wary of using one as a metaphor for the other.

Anderson is not just talking about the difference between neurological hardware and electronic hardware, but about differences in capacities. Computers are fast and accurate, and able to retain information for indefinitely long periods of time and retrieve it on demand. By comparison, humans are slow processors, make more errors, and have difficulty in retaining and retrieving stored information. On the credit side, humans have greater versatility and adaptability, and greater tolerance for variability in the task and distortion in the input. Because of these differences, processes that are optimal for the human system are liable to be nonoptimal for the computer, and vice versa.

In practice, the AI/CS distinction may become slightly blurred. A CS may be forced by technological constraints to depart from psychological theory in some respects; and an AI system may reflect psychological theories when these happen to suggest a feasible way to do the job. AI may also yield psychological insights in the course of developing and refining a system.

AI and Sufficiency Conditions

One of the ways in which AI systems can help the cognitive psychologist is by revealing what are the minimally sufficient conditions for successfully performing a given task, what elements and processes have to be incorporated in the system if it is to work to a specified level of efficiency. While it may be helpful to know the sufficiency conditions a psychological model should fulfil, problems arise because AI systems tend to throw up a multiplicity of different sufficiency models. In language processing and speech recognition, for example, radically different systems do similar jobs. It is difficult for the psychologist to know which set of sufficiency conditions is the appropriate one to adopt in a psychological model. One contribution that AI makes to psychology is undeniable. To the extent that an AI program does draw on psychological theories, these have to be made explicit, precise and logically coherent. Gaps and deficiencies in the theories, fuzzy and poorly specified parameters, and lack of constraints are all exposed. At the very least, AI models set an example of clarity and completeness. The psychologist is forced to clean up his act if he wants to join in the game.

In computer simulation, the analogy with human performance is, by design, much closer. CS is potentially a powerful tool for testing and refining psychological theories. It is the only way to find out whether a theory about how a given task is performed will actually work. Moreover, if the theory proves to be inadequate, simulation will often reveal the source of the weakness. The aim of computer simulation is to make machines perform tasks in ways that are functionally equivalent to the ways in which humans carry out the same tasks. But what is to count as functional equivalence?

The Problem of Functional Equivalence

Criteria for equivalence

The criteria which are appropriate and sufficient to permit a claim of functional equivalence will necessarily depend on how complete, detailed and exact a reproduction of human behaviour the CS worker is aiming to create. Because this has not always been made clear, misunderstanding and confusion have arisen, and computer simulation has been severely criticised (e.g. Dreyfus, 1972) for failing to attain levels of equivalence that are not strictly necessary or relevant. Pylyshyn (1975) makes this point when he comments:

> The relation of model to system-being-modelled must be partial and in-complete in important ways. As Sellars (1963) has put it, the interpretation of the model as some kind of analogue of a system is possible only if the model is accompanied by a commentary which tells the user which aspects of the system are mapped onto the model, and which aspects of the model are relevant to its analogy with the system. Dreyfus wants the relation of "representing" to be so complete and transparent that no such commentary would be necessary. But this is impossible unless the model and the system are so close to being identical that the model can no longer serve as an instrument for understanding the system—which, in the case of CS, is its sole purpose.

Given, then, that the object of CS is not to produce entities which are virtually identical with human beings, but only to produce analogies which are equivalent in some respects, it is vital to specify the kind of equivalence which *is* essential if computer models are to prove an informative method of investigating human behaviour.

The goodness of fit between the mind and the machine depends largely on the level of description at which they are compared. There is general agreement that the appropriate comparison is not at the level of electronic hardware and neuronal tissue. A more abstract level of description is required, but at the highest level of description where only the most general principles are specified, there is a danger that the comparison may be vacuous. If it is to be illuminating, it is necessary to choose a level of abstraction at which specific procedures and representations are described. Information Processing Theory provides a common language which enables human and machine performance to be described in comparable terms at about the right level of detail. Other problems that arise in evaluating man–machine equivalence are discussed below. It is perhaps surprising to find that these are exactly the same problems that arise when we try to formulate general theories of human performance on the basis of experimental testing of human subjects.

Equivalent to whom?: the problem of individual differences

Should a CS program yield a result which is equivalent to the best human performance, to the average human performance, or to the performance of some individual of normal intelligence? Should it be equivalent to a skilled and practised human performer, or to an untutored beginner? Since the range of human performance at complex tasks like chess playing, mathematics or logical problems is very wide, this question needs to be answered. Dreyfus cites one CS worker (Gruenberger, 1962) as aiming for a program that plays chess better than any man, and regards the achievement of only "reasonably competent" chess playing programs as evidence for the failure of CS. However, if the aim of the programmer is to reproduce the mental operations involved in the chess playing of an average or novice player, then a reasonably competent machine performance might well constitute a successful simulation. Attempts to simulate "average" performance might fail for the reason that the average performance in tasks like problem solving and concept formation does not necessarily reflect the performance of any single individual. Why should the computer mirror average performance if no individual subject in the experimental task does? If the gap between machine performance and average human performance is no greater than the differences between one human individual and another, it is hardly justifiable to conclude that the simulation is unsuccessful. Turing's test (Turing, 1950) evades the problem of individual differences by requiring that the output of a computer simulation should be such that an observer could not distinguish it from the output of a human performer; that is to say, it should be equivalent to the output of *some* human individual. Even so, it might be necessary to instruct Turing's observer that some aspects of the comparison were relevant and others irrelevant. In judging the equivalence of mathematical calculations, for example, it might be desirable for him to confine his comparison to the accuracy of the solutions, and ignore differences in speed. Arguably, the most satisfactory equivalence would be achieved if systematic variations in the program produced variations in the machine performance so as to mimic the whole range of human individual differences.

General equivalence or specific equivalence?: the problem of generalizability

Humans possess cognitive abilities which enable them to perform a wide range of different tasks. Most CS programs are designed to carry out only a limited set of specific tasks. This limited generality has led some critics, such as Bolton (1972) to assert "A computer which performs one specialist task very well, but is helpless at any other problem is not therefore representative of human problem solving". A number of arguments can be advanced for not accepting Bolton's stricture. Lack of versatility is not necessarily a fatal flaw in computer simulation. Even if we accept Spearman's (1927) conclusion that there is a general ability factor in human intelligence, as well as specific ability factors, common sense insists that human versatility is not unlimited. People can be excellent scientists, and poor bridge players. It is not clear what degree of general ability a CS program ought to manifest if it is to be analogous to human intelligence.

Some CS programs have in fact achieved a measure of generality, notably the *General Problem Solver* of Newell *et al.* (1959), a sequentially organized program which proceeds by setting goals, detecting differences between the prevailing state and the goal, and generating moves to reduce these differences. Technological difficulties of incorporating sufficient specific data to cope with a wider range of problems have proved to be one of the main limitations to the generality of this program. It did succeed in solving a variety of logical and mathematical problems, and was in principle extendable to other problems.

Dresher and Hornstein (1976) have argued that AI models of language processing are of no psychological relevance whatsoever, because they lack the generality of the human system and the universality of linguistic theory. It is true that working models of language processing do tend to be both task specific and material specific. They can carry out a particular task within a particular semantic domain, with a limited vocabulary and a limited range of sentence structures. So one system may be able to describe layouts of geometrical shapes, another to write fables, another to answer queries about train timetables. There is, at present, a sharp trade-off between generality and efficiency. The more delimited the task and the input, the better the system works. Models that do have greater generality (like Schank's Conceptual Dependency model, p. 211) tend to be programmatic, rather than fully implemented working models. The psychologist must try to assess how far lack of generality detracts from equivalence. Much depends on whether the specific models are in principle extensible and generalizable.

At present, there exists a "complexity barrier" in machine intelligence. That is, once a data base is expanded beyond a fairly small size and degree of complexity, problems of organization, and of heuristics for accessing information within the data base, become acute. The system must have procedures for determining where to start searching, and for selecting the elements in the data base that are most relevant. It must have procedures for determining the order of search, and it must have procedures for determining when to stop searching,when to accept that only a poor match, or no match at all, is in store. In a large data base, items need to be organized and related so as to facilitate whatever search procedures are employed. So far, these problems have not been solved. And, even if machines could operate efficiently with very large data bases, they need not necessarily operate in the same way as the human system.

If a model with broad general language processing skills could be developed, would it be radically different from the small scale specific models? There are some reasons to suppose that in language systems more means different: quantitative differences involve qualitative changes. For example, psycholinguists have been doubtful whether the communication systems learned by chimpanzees (described in Chapter 5) can be considered as language, and one of the grounds for doubt is the limited generality and complexity they display. It seems intuitively that a language user, whether machine, animal or human, which had a vocabulary of only a few hundred words would be qualitatively different from one with a vocabulary of many thousand words. The level of complexity required in the organization of the storage system, and in the retrieval procedures would be greater, and the number of combinatorial possibilities would necessitate more complex rules to govern and constrain them. Studies of semantic organization in children (reviewed in Chapter 2, p. 23) showed a developmental trend of this kind as the child's language system expanded. So there is some force in the argument that the limited and highly specific machine systems are not representative of human cognition because they lack generalizability. On the other side, it can be argued that a CS program does not always need to be generalizable if it is to be a useful analogy to human performance. Whether this is so, or not, depends on the aims of the simulation, and the claims that are based on it. If the aim of a CS program is to test a model of letter recognition by simulating the hypothesized stages of processing, and comparing them with human performance, the validity of the simulation is not affected if the program cannot also recognize faces. The lack of generality would be crucial only if the program claimed to exemplify a general mechanism of pattern recognition; or, if we could assert as an empirical fact that humans employ the same processing stages in all pattern recognition tasks. In fact, the whole trend of the experimental work on human information processing over the last decade or so has been to reveal that processing stages are task specific, rather than being uniform across different tasks. It is hardly fair to castigate computer simulation for failing to display a generality which is also lacking in theoretical models of cognition, and in experimental results. Most CS workers are far from claiming a generality and completeness that their programs do not possess. Anderson and Bower (1973) explicitly state that they "try to abstract from the real world significant components of the phenomena at hand". Whether or not they manage to identify the significant components is a much more important issue than generality *per se*.

Equivalence of structures and equivalence of strategies

In cognitive psychology it has been found useful to distinguish between structures and strategies, or states and processes. Pylyshyn (1980) has also distinguished between what he calls the cognitively impenetrable fixed capacities of the mind, and the particular representations and processes that are flexibly deployed on specific tasks, which are described as cognitively penetrable. They can be changed and influenced by factors like beliefs, tacit knowledge about the task, expectations and goals. Models need to distinguish between the fixed and variable elements and processes in the system. Pylyshyn argues that separate validation is required for each.

It is characteristic of human performance that a variety of different strategies can be employed on most tasks. Besides applying different processing operations in different tasks, a single human performer typically has a range of possible strategies available for any single task. To take a simple example, he may choose any one of several methods in order to multiply 346 by 24. Computer programs do not always have this flexibility. However, there is in principle no obstacle to programming a simulation with alternative strategies. The *Logic Theorist* of Newell *et al.* (1958), for example, has three heuristics available for proving theorems. The fact that different strategies can be used to perform the same task does, however, raise some problems for computer simulation. Firstly, it is extremely difficult to identify and represent the factors which incline a human performer to prefer one strategy over another, or to abandon one strategy and shift to another. Individual preferences are liable to be determined by past experience, intelligence, practice, the relative values placed on speed and accuracy, and the cost in terms of cognitive load. These determinants of strategy selection are not sufficiently well understood, and are too complex and variable to be accurately simulated. Secondly, it is difficult to judge whether functional equivalence between human and computer has been achieved if different strategies can yield the same result, or to infer nonequivalence if the same strategy could yield different results. It should be noted, though, that the tendency to assume uniformity of strategy is not confined to CS work. Many models of human performance (for example, models of memory) based on experimental data also make this assumption, and are open to the same criticism.

Automatic and attentional processes: the problem of consciousness

Another problem for machine simulation arises because mental operations in humans can be classified as either attentional or automatic (Shiffrin and Schneider, 1977), and these two kinds of operation exhibit qualitative differences. With practice, many mental operations become automatic. It is characteristic of automatic processes that they do not require continuous monitoring, and are not accessible to conscious awareness. Automatic processing is fast and may be combined with other concurrent mental operations without interference. Novel or unpractised tasks are more likely to require attentional processing. Attentional processes are under conscious control, are slower, and cannot be combined with other concurrent operations without some loss of efficiency. So, for example, changing gears while driving (with a manual shift) is usually an automatic process; negotiating traffic junctions is an attentional process. It has been objected that there is no parallel in machine intelligence to this distinction between automatic and attentional, unconscious and conscious processes. Simon (1979) counters this objection with the suggestion that the difference between conscious and unconscious processing in humans is analogous to the distinction between interpreted and compiled processes in a program. A precompiled program, or part of a program, is already translated *en bloc* into machine language, and is run out ten times faster than an interpreted program, in which the preconditions for each step are checked before it is executed. This step by step control is functionally analogous to conscious attentional processing in humans. Gear changing is precompiled; responding to traffic conditions is interpreted.

Declarative and procedural knowledge

A distinction commonly applied in machine intelligence is that between declarative and procedural representations of knowledge (Winograd, 1975). The philosophical distinction between "knowing how" and "knowing that" has been revived. Proceduralists maintain that all knowledge consists of knowing how, and can be represented as sets of processes; while declarativists consider that knowledge consists in stored propositions (knowing that) as well as general procedures for manipulating them. The declarative form of representation appears intuitively to be more appropriate for human knowledge. It has the great advantage that it can be easily modified, added to or altered. Modification of a specific domain of knowledge need not cause knock-on effects elsewhere in the system. The knowledge that today is Thursday is easily updated. Procedural knowledge is less likely to be so domain specific; some procedures are common to many domains of knowledge, so modification of procedures can have far reaching effects to other parts of the system. However, some procedural knowledge, such as knowing how to do arithmetic subtraction can be represented as a specific production system that is not necessarily inter-dependent with other production systems. While procedural knowledge necessarily entails that the uses for each piece of knowledge are specified, declarative knowledge is more versatile, and can be used for any judgements, inferences, comparisons, classifications or whatever, as required. In humans the knowledge base is being acquired, updated and modified throughout the life span, and old knowledge is often put to new uses, so it is arguable that a declarative form of representation would be more advantageous. In computers, knowledge is more often built in from the start for a specified purpose, so a procedural form of knowledge may be more appropriate. If humans and computers do differ in the form of knowledge representation that is characteristic, equivalence breaks down, and this is an important man–machine disparity.

Analogue and digital processing

It is often claimed that analogue functioning is a characteristic of human performance. That is, information is represented as a continuously graded quantity rather than an all-or-none, yes–no, discrete state. Most computers operate on the digital principle, with elements assuming the discrete states of 0 or 1, whereas the human nervous system can transmit continuously graded analogue information. Dreyfus (1972) has argued that computers cannot operate in analogue form, and that their failure to do so invalidates claims of equivalence. Several arguments can be advanced in refutation of this objection. Firstly, it is not impossible to incorporate analogue devices in computers, although it may be complex and time-consuming to do so. Secondly, if the size of the discrete steps is sufficiently small the difference between analogue and digital forms becomes negligible (Pylyshyn, 1975). Thirdly, Sutherland (1974) has pointed out that, while analogical functioning is typical of physical processes in the human brain, it is not typical of cognitive processes. Humans are poor at categorizing analogue information, since we can only identify about seven different pitches in a range of tones, while our ability to categorize discrete information such as verbal stimuli is virtually unlimited. It is more accurate to describe the brain as an analogue-to-digital transformer than a strictly analogue processor, since continuously graded signals such as speech sounds are transformed to digital responses. Finally, the analogue–digital difference between man and machine would only be important if physical equivalence rather than formal equivalence was required.

Competence equivalence or performance equivalence?: the problem of phenomenology

Critics of CS, including Dreyfus (1972) and Neisser (1963), have argued that the man–machine analogy breaks down in so far as machines fail to incorporate the performance factors which influence human processing, and so lack "psychological reality". Their objections are, for the most part, misconceived. The same criticisms could equally well be levelled at information processing models which ignore emotional, motivational and experiential factors just as much as CS does. The criticisms may be justified either if a model claims to be a performance model, when in fact it is a purely competence model; or, if competence models are considered too restricted to be illuminating. In practice, most models, whether they take the form of computer simulation models, or theoretical models based on experiments with human subjects, select and incorporate some performance factors and ignore others. Early versions of the Collins and Quilian model of semantic memory described in Chapter 2 failed to incorporate effects of familiarity and experience. The *Logic Theorist* of Newell *et al.* (1958), on the other hand, does include effects of experience, being biased towards choosing moves which gave successful solutions in previous problems. What needs to be justified is the criterion for selection of some performance factors and the omission of others.

A major plank in Dreyfus's critique is his contention that it is *a priori* impossible to formalize in CS the phenomenological aspect of human performance. Human problem solving is accompanied by subjective feelings such as boredom, fatigue, interest, frustration and understanding. Neisser (1963) also emphasized the motivational differences between man and machine. A man playing a game of chess is seldom motivated solely by the desire to win the game. More commonly he has a multiplicity of motives, and may be concerned with the elegance and novelty of his strategies, the quality of social interaction with his opponent, and the time within which he would like to conclude the game so that he can go away and do something else. The values he attaches to these various goals may shift throughout the game and change his behaviour. Human goals are multiple, interactive and flexible. Computer goals are more often simple and fixed. Computer output does not exhibit the fluctuations caused by feelings of boredom, fatigue and lack of perseverance, and in these respects, is not, according to the phenomenologist view, equivalent to human behaviour.

The phenomenologist attack on CS also claims that the man–machine analogy is invalid because the machine does not "understand" what it is doing. In answer to this objection, Wilks (1976) remarked that:

> if I am asked for the phenomenology of anyone else's understanding, I have, of course, no feelings and immediate assurance to fall back on, and I am out in the cold world of watching his behaviour for appearances of understanding. . . . What kind of criteria of phenomenological reassurance about the understanding of another can I have that I do not have for a machine—the criteria are and must be behavioural in both cases.

In other words, the existence of subjective understanding is just as much a problem for the human experimental psychologist as it is for the CS worker. The cross-cultural comparisons of cognitive tasks reviewed in Chapter 7 showed how difficult it can be to ensure uniformity of understanding across human subjects. Nevertheless, it is arguable that the problem of understanding is an order of magnitude greater in machine–human comparisons than in human–human comparisons. It is usually possible to test human understanding by examining a much more varied and extensive repertoire of verbal and nonverbal behavioural responses than a machine can produce. The importance of the question of "understanding" is illustrated by the specific examples discussed later in this chapter (pp. 211–218).

Dreyfus also claims that the exercise of human intelligence is critically dependent on having a body, because it is based on knowledge acquired by means of the perceptual and motor systems. This objection is only partly countered by Pylyshyn (1975) who, while admitting that the body is necessary for the acquisition of knowledge, maintains that there is no reason why the formal conceptual structures so acquired cannot be represented in a machine. According to this view, the machine could accurately represent human capacities at the point in time when a task was begun. But most human performance involves continuous processing of perceptuo-motor feedback during the task, so the bodiless machine would not be equivalent in this respect. In fact, since it is now possible to equip machines with sensor and effector mechanisms, there is no reason why perceptuo-motor modifications of ongoing performance cannot be programmed to occur during the course of the task. When this is done, it turns out to enhance the "understanding" of the machine in important ways.

Some performance factors such as familiarity, set, practice, intentions, distractability and limited persistence can be incorporated in CS systems in so far as they can be defined in formal terms. If intentions are defined as the selection of operations so as to produce a predetermined goal state; or familiarity is defined as the occurrence of a positive match between a new input and a stored representation of a previously encountered input, these factors can be adequately represented in CS, although the subjective emotions that accompany them are absent.

In general, it is neither necessary nor desirable for a CS model to incorporate phenomenological aspects of behaviour. The selection of which performance factors should be included in a model is entirely dependent on its aims and claims. If the aim is to represent one of the possible sets of operations that a human could employ in carrying out the task (a weak equivalence), it would be important for the CS model to incorporate human performance factors that are fairly fixed and uniform such as limited memory and limited information processing capacity. It would be less necessary to incorporate performance factors like values and motives that are more variable. If the aim of the CS is to mimic the *actual* performance of a human subject (a strong equivalence), then failure to include the variable performance factors would be more damaging.

Weak equivalence and strong equivalence

Selection of the appropriate criteria will depend on whether the aim of the CS is to demonstrate a weak equivalence or a strong equivalence. It might seem that a claim of weak equivalence, that is, that the machine represents a possible model of human performance, is justified if the machine succeeds in performing the task. But this is only true if certain *a priori* criteria are also fulfilled. A machine which plays a passable game of chess, but selects its moves by testing the outcomes of many thousands of possible moves, cannot be even weakly equivalent to the human player, since we know *a priori* that such a method is beyond the capacities of the human information processing system. If the CS is designed to test for strong equivalence, and to represent the operations actually employed by human performers, much more stringent criteria are required. In addition to performing the task successfully, and having a processing capacity that falls within the range of human abilities, the machine should also give some further evidence of using the same operations as human subjects. Such evidence may be forthcoming if, for example, a set of problems yields the same order of difficulty for the machine and for man, and if the errors made by the machine are qualitatively similar to the errors of the human subject. Although comparison of speed of processing in itself tells us nothing except that machines are faster than the human brain, patterns of variation in speed can prove informative. It has been common practice in cognitive psychology to assess and compare the complexity of different tasks by examining the pattern of reaction times, on the assumption that additional operations are reflected in increments to response times. Patterns of variation in speed of processing by machine and human can be compared, and correspondence of these patterns provides evidence of functional equivalence. A claim of strong equivalence would be further reinforced if the steps of the CS program are reflected in the protocols of human subjects. Although "thinking aloud" may provide only an incomplete record of the stages of human reasoning, it does indicate some of the processes of hypothesis selection, testing, revision and rejection which occur before solution is reached, and comparison of protocol and program provides one of the most powerful tests of man–machine equivalence.

When these criteria are not satisfied, are we entitled to claim non-equivalence, and to infer that the model of human behaviour being tested in the CS must be rejected? In making a judgement of nonequivalence it is necessary to locate the source of the difference. Does the CS differ from the human performer because it does not incorporate the same sequence of operations? Or does the difference lie in the performance factors such as differences in speed, memory capacity, motivation and past experience? While comparison of final outputs may fail to shed any light on the source of nonequivalence, ongoing comparison of protocol and program is more likely to pinpoint the difference and show whether the model being tested is wholly mistaken, or only wrong in certain details.

In this discussion it has become clear that, while some of the objections raised by critics of CS are not very relevant, there are serious problems of interpretation when CS studies are used to test psychological models. It is also apparent that most of these same problems arise when the psychological models are tested against experimental data derived from human subjects. Here the difficulties of interpretation arouse less chauvinistic passion, and too little attention, but are just as acute.

The remainder of this chapter is devoted to consideration of a few examples of AI models. Some other models (of semantic memory, of visual imagery, or problem solving, etc.) have already been discussed in earlier chapters. The ones that follow have been selected as illustrating the problems of the computational metaphor.

Models of Speech Recognition

Two systems that have been developed for recognition of continuous natural speech work on very different principles. It is therefore instructive to compare them, and to consider which system is more likely to resemble human speech recognition. Both were developed as artificial intelligence programs, and not as simulations of human performance. Although functional equivalence was therefore not the goal, the fact that each model reveals a different set of sufficiency conditions for speech recognition has caused some rethinking of psychological theories.

Both HARPY and HEARSAY II were designed to meet the specific goals of accepting connected speech from different speakers; of handling a vocabulary of at least 1000 words with an artificial syntax; making less than 10% errors; and responding rapidly. Both operate over limited semantic domains, such as a document retrieval task.

HEARSAY II

This system (described by Reddy, 1980; Lesser and Erman, 1979) works by "co-operative computation", whereby asynchronous parallel processes interact co-operatively. Twelve different knowledge sources (KSs) operate at different levels. The KSs include acoustic-phonetics (the characteristics of speech sounds); phonology (variability in pronunciation); prosodics (stress and intonation patterns); morphology; vocabulary; syntax; semantics; and pragmatics. The input sentence is segmented, and acoustic analysis of the wave form yields hypotheses about the identity of the phones in each segment. From the phone hypotheses, syllable hypotheses and word hypotheses are generated at higher levels. Human speech is very variable, and is liable to contain errors and gaps. Function words such as articles and prepositions are especially likely to have an imprecise acoustic realization. As a result, the ability of the system to identify words on the basis of acoustic characteristics is quite poor. The system focusses on the longer words, which tend to be more distinctive, and using the strongest hypotheses as anchor points, or "islands of reliability", works outwards from these, rather than in a strictly left to right direction. The initial word match processes yield a lattice of entries, with alternative possible matches for some segments. Some of these are strong matches with a high likelihood value; others are only proposed with low likelihood values. At this stage the lattice contains errors and gaps, as well as multiple hypotheses.

The higher level KSs such as syntax, semantics and pragmatics working top-down, both separately and in interaction, progressively revise, refine and verify current hypotheses. A central component is a global data structure called the "Blackboard" which displays and keeps track of the status of current hypotheses. All KSs have access to the blackboard. Some KSs are activated by the input; some are activated by other KSs. Hypotheses of one KS, at one level, are used to generate other hypotheses at other levels. One of the main problems with HEARSAY is in the control of order of testing hypotheses, and of co-operation between KSs. A KS scheduler selects a few out of the multiple competing hypotheses at different levels. At some stage the system must stop and decide to accept the strongest hypothesis. HEARSAY II has achieved an accuracy of 91%. It is characteristic of the system that errors which are syntactically legal and semantically acceptable are unlikely to be corrected, because the acoustic information contributes relatively little to the final identification.

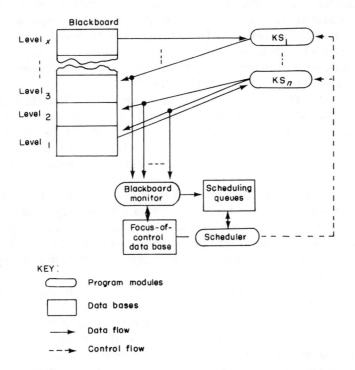

FIG. 33. *HEARSAY II architecture. The blackboard is divided into levels. Each KS interacts with just a few levels. A KS becomes a candidate for application if its precondition is met. However, to avoid a "combinatorial explosion" of hypotheses on the blackboard, a scheduler is used to restrict the number of KS's that are allowed to modify the blackboard (Lesser and Erman, 1979).*

Does HEARSAY resemble the human speech recognizer? One of the most striking features of the HEARSAY system is that information derived from the initial acoustic analysis of the wave form is quite crude, sketchy and error prone. Recognition is heavily dependent on the refinement and amplification of this information by higher level hypothesis-and-test procedures, and top-down application of syntactic and semantic constraints. Essentially this is a top-heavy system. In the human speech recognizer, the lower level stages of acoustic analysis are considerably more efficient. Information derived from the input alone is sufficiently rich and detailed that humans can identify sentences spoken out of context; sentences that are ungrammatical or anomalous; random strings of words, or even nonsense syllables. For inputs of this kind, top-down constraints are minimal, and identification rests on bottom-up processing.

Of course, human speech recognition is facilitated when the input conforms to syntactic and semantic constraints. It is faster, more accurate, and can survive noise and degradation better. Nevertheless, it is true to say that the ability to extract relatively rich and unambiguous information from the acoustic wave form renders the human system much less dependent on top-down hypothesis testing than HEARSAY.

Another difference arises out of capacity limitations. The HEARSAY system makes heavy computational demands. It requires very rapid and accurate processing, and also places heavy demands on the monitoring component. The machine system is able to generate and test and keep track of large numbers of hypotheses, but could the human recognizer do this fast enough to keep pace with the continuous speech input? At an average speech rate of 150 words per minute, there is not a lot of time to construct, test and revise alternative hypotheses. Woods (1980) argues that these processes occur unconsciously and are therefore not subject to capacity limitations. In listening to foreign languages, when we do become con-sciously aware of hypothesis testing, we often find we fall behind, and parts of the input are lost.

Even if humans could process fast enough, memory limitations would almost certainly make a HEARSAY type of system unworkable. The rapid decay of memory for acoustic information means that it would quickly become unavailable for re-testing against revised hypotheses. The book-keeping capacity of HEARSAY to store and schedule multiple hypotheses far exceeds the capacity of human working memory. The human speech recognizer is capable of revising hypotheses to a limited extent, as we are conscious of doing in the "garden path" type of sentence like

"I was afraid of Ali's punch especially as it had floored many strong men who boasted of their ability to handle alchohol."

but it is very doubtful if we could handle multiple backtracks.

The garden path effect also reveals another aspect of human speech processing. While HEARSAY operates bidirectionally outwards from islands of reliability, humans operate in a much more left to right direction. We do not suspend identification of the early part of a sentence. We begin at the beginning, and revise the interpretation later if necessary. The human ability to utilize acoustic information makes this possible. A machine system that relies on syntactic and semantic constraints needs a larger sample of input before it can begin identification, because these constraints only apply over larger units.

Obviously, another difference between human and HEARSAY lies in the size of the data base. By contrast to the restricted vocabulary and semantic domain of HEARSAY, the amount of knowledge, linguistic, semantic and pragmatic accumulated by an average human language user over a life time is enormous. The set of possible hypotheses is so large that, if an AI system were equipped with KSs on a comparable scale, problems of search, and of selecting, scheduling and rating hypotheses might well prove to be intractable. In human speech recognition, the range of possible hypotheses at a higher level is narrowed by the information derived from low level analysis. In HEARSAY, the relatively sketchy information extracted from the signal does not serve to constrain hypothesis generation to the same extent. It is doubtful if a top-heavy system like HEARSAY could function if the KSs were expanded to the human scale. Another feature of HEARSAY that seems alien to human functioning is the way the system entertains contradictory, mutually exclusive hypotheses at the same time.

A final objection is that in humans a top-heavy system would be liable to produce greater individual differences in speech perception than are commonly observed. Individuals would be more liable to disagree about the correct identification of a spoken utterance. A system that relies on stored knowledge for recognition would produce this disagreement, because knowledge and experience vary considerably from one individual to another. A bottom-up system relying more on sensory analysis is less likely to produce individual differences. While this problem does not arise for AI systems where the stored knowledge is controlled and standardized, it could cause difficulty if human speech recognizers worked like HEARSAY.

Although the HEARSAY model with its flexible interaction between different sources of information seems to resemble some psychological models of an interactive general cognitive system, it is unlikely that such a model is applicable to human speech recognition. It may be better suited to general decision making. Hayes-Roth and Hayes-Roth (1979) developed a model of cognitive planning on the same principles as HEARSAY. Interactive specialists decide how to plan a day's errands around the town on the basis of spatial proximities and priorities (getting medicine from the chemist is important, and the dry-cleaners is near the chemist so go there next).

HARPY

The HARPY model developed by Klatt (1977, 1980) had the same goals, and has outperformed HEARSAY, achieving 95% accuracy, and accepting connected speech from several male and female speakers. It differs from HEARSAY in a number of important respects. It is primarily a bottom-up system in which the role of higher level knowledge is minimized. It operates by so-called direct lexical access using a "table look-up" without analytic decomposition of the input. Perception is a process of search-and-match. HARPY stores precompiled sets of acoustic representations of all the lexical items in its vocabulary. Knowledge about acoustic–phonetic relations, word boundaries, phonological variations and speaker voice characteristics are all built into precompiled expected spectral sequences. Word recognition is by a process of pattern matching. The acoustic wave form of the input is matched against the precompiled patterns, and matches are located by a process called beam-search which focusses on likely and near-miss candidates. Processing is left to right. Syntax is also precompiled as sets of syntactically legal structures. The word sequence that is the best match is selected, and alternative candidates discarded, when processing more of the wave form ceases to increase the probability of any candidate. Hypothesis testing and interaction between levels is minimized, so the amount of computation is much less than in the HEARSAY system. The essential feature of HARPY is that identification is by matching the input directly to the stored lexical representation, and not by analysis. There is no phonetic transcription stage. Klatt argues that phonetic analysis introduces too many errors and is best omitted.

Does HARPY resemble the human speech recognizer? Although HARPY works better within its own task domain than any other AI system, some obvious limitations are apparent. It cannot handle novel words, or ungrammatical utterances; it cannot cope with much in the way of distortion; it cannot recover from errors; it is not very flexible, and it may be difficult to expand. The reason for this last shortcoming is that the system entails storing a large number of expected spectra. Increasing the vocabulary and the number of speaker voices would enormously multiply the number of items that had to be stored. The search procedures that work well enough with a small system may be inadequate for an expanded version.

The human system does operate effectively with a large vocabulary, accepting speech from any speaker, on any topic, functioning robustly in noisy conditions and operating over more than one language. Could this kind of performance be achieved if humans worked like HARPY? While HEARSAY appeared to be excessive in computational demands, HARPY may be excessive in memory storage demands. Norman (1980) considers it may be feasible to suppose that humans could store 10–20 spectral patterns for each word, but could search processes be successful in a store of this magnitude? Klatt himself has suggested that the search for acoustic pattern matches would need to be constrained by interactive semantic and syntactic predictions acting to narrow the search space. Alternatively, a strictly bottom-up system could be supplemented by higher level knowledge if direct access failed. These modifications make HARPY more plausible as a model of human speech recognition. Essential aspects of the model such as precompiled knowledge; the use of direct search and match at the word level, instead of lower level feature analysis; left to right processing; and a reduced role (relative to HEARSAY type models) for higher knowledge, would be retained in the modified version. HARPY type models substitute prestorage for computation, representations for rules, declarative knowledge for procedural knowledge. Norman suggests this type of system might be better attuned to human capacities than HEARSAY. Since it does not require multiple hypothesis testing and backtracking, demands on working memory are minimized. Precompiled knowledge operates automatically without the need for conscious processing which, in humans, is so limited in capacity. The system is modular rather than interactive, so component parts can be modified without causing widespread knock-on effects. Psychological experiments on speech recognition also offer some support for the conclusion that phonemes are not necessarily analyzed and identified; the normal unit of recognition is a larger one such as the syllable or the word.

HARPY has suggested new possibilities for theories of human speech recognition. While it is clear that it could not stand as a model of human performance without modification, it has a number of features that seem well suited to human capacity.

Models of Language Understanding

The speech recognition models, though sometimes described as "understanders", identify language inputs rather than understanding them. They translate a speech input to a typed output. This section is concerned with some models that have been designed to go beyond recognition, and to understand language. Most models of language understanding are in the AI tradition rather than being simulations of human performance. Early failures made apparent the need for extensive semantic and world knowledge, without which "understanding" is no more than a superficial decoding. Although Dresher and Hornstein (1976) have argued that these AI models have no psychological relevance, they have in fact been valuable in revealing the sufficiency conditions for achieving different levels of understanding. A few of these models are described below.

Schank's conceptual dependency model

Schank's is a programmatic model rather than a fully implemented working model. As such, it can aim at greater generality, and is unrestricted as to task and semantic domain. In this it differs from the working models which are all sharply restricted. Schank's model (Schank, 1972) minimizes the role of syntax, and emphasizes the importance of stored knowledge. Sentence meaning is derived almost entirely from semantic analysis of lexical items, not analysis of syntactic structure. The system employs a verb-based parser guided by a conceptual analyser. It parses sentences by a method which is intuitively rather similar to the way we understand foreign languages, when we have only an imperfect or halting grasp of the grammar. The model has a conceptual base consisting of stored knowledge about conceptual relationships. There are four main conceptual cases: objective, directive, recipient and instrumental. These are illustrated in the following sentences.

I sent Mother money.

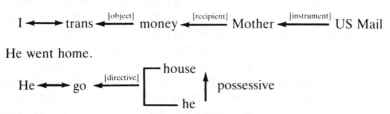

He went home.

He went home.

In the network of conceptual dependencies, concepts are linked by dependency relations like change of state, causation or trans (the transfer of objects, changes of location or possession), time, negation, etc. All the verbs that occur in everyday speech are rendered into 12 primitive actions like propel, move, ingest, expel, grasp, etc. The network specifies what arguments a particular predicate requires. For example, it specifies that the word "go" implies movement by an actor or object and a change of location. This stored knowledge is used to guide the parser in interpreting the input, and to generate expectations. The parser begins by isolating the main verb, and refers this to the conceptual dependency network. The conceptual relations associated with the verb are used to determine the role of other words in the sentence. The output of the parser is a network with the components of the sentence mapped on to an abstract representation of labelled nodes and links. In one of Schank's examples, the sentence "the big man took the book" is mapped as:

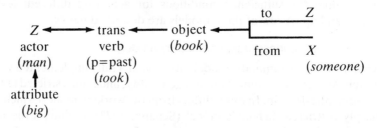

The parser has added the inference that the act of taking involves transfer of possession from someone (*X*) to the actor. In practice, the initial verb-finding process might be expected to run into difficulties, since it employs syntactic cues to identify the verb such as inflections, and these may not always be present. As a model of human understanding it is not entirely plausible, since it is intuitively obvious that in reading, or listening to speech, comprehension is not suspended until the arrival of the main verb.

One problem is that the conceptualization derived from a given input sentence may be only one of several possible interpretations. In one example, Schank analyses the sentence "John ate ice cream with a spoon" to

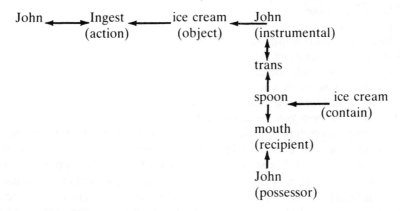

Dresher and Hornstein object that there is no reason to choose this particular conceptualization. Why stop there? Why not include John's muscular movements, thoughts and reactions as well as his mouth? They criticize the lack of any principles to select, constrain and terminate a particular conceptualization, and to control the amount of implicit information that is unpacked, and decide the level of detail necessary for understanding. This is an important and difficult problem. To some extent, it is solved by incorporating the idea of "scripts" into the system. Proliferation of inferences is limited to the domain of the relevant script. Inferences about John's neurophysiology are excluded from a restaurant/ ice cream eating script. Dresher and Hornstein also criticize the way semantics dominates syntax in Schank's model. However, many psycholinguists would disagree with them about the importance of the role of syntax.

The model does capture the predictive character of language understanding, and the way unfinished utterances can be anticipated. The model is being developed for understanding and generating stories. The conceptual dependency network is potentially unlimited in complexity, but problems of access within it have not yet been fully worked out.

Models that answer questions and hold conversations with a human by teletype have improved considerably since Weizenbaum's DOCTOR was introduced. This early model (long since repudiated by its originator) is included to show how much progress has been made.

Weizenbaum's DOCTOR

Weizenbaum (1968) describes a program called DOCTOR which performs the role of psychiatrist in a conversation with a patient. Weizenbaum supplies a transcript of a conversation with a human subject acting as patient. The machine responses are given in italics.

Men are all alike.
In what way.
They're always bugging us about something.
Can you think of a specific example.
My boyfriend made me come here.
Your boyfriend made you come here.
He says I'm depressed much of the time.
I am sorry to hear you are depressed.

The program operates by selecting a key word in the input, and applying a transformation rule contextually associated with that key word. In the absence of a key word, a standard filler type of output is supplied, or an earlier transformation is reiterated. Weizenbaum asserts that in human–human interaction "there can be no total understanding and no absolute test of understanding". In his simulation, the "naturalness" of the conversation is the test of the machine's understanding. We need not be pheno-menologists to feel there is something unsatisfactory about DOCTOR's understanding. DOCTOR's success seems to stem mainly from the choice of format in which the machine plays the traditionally restricted, and some-what unresponsive, role of the psychiatrist. Clearly, as a dinner-table conversationalist he would be much less acceptable. DOCTOR's conver-sation breaks down if the human participant deviates from the role of patient, but it could be argued that human–human conversations de-generate similarly when contextual assumptions are not shared. This parallel is hardly sufficient to conceal the vast difference between ordinary human–human conversation, and the DOCTOR–patient conversation. Most humans share enough cultural context to be able to converse satisfactorily over a wide range of topics and, most importantly, misunder-standings can usually be remedied by explanations, or by backtracking until a common ground is found, and establishing a new shared framework from that point. Indeed, if this were not so, it would hardly be possible for teachers to impart new ideas to their pupils.

Winograd's SHRDLU

This model is recognized as a milestone in natural language understanding by machines. The understanding of computers is limited not only by the restricted context available to them, but also by the restriction of their input and output modalities. In relation to understanding, there is some point to the argument that functional equivalence cannot be achieved by machines lacking some kind of a body. Human–human understanding is not dependent solely on linguistic interchanges, but is also mediated by shared sensory information, and demonstrated by appropriate actions. SHRDLU manifests a deeper level of understanding because it incorporates analogues of perceptual and motor functions as well as language processing. In the philosopher's terms its use of language has reference as well as sense. Winograd's program operates within its own "real world", which is an internal representation of an array of blocks of different sizes, shapes and colours displayed on a screen (Winograd, 1972). It is equipped to "perceive" and "manipulate" these objects by consulting or by changing the internal representation, and can store new information and answer questions about the state of this world, and also carry out commands to move the objects around as well as describe and explain its own previous moves. It can add new facts to its store, and use the information later. It can ask questions to elucidate uninterpretable commands, and employ inferential reasoning. It can use the perceptual context to identify the referents in the questions and commands, and can infer the intended referent when the description is ambiguous. Given a command like "put it on top of the red one", it identifies the referent of "it" as the last mentioned object, and searches the scene for the most likely referent to fit the description "the red one". This kind of behavioural evidence of understanding is more satisfactory than a purely verbal output, and is the kind of evidence we often demand from children and pupils when we suspect that parrot-like replies may conceal a lack of understanding.

The system operates with flexible interaction between the syntax and semantics of the input sentence, and stored knowledge about the current state, and general properties of the blocks world. Three programs, syntax, semantics and deduction, work in a heterarchical combination. The parser operates from left to right, backtracking to revise when semantic considerations rule out the initial parsing. Identification of the sentence mood (imperative, declarative or interrogative) is basic to the parsing process. All SHRDLU's knowledge, including syntax and semantics, is represented as procedures, and words in its vocabulary are defined by semantic markers. SHRDLU responds to questions like:

Why did you do that?

To get rid of the green block

How many objects have you touched?

Four

What colour is the smallest block?

Green

and to commands such as:

Put a small one onto the green cube which supports a pyramid

and, Put the blue pyramid on the block in the box.

The ability to respond to the first of these commands demonstrates that the program can solve problems of anaphoric reference. That is, it can determine the referent of "small one". The second command is ambiguous, since it can mean either

Put the blue pyramid (which is) on the block in the box

or, Put the blue pyramid on the block (which is) in the box.

In the context of the scene displayed in Fig. 34, SHRDLU selects the second meaning as making better sense.

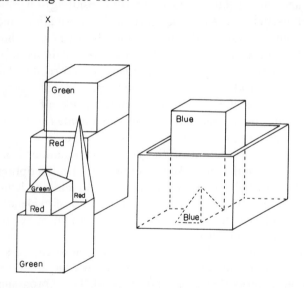

FIG. 34. *A Blocks World display (adapted from Winograd, 1972).*

As in children, SHRDLU's ability is greater in comprehension than in production. Only simple sentence structures can be generated. Although its exchanges appear strikingly sensible, SHRDLU's understanding is still limited, even within its own blocks world. It does not even know all there is to know about blocks (e.g. their weight, material, possible uses). According to Dresher and Hornstein, whereas Schank's model suffered from vagueness and lack of specificity, Winograd's is too specific and lacks generalizability. Such wholesale rejection is certainly premature. The potential generalizability of a system like Winograd's has yet to be fully explored. What is clear is that a system which is capable of scene representation as well as simply decoding linguistic inputs, and has a cognitive system capable of reasoning as well as language recognition devices, achieves greatly improved understanding; and that ability to act, as well as to generate linguistic responses also provides stronger evidence of that understanding.

Norman's questions

Norman (1973) has listed a number of types of question which are typically handled in different ways by men and machines, and so serve to show where equivalence breaks down. One is the telephone number problem. If asked to give the telephone number of Charles Dickens, a human subject would most probably reject the query outright as a stupid question. The computer would search its memory and eventually signal "Not known". Humans apply general knowledge of literature, and the history of technological progress, and can reject this anomalous input at an early stage of processing. The three drugstores problems is rather similar. Given the input sentence "I went to three drugstores" the computer stores this information. The human would ask "whatever were you looking for?". The input is not rejected outright, but some further clarification is requested because the original statement does not make complete sense on its own. In another example, The Empire State Building problem, the question "Where is the Empire State Building?" elicits different answers from humans depending on whether the questioner is two blocks away from the Empire State Building, or in the middle of Europe, and on whether his intentions are interpreted as a wish to go there, or to know the approximate location, or the postal address. The human answer is adapted to the contextual setting of the question and the inferred purposes of the questioner, whereas the computer's answer would be a standard one. What is apparent in these three examples is that the range of knowledge that the human thinker can bring to bear on the question spans his entire life experience, not just the immediate local context: that he is able to perceive what, in all his stock of information, is relevant to the question being asked, and that his responses are flexibly determined, not fixed. It is the restricted use of contextual information which is the chief source of nonequivalence in the understanding of computers. It is worth noting, however, that the ability to modify responses in accordance with contextual information is typical of *adult* human question answering, and that young children behave rather more like computers. The child who gets lost at a football match, and tells the policeman that his name is Johnny and he lives at number 29, is behaving like the computer answering the Empire State Building problem.

In this discussion of language understanding systems a variety of criteria for understanding have been applied including the ability to answer questions naturally; to answer appropriately; to perceive implications; to disambiguate. Some of the systems fulfill some of the criteria. None approaches a human level of understanding, so even if we concatenate the models, we still do not have a complete set of sufficiency criteria for achieving full understanding.

Expert Systems: MYCIN

An area of growing importance in the field of AI is the development of expert systems. An expert system incorporates the knowledge of a body of experts about a particular subject such as organic chemistry, mineralogy or diseases. The system then acts as an intelligent assistant to workers in that subject. It does not simply store the information, but is capable of utilizing the information to make judgements. In order to be able to form judgements the system incorporates rules of scientific reasoning, and can apply these to new input data in combination with its store of expert knowledge. Expert systems are problem solvers, not just data banks.

MYCIN is a medical diagnosis system (Shortliffe, 1976) designed to identify the organisms in bacterial infections. It has four inter-related functions; to make a diagnosis of the infection; to select an appropriate therapy; to make a prognosis; and to act as a medical tutor. It is designed for interaction with a physician as user. The questions considered by the system include whether the infection is significant (relevant data are the list of the patient's symptoms entered by the physician); what is the organism's identity (results of analyses of blood samples, swabs, etc.); what are the potentially useful drugs (statistical probabilities associated with use of different drugs); and which drug is suitable for the particular patient (considering age, other medication, diseases, allergies, etc.). The system incorporates 200 decision rules which correspond to sets of productions (see Chapter 7, p. 162). Rule 085 given below is one such production. The patient data are input by the physician-user in response to questions generated by MYCIN. The system creates a dynamic data file during the consultation which is an ongoing record of its deductions and conclusions. Figure 35 shows the flow of control in the system, and the three subprograms, consultation (which gathers the patient data, and outputs advice and conclusions); explanation (which answers the user's queries and explains the reasons for its conclusions); and rule acquisition (a subprogram for adding new rules to the knowledge base when an expert user detects gaps in the system). MYCIN accepts and outputs ordinary clinical language, so that the user needs no special skill, but MYCIN's language understanding is extremely simple. It operates by identifying key words (rather like

DOCTOR), and syntax and semantics are more or less ignored. The user must employ special prefixes which indicate to MYCIN what type of question is being asked. In a typical interaction, MYCIN asks questions and the user enters the patient data. MYCIN uses the knowledge base to process the information and select further questions, and finally outputs a treatment recommendation. The physician can ask MYCIN to explain the reasons why particular questions are being asked, and why a particular conclusion is reached. In a typical exchange:

User	What is the identity of the organism?
MYCIN	*The identity of the organism is E.coli (·43), Proteus (·22), Pseudomonas (·22), Klebsiella (·13)*
User	How did you decide it might be *Pseudomonas*?
MYCIN	I used Rule 085 which gave a certainty of ·6
User	What is Rule 085?
MYCIN	If the strain of organism is gramneg and the morphology is rod and the patient is a compromised host
	Then with a certainty factor of ·6 the organism is *Pseudomonas*

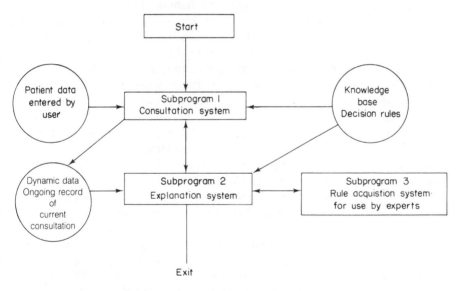

FIG. 35. *The flow and control of information in MYCIN (Shortliffe, 1976).*

A decision is made by cumulating the certainty factor ratings, ordering possible hypotheses, and selecting the highest rated alternative. In 1976 experts who evaluated MYCIN's performance approved of 72% of its decisions. The system is still able to operate and produce a conclusion when the patient data are incomplete, but becomes less reliable. Attempts to make a system to diagnose a large number of different diseases are also less successful. Expert systems work best over limited knowledge domains that have an agreed and precisely defined classification system. The rule acquisition component allows the system to keep improving as new rules are added to rectify weaknesses. The modularity of the system makes it easy to modify, or add to it.

Expert systems like MYCIN are not intended to model human cognition, or to supplant it, but to complement it. As with other AI research, however, it has produced new insights into the nature of scientific reasoning, and clarified the way in which evidence is weighted and combined in probabilistic decision making.

Many of the limitations of computer simulation that have been noted throughout this chapter are both technological and theoretical. There are limits on the size of the data base that is practicable, so the computer can only store and access a restricted local context. This handicap imposes limits on the versatility, flexibility and depth of understanding that the simulation can attain. It follows that the computer cannot simulate the human thinker, but only an arbitrarily defined subset of thinking operations. The extent to which computers succeed in simulating human thinking forces us to reconsider questions about the relationship of language and thought discussed in Chapters 5 and 6, and to acknowledge that the language of the computer program can be adequate for many kinds of thinking.

Besides these limitations of scope and complexity, the main barrier to successful computer simulation is our ignorance of many aspects of human performance. We cannot simulate processes which we cannot describe. We cannot specify, for example, exactly how practice and familiarity bring about improvement in performance, nor how conscious rule-following gives place to automatic unmonitored skilled performance. We don't understand how we decide which are the essential features of a pattern or a problem, and which are inessential or irrelevant; or how we decide what aspects of past experience, and what kinds of contextual information, are applicable to a new problem. We don't understand what governs shifts between verbal and visual coding, or serial and parallel processing or how attention operates to produce in-depth processing of focussed information, and rough monitoring of objects and events outside the focus. We are not able to say very precisely what we mean by creative thinking, or insight. The kind of thinking which is most difficult to formalize is the kind that is not language based. In all these areas, the success of computer simulation is curtailed by the shortcomings of theoretical psychology, rather than the shortcomings of CS techniques.

Ideally, experimental testing of human subjects, machine simulation and theory building ought to constitute a three-way interaction. Rumelhart and Norman (1975) express this policy in describing their methods:

We postulated a procedure: then we put the components together, modifying the parts to make this possible: then we used the system for a while, discovering the strengths, weaknesses and conceptual errors. we then repeated the entire process, each time learning more about our underlying theoretical conceptualizations.

The ELINOR model of semantic representation described in Chapter 2 was developed by applying these methods. Their initial postulates were derived from theories which in turn were based on human data. The computer simulation provides a method of discovering whether theory is fully specified, since the exercise of formalizing the theory exposes any vagueness or inconsistency, and the results of the computer simulation are a test of the predictive power of the theory. Thus experimental testing of human subjects, and machine simulation provide two complementary ways to test the validity of psychological models. By comparison with human testing, the CS method allows better control of variables, and, although the problem of equivalence makes the interpretation of the findings more difficult, the methodology of cognitive psychology gains in power and precision from the technique of computer simulation.

Recommended reading

Margaret Boden's book *Artificial Intelligence and Natural Man* gives an excellent introduction to this area. Bobrow and Collins *Representation and Understanding* is a collection of interesting papers. Read Shortliffe's book for a detailed account of a medical diagnosis system. Winograd's 1972 paper is a classic, and Simon's 1979 review is full of perceptive insights. Barr and Feigenbaum's *Handbook of Artificial Intelligence* is detailed and useful, with a section on speech recognition systems.

9 HEMISPHERE DIFFERENCES

It has been known since the nineteenth century that the two cerebral hemispheres are functionally asymmetrical. Broca (1865) and Hughlings Jackson (1880) noted the tendency for language disorders to occur following left hemisphere damage, and since then a growing body of clinical evidence has accumulated confirming their observations, and also revealing a right hemisphere specialization for a variety of nonverbal visuospatial cognitive processes. Currently there is a marked upsurge of interest in cerebral asymmetry among cognitive psychologists. Several factors have triggered this development. The intrusive effect of hemisphere differences has to be taken into account whenever experimental procedures involve the presentation of visual or auditory material which is spatially extended to the left or right of the subject. In dichotic listening or tachistoscopic recognition experiments, performance differences between left and right ears, or left and right sides of the visual field reflect differences in the processing capacities of the two hemispheres, and researchers must necessarily take account of this factor in interpreting their results. There has also, perhaps, been some unease at the extent of the gulf between theories of higher mental processes abstractly represented in flow-chart models, and the underlying brain mechanisms. In some ways, the study of hemisphere differences represents an attempt to bridge this gulf and to forge closer links between cognition and neurophysiology. It holds out the fascinating prospect of mapping the words, images and conceptual processes of human thinking on to actual physical locations in the brain. As a result, a great deal of recent research has been devoted to the detection and characterization of functional differences between the hemispheres. There are now three main sources of evidence for hemispheric specialization in humans. Firstly, the study of the brain-injured allows comparisons to be made between the performance of patients with localized damage in one hemisphere, and patients wth similar damage to the opposite hemisphere. Alternatively, patients with unilateral damage can be compared with normal intact subjects. Secondly, studies of a group of split-brained patients, who have had the two cerebral hemispheres surgically disconnected, have yielded comparisons of the performance of each of the isolated hemispheres. Thirdly, studies of normal intact subjects

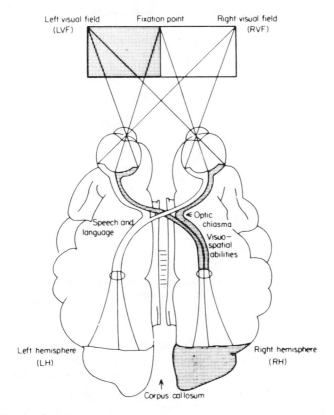

FIG. 36. *Visual pathways.*

employ procedures whereby information is channelled so as to reach one hemisphere before the other.

In visual perception (see Fig. 36), stimuli are placed to the left or right of a central fixation point, so that they are projected to the contralateral hemisphere. Stimuli in the left visual field fall on the nasal hemiretina of the left eye and the temporal hemiretina of the right eye, and project to the right hemisphere. The right visual field stimulates the temporal hemiretina of the left eye and the nasal hemiretina of the right eye and projects to the left hemisphere. With auditory perception, material presented to the left ear is projected primarily to the contralateral right hemisphere and the right ear transmits primarily to the left hemisphere. Each ear has pathways to both hemispheres, but the contralateral paths are stronger, and when both ears receive input simultaneously, as in dichotic listening, the ipsilateral paths are inhibited (Kimura, 1967; see Fig. 37).

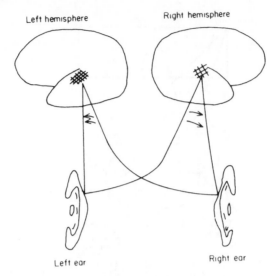

Left hemisphere   Right hemisphere

Left ear   Right ear

FIG. 37. *Auditory pathways. The arrows indicate the inhibition of the ipsilateral pathways when both ears receive input simultaneously.*

Comparisons can be made between performance in conditions when the input is directed to the left hemisphere, and conditions when it is directed to the right. In all these comparisons, problems of methodology and of interpretation of the findings arise, so that the evidence from each of these three sources can be criticized. Nevertheless, the results have converged to a considerable extent, and produced a consensus such that although some of the details may be disputed, the general conclusions that different cognitive processes are subserved by different hemispheres are not in doubt. This chapter will review the particular difficulties that attend each method of investigating hemispheric specialization, summarize the findings, and assess the theories.

Clinical Studies of the Brain Injured

Problems of assessment

When unilateral brain damage is sustained the effects are specific to the side of the lesion, and the kinds of deficit that are observed following lesions of the left hemisphere are different from those that are associated with lesions of the right hemisphere. This relationship between the side of the lesion, and the type of disorder, provides evidence of the functional specialization of the hemispheres, but there are numerous reasons why the pattern does not always emerge very clearly and consistently.

In many cases the nature, locus and extent of the damage cannot be very accurately ascertained. When the observations are based on the effects of tumours, cerebro-vascular damage or closed head injuries, the lesions tend to be diffuse, and to have quite widespread secondary consequences such as oedema, infection and intra-cranial pressure, so that it is more difficult to establish a precise relation between the site of the damage, and the kinds of deficit that result. Another problem arises when patients have been suffering from pathological conditions, such as focal epilepsy, prior to surgical intervention. In these cases the epileptic condition may have produced changes in cerebral organization, and the post-operative deficits cannot be taken as a reflection of normal brain organization.

Newcombe (1969) has pointed out that these problems are minimized in studies of brain injuries resulting from gunshot or missile wounds. The lesions are usually quite circumscribed; they receive early treatment, so that the possibility of infection and generalized damage is reduced; and they are usually incurred by soldiers, who are young healthy adults of normal intelligence at the time of injury.

Comparisons between the effects of left brain injuries and right brain injuries require careful matching, not only of the nature and extent of the lesions, but also of other factors such as the age, sex, IQ, handedness, general health and medication of the patients. The time elapsed since the injury was incurred, and the degree of recovery of function achieved also have to be taken into account.

The effects of handedness

The effects of unilateral brain injuries are in any case different for left- and right-handers. There are individual differences in the direction and degree of lateralization of brain function, which are linked, to some extent, with hand preference. While the majority of individuals have language ability lateralized in the left hemisphere and visuospatial abilities in the right, this pattern is not universal. Rossi and Rosadini (1965) used sodium amytal injections to anaesthetize a single hemisphere. With this technique a temporary disruption of language occurs if the anaesthetized hemisphere is the one which is functionally specialized for language. Their results indicated that approximately 90% of right-handed subjects had language lateralized to the left hemisphere, while only about 64% of left-handers conformed to this pattern. It appeared that, of the remaining 10% of right-handers and 36% of left-handers, some had the reversed pattern of organization, with language functions represented in the right hemisphere, while some showed a much greater degree of functional symmetry (sometimes called bilaterality, mixed dominance or mixed-brainedness) with language being represented in both hemispheres.

Levy and Reid (1976) claimed that the pattern of brain lateralization in left-handers could be reliably inferred from hand posture in writing. The so-called "hook" writers with inverted hand posture displayed a left hemisphere superiority for language, and a right hemisphere superiority in a visuospatial task. Levy and Reid concluded that hook writers were those with the brain lateralization pattern characteristic of most right-handers. Left-handers with normal noninverted writing hand posture appeared to have the reversed pattern of lateralization. Although this claim was received with a good deal of credulity at the time, subsequent attempts to replicate it have failed (Corballis, 1978; McKeever and Van Deventner, 1978), and hook writing is no longer regarded as a reliable indicator of brain organization.

Attempts have been made to link handedness and brain lateralization with measures of cognitive ability. Levy (1969) found that when left-handers were given verbal and visuospatial performance IQ tests, they were significantly worse at the visuospatial tests, and suggested that the bilateral representation of function sometimes associated with left-handedness is less efficient than a pure, well-lateralized representation. This "invasion hypothesis" assumes that bilateral representation of verbal functions involves invasion of the right hemisphere, and is therefore detrimental to the visuospatial ability, which is displaced. More recent and larger-scale studies (Roberts and Engle, 1974) of nearly 8000 school children have reported no indication of differences between right- and left-handers in either verbal or nonverbal test scores. Whether left-handers are liable to be cognitively handicapped, or cognitively gifted in any specific ways is still disputed (see Herron, 1980, for a review of the evidence).

It is generally agreed, however, that left-handers are not a homogeneous group. Some are classified as familial left-handers, whose handedness is considered to be genetically determined. Those with no family history of left-handedness may have acquired their hand preference as a result of birth traumas. Genetic left-handers and traumatic left-handers would not necessarily have the same brain organization. Further confusion arises because the classification of handedness is not always accurate. In the 1930s only 2–3% of the population in Britain and America was classified as left-handed, as opposed to 10–11% at the present time. Substantial numbers of crypto-left-handers were submerged by educational practices that deliberately reformed their natural hand preference. The power of such cultural factors is still evident today. In Japan only about 1% of the population is reported as left-handed. Because of these disparities, apparently anomalous effects of brain lesions may be due to misclassification of handedness, as well as variations in the pattern of cerebral organization.

The effects of maturation

Cerebral asymmetry also varies with age. In early childhood, localization of function is less evident and less rigid. Until recently it was believed (Lenneberg, 1967) that both hemispheres were completely equipotential in the first years of life. This "equipotentiality hypothesis" claims that damage to either hemisphere will disrupt language development to an equal extent. It also claims that following unilateral injury or hemispherectomy in early childhood, functions re-locate in the undamaged hemisphere. Either hemisphere is capable of subserving any cognitive function. This plasticity of cerebral organization diminishes with age, and is lost by the early teens.

The equipotentiality hypothesis has been challenged (Dennis and Whitaker, 1977; Dennis, 1980). Dennis believes that even before the age of 2 years, left hemisphere lesions are more likely to affect language development than right hemisphere lesions. She has compared language development in children who have had left hemispherectomy (left hemidecorticates) with those who have had right hemispherectomy, before the onset of speech. If the equipotentiality hypothesis were true, the right hemisphere should provide as good a substrate for language development as the left. Dennis found that left hemidecorticates do less well at complex syntactic discriminations (such as active–passive distinctions); at utilizing rhyme cues for word retrieval; and at organizing words into conceptual clusters. No differences were found between left and right hemidecorticates on other tests including naming and fluency. So Dennis's case against equipotentiality rests on quite small differences in a few tests with very small numbers of children. Given the variation in the normal range of children's language ability, it is not a very strong case.

Whether or not the hemispheres are developmentally equipotential, recent studies by Entus (1977) have produced evidence that functional lateralization is already present in infants soon after birth. Entus conditioned a sucking response in infants aged 3–20 weeks to pairs of sounds presented dichotically (that is simultaneously in both ears).

The pairs of sounds were either two different speech sounds (ba and da) or two musical sounds. After the rate of sucking had habituated to a particular pair, the sound in one ear only was changed. Recovery from habituation was greater for speech sounds when the right ear stimulus was changed, and for musical sounds when the left ear stimulus was changed.

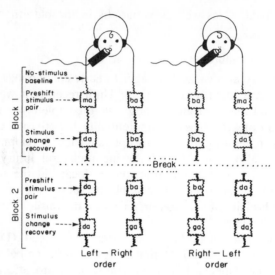

FIG. 38. *Schematic representation of the experimental procedure showing stimulus sequence and ear order (Entus, 1977).*

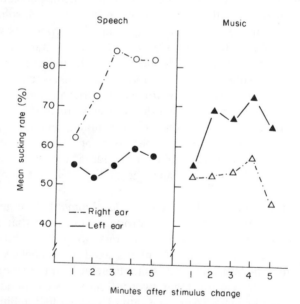

FIG. 39. *Mean number of sucks per minute, as a percentage of the maximum predecrement sucking rate, for 5 min after the decrement criterion of 16 infants who participated in both experiments.*

Figures 38 and 39 illustrate the paradigm and the results. The assumption is that the ear showing the greater recovery is contralateral to the hemisphere that is already more proficient at dealing with that type of stimulus.

The general developmental trend in normal intact children is for cerebral asymmetry to increase with age, as the functions become more strongly lateralized.

The effects of sex

The nature and existence of sex-related differences in patterns of cerebral organization are also contentious issues. A substantial amount of evidence has been marshalled (see McGlone, 1980) suggesting that the male brain is more asymmetric for verbal functions, and possibly for visuospatial functions as well. In the female brain, these functions are, it is argued, less strongly lateralized. The evidence for these assertions includes the claim that there is a greater incidence of severe speech disorders following lesions of the left hemisphere in males than in females, and that a larger proportion of males exhibit a right ear (left hemisphere) advantage for speech in dichotic listening tests. Applying the invasion hypothesis, it is claimed that in women the greater involvement of the right hemisphere in the representation of language displaces visuospatial ability, and causes females to be less efficient at visuospatial processing. All the findings and their interpretations are contested. Even if the reported sex differences are reliable, they may be reflecting sex-linked strategy differences rather than sex-linked brain organization.

Deficits following unilateral lesions

In spite of these difficulties and discrepancies there is good general agreement that, in the majority of cases, different kinds of deficit are associated with lesions of the left and right hemispheres. Newcombe's study of missile injuries reveals a dichotomy between left-brain-injured and right-brain-injured, persisting many years after the injuries were incurred. The left hemisphere group were consistently poorer at tasks requiring learning and retention of verbal material, and in tests of verbal skills such as vocabulary, spelling and word fluency, while the right hemisphere group showed no impairment on these tasks. Instead, the right hemisphere group were consistently poorer at learning visually guided mazes, at drawing or reproducing block designs, at estimating the number of cubes in a diagrammatic arrangement, and at recognizing incomplete patterns, especially fragmented faces. A double dissociation of the site of the lesion and the nature of the deficit emerges clearly from the data, and is complemented by the observations of many other researchers. Patients with unilateral right-sided damage typically show deficits in visuospatial tasks including face recognition (De Renzi *et al.*, 1968), discriminating the position and slopes of lines (Warrington and Rabin, 1970), estimating a number of dots, and recognizing nonsense figures (Kimura, 1966). Corsi (cited in Milner, 1971) designed a verbal and a nonverbal version of a memory test, and found that patients with left fronto-temporal lobectomies were poor at recognizing recurring words in a series of words, but could recognize recurring pictures in a series of abstract pictures. The right fronto-temporal group could recognize words, but not pictures.

Disorders of verbal information processing are associated with left-hemisphere damage whether the material is represented in a visual or an auditory form. Milner (1962) has reported evidence showing that auditory functions are lateralized in a way that corresponds to the verbal/nonverbal dichotomy in visual tasks. Normally, verbal material is better perceived by the left hemisphere, and nonverbal material, such as musical and environmental sounds, is better perceived by the right hemisphere. Kimura (1961) found deficits in the auditory perception of verbal material after left temporal lobe damage, and Milner (1962) found recognition of melodies, timbre and tonal patterns was impaired after right temporal lobectomy.

Complete or partial specialization?

Although these observations clearly indicate that the hemispheres are functionally specialized, it is not necessarily the case that specialization is absolute. Even in the adult, right-handed male with the left hemisphere specialized for language, the nonspecialist right hemisphere may exhibit some language ability. Searleman (1977) has reviewed case studies of patients following left hemispherectomy. The residual language ability displayed by these patients is thought to represent the performance of the right hemisphere. However, in some of these cases it is possible that the diseased condition of the left hemisphere could have induced an abnormal reorganization at an earlier stage. In these patients, speech is very limited, and mostly consists of single words or stereotyped phrases. Propositional speech is extremely rare. Comprehension is preserved much better than production. Patients can generally follow spoken instructions, and give yes or no answers to simple questions. Further evidence of right hemisphere language ability can be inferred from careful examination of the effects of right hemisphere lesions. In patients with right-sided damage, Wapner *et al.* (1981) found subtle defects in story recall such as confabulation, mis-sequencing, recall of verbatim details rather than gist information, and failure to appreciate humour and emotional tone. They concluded that in the intact normal the right hemisphere controls the formation of a global representation of the story, and processes affect. These findings are difficult to reconcile with a theory of absolute specialization.

Evidence of interactive organization

Recent emphasis on hemisphere differences, and on asymmetry of function, has tended to obscure the existence of hemispheric interaction. While the evidence from unilateral lesions indicates that each of the two hemispheres is specialized for the performance of particular tasks, the normal brain does not function as two isolated units, but as a closely integrated system. The interactive nature of hemispheric organization is shown by the fact that unilateral lesions may have bilateral consequences, and the results of bilateral lesions do not simply represent the sum of the effects that would arise from each of the lesions alone. Teuber (1962) has reported that the effects of unilateral lesions in the visual system may not be confined to the contralateral visual half-field, and subtle changes may occur in both halves of the visual field. Similar changes may occur in the tactile sense of both hands, and are not confined to the hand contralateral to the lesion. In hearing, unilateral lesions impair binaural judgements of localization, and binaural synthesis of sounds of different frequencies. In these tasks the normal interactive operation of the hemispheres is disturbed. Newcombe and Ratcliff (1973) studied the effects of bilateral brain injuries, and noted some specific deficits which had not been detected with unilateral injuries of either hemisphere. In object naming and judgements of left–right orientation, the bilateral group took significantly longer to respond than those with unilateral injuries, as if the rate of processing was slowed by the bilateral injuries. Teuber (1962) reported that while unilateral injury of either hemisphere slowed down the rate at which ambiguous figures like the Necker cube reverse, bilateral injuries speed up the reversal rate. Even if the effects of bilateral injuries are not very consistent, they do provide evidence of a mutual influence of one hemisphere on the other.

Studies of Split-Brain Patients

The evidence for functional specialization of the hemispheres which comes from the effects of lesions is complemented and reinforced by the results of studies of patients who have undergone cerebral commissurotomy, so that the two hemispheres are disconnected (Gazzaniga *et al.*, 1962; Gazzaniga, 1967). In these cases, it is possible to examine the functions of each single hemisphere in isolation, by testing the response capacities when sensory inputs have been confined to one hemisphere.

Disturbances of sensory–motor integration in these patients have been observed when the response must be made with the hand contralateral to the side stimulated. For example, when sensory information is presented on the right side and so transmitted to the left hemisphere, responses can be made with the right hand since this is primarily controlled by the left hemisphere. Responses by the left hand (controlled by the right hemisphere which did not receive the sensory information) are impaired. The patient is typically able to point to body areas that have been touched, using the right hand to point to locations on the right side of the body, and the left hand to indicate locations on the left side of the body, but he has difficulty in using the hand opposite to the body location. Similarly, the patient can point to the location of a light source in the right visual field with his right hand, or in the left visual field with his left hand, but the crossed integration proves more difficult. Individual patients vary in their ability to mediate crossed responses.

The lateralization of language functions to the left hemisphere, and visuospatial functions to the right, is reflected in the patterns of deficit exhibited by the split-brain patients. Figure 36 shows how left and right visual fields project to right and left hemispheres, respectively. The patient cannot name or describe objects or words presented in the left visual field, nor can he name objects which are placed in the left hand. The right hemisphere appears to be mute, and, after disconnection, has no access to the speech mechanisms of the left hemisphere. Further tests have shown, however, that the right hemisphere is not wholly alinguistic, and is capable of analysing and encoding verbal material to some extent. When simple words are presented in the left visual field to the right hemisphere, the patient can point with his left hand to a corresponding object or the corresponding word in a display. More sophisticated language comprehension has been shown by the ability to select the word "clock" out of five words presented to the left visual field after hearing a definition such as "used to tell the time", and this suggests that the right hemisphere is capable of some semantic analysis. Even so, the linguistic abilities of the right hemisphere are restricted to fairly rudimentary processing of concrete words in simple choice situations. The disconnected right hemisphere is apparently able to recognize nouns and adjectives better than verbs, while comprehension of function words, and of syntactic relations is negligible. Levy and Trevarthen (1977) showed that while the right hemisphere was capable of carrying out visual word matches (when a word was presented in the left visual field, the identical word could be correctly selected from a set of alternatives), the ability to carry out a phonological match was lacking (when a word was presented in the left visual field the patient could not select a rhyming word from the alternatives). These findings necessitate some modifications in the view that the language function is lateralized in the dominant hemisphere. To regard language as a single unitary function is clearly an oversimplification. Instead, the split-brain results force us to consider language as a set of interrelated component functions, which can be lateralized to varying extents. While speech and phonological encoding are reserved to the left hemisphere, the right is capable of some verbal analysis. However, a recent study of aphasic patients (Kinsbourne, 1971) has shed a different light on the language capacities of the right hemisphere. Kinsbourne's patients were suffering from aphasia following lesions of the left hemisphere; and were producing fragmentary and disordered speech. In order to decide whether this aphasic speech was the output of the damaged left hemisphere, or of the undamaged right hemisphere, the left side was anaesthetized. Since the speech showed no changes as a result of anaesthesis, it was possible to conclude that the right hemisphere was mediating the aphasic speech. So, although in the split-brain patients the right hemisphere appeared totally incapable of speech, in Kinsbourne's aphasics, the right hemisphere was producing disordered speech.

The specialization of the right hemisphere for visuospatial functions has been confirmed by the performance of the split-brain patients. Geometric designs are copied better by the left hand after commissurotomy, and Milner and Taylor (1972) found that the left hand was strikingly superior in matching complex tactile patterns. With the left hand, patterns could be correctly matched after intervals of up to two minutes, while with the right hand, five out of seven patients could not match the patterns even with a zero delay interval.

In spite of the good agreement of the results of the split-brain studies with the conclusions based on unilateral lesions, there are serious problems in the interpretation of these results. The capacities of the disconnected hemispheres may not give an accurate indication of the lateralization of functions in the normal intact brain for various reasons. Firstly, the commissurotomy patients had suffered from severe long-standing epilepsy prior to surgery, which may have caused abnormal reorganization of their brains. Levy and Trevarthen (1977) have argued that the uniformity of the patterns of deficit exhibited by these patients is not consistent with a pathological origin. They claim that if the epileptic condition had caused reorganization, more diverse patterns of deficit would have been produced. In their view, the similarity of the observed disorders is more plausibly attributed to the surgical intervention which was the same for all these patients. A closer look at the individual data casts some doubt on this argument, since the performance of the split-brain patients is not in fact very uniform, and a considerable range of individual differences is apparent. The possibility that the functioning of the disconnected hemispheres is not representative of normal hemisphere specialization cannot be altogether dismissed. Secondly, the possibility that some information can still be transmitted from one hemisphere to the other via remaining pathways in the midbrain cannot be wholly ruled out. Thirdly, since the disconnected hemispheres are not subject to the mutual facilitation and inhibition that occurs in the intact brain, their functioning must necessarily be different. And, finally, the ability of these patients, after years of testing, to "cross-cue" between hemispheres, by-passing the severed callosal route, and transmitting information by bodily gestures and orienting responses, has been noted by most researchers, although it is difficult to assess the effectiveness of such methods of inter-hemispheric communication. However, it does mean that the two hemispheres in the split-brain are not totally isolated from each other and can communicate indirectly to some extent. For all these reasons, the study of split-brain does not itself provide definitive answers to questions about hemispheric specialization in normals, but it does strengthen and amplify the evidence from other sources.

Studies of Hemisphere Differences in Normal Subjects

Techniques and methodological problems

Techniques have been developed to explore functional differences between the hemispheres in normal subjects by channelling sensory inputs so that they are projected primarily, or most directly to one or other hemisphere. Accordingly, superior performance, in terms of accuracy or latency response, is predicted when the material is projected directly to the hemisphere specialized for processing that type of material. For example, we predict that verbal material should be better perceived when presented to the right visual field or the right ear, and nonverbal material should be better perceived when presented to the left visual field or left ear. Of course, in normals the two hemispheres are not disconnected and information can be rapidly relayed across the corpus callosum from one hemisphere to the other. These techniques do not therefore allow the functioning of each hemisphere to be examined in isolation, and we cannot tell whether stimuli are processed within the hemisphere to which they were initially projected, or whether the input has been transmitted across the transcallosal route for processing in the other hemisphere. When hemisphere differences are obtained, two interpretations are usually possible. If, for example, verbal inputs are processed faster and more accurately when projected to the left hemisphere, and more slowly and inaccurately when presented to the right, the inferior performance of the right hemisphere may be due to the less efficient language-processing capacities of the right side. Alternatively, it may be explained on the assumption that the nonspecialist right hemisphere sends the information across to the language hemisphere for processing, and some delay and loss of information is incurred in transit. So obtained hemisphere differences might be due either to the unequal efficiency with which the input is processed within each hemisphere, or to the crossing-over between hemispheres. Experimental data do not usually discriminate between these alternatives. Two questions need to be asked in considering this issue. If we favour the unequal efficiency explanation, we need to ask whether the evidence from unilateral lesions suggests that the nonspecialist hemisphere would have the capacity to perform the task at the observed level of efficiency. If, on the other hand, we prefer the crossing-over explanation, we need to ask whether the estimates of the time required for transcallosal transmission are consistent with the differences in reaction times obtained for left and right hemisphere presentation. Estimates of interhemispheric transmission time (IHTT) derived from neurophysiological studies range from 3–15 ms (Ledlow, 1976), but dichotic listening and divided visual field methods generally yield much larger left–right differences, often in excess of 50 ms. The magnitude of the difference also varies from task to task, from individual subject to individual subject, and from trial to trial. This variability can only be reconciled with a crossing-over explanation by making the additional assumptions that more complex stimuli would take longer to transmit, and that loss of information during crossing may make the final processing more difficult.

Further methodological problems in the techniques for studying hemisphere differences in normal subjects have been reviewed by White (1972). In presenting visual stimuli, it is essential to ensure that the subject maintains fixation on the central point during the stimulus presentation so that the stimulus falls outside the foveal area of vision. Even if fixation is strictly controlled, Posner (1980) has shown that subjects are still able to orient attention toward left or right visual field, and improve performance in the attended field. In most divided visual field studies, orientation of attention is neither controlled nor monitored. The exposure duration of the stimulus should also be limited to a time less than the latency of eye movement, which is estimated at about 180–200 ms, depending on the extent of the movement. When longer stimulus durations are employed, eye movements may take place after the stimulus onset with the result that the stimulus is not confined to the contralateral hemisphere.

Even in the best controlled studies, the results obtained with these methods appear unreliable. In divided visual field tasks, only about 70% of individuals who have left hemisphere dominant for language (established by sodium amytal tests) show the predicted right field advantage for verbal material. In dichotic listening, somewhere between 65% and 85% show the predicted right ear advantage. Colbourn (1978) has pointed out that the analysis of the data from such studies is frequently statistically invalid.

When reaction times are used to measure hemisphere differences, problems relating to the statistical significance of the results arise because of the large variance that is inevitably associated with reaction times. The effects of practice, fatigue, fluctuations of attention, false or correct anticipation, repetitions, and stimulus–response compatibility all contribute to produce this variability in the speed of response, and the relatively small effects of functional differences between the hemispheres are easily obscured. When accuracy measures are employed instead of reaction times there may be other problems. It is usual to examine the performance of left and right visual fields for recognition of stimuli exposed very briefly at near-threshold durations and to compare the number of errors for left and right presentations. Recognition thresholds vary from subject to subject, and tend to decrease as the subject becomes more practised, so that it is hard to select an exposure duration that will produce a uniform level of difficulty.

The variability in hemisphere differences which is often found in experiments with normal subjects may be due to lack of precision in the techniques of testing, strategy differences, or individual differences in the degree and direction of lateralization. It is common to find that not all the subjects in an experiment exhibit the predicted asymmetries of performance, or that asymmetries shift at different stages of practice, or with small changes of instructions, type of material and experimental design. Although considerable consensus of results seems to have been achieved, the extent of this apparent agreement may be misleading, since results that run counter to predictions are seldom reported, and the practice of discarding negative results means that an artificially high level of support has been claimed.

In experiments which use dichotic listening to explore hemispheric differences in processing auditory material, there are also some methodological problems. The assumption that an input is primarily transmitted to the hemisphere contralateral to the ear of presentation is only justified if it is exactly synchronized with the competing input in the ipsilateral ear. Asymmetries in auditory processing have sometimes been obtained with monaural stimulation, but only in a few tasks with a high level of difficulty (Bakker, 1970; Cohen and Martin, 1975). It is also essential that the subjective intensity of the signals be equated for both ears, so that differences are attributable to functional specialization rather than to differences in acuity.

Berlin (1977) points out that in dichotic listening, left–right differences are very unstable, and vary with the relative intensity of the two channels, with practice, and with overall level of accuracy. When comparisons are made between the magnitude of the observed hemisphere asymmetry in different conditions, or in different populations of subjects, the proportion of correct responses to left and right ear stimuli must be related to the proportion of "double correct" responses, when the subject reports both stimuli accurately.

Interpretation of the observed asymmetries

The predicted hemisphere asymmetries will depend on whether the stimulus is classified as verbal or as nonverbal. Although it may seem a simple matter to decide whether or not a given task is a verbal one, in practice it is not so easy. Subjects often transform or recode the stimuli from one form to another. They construct images for words, and give names to faces or nonsense figures. Beaumont (1982) reviewing the results of divided visual field studies with verbal stimuli, notes that the right visual field advantage is sensitive to word concreteness, imageability, word frequency and syntactic class, and that these factors may interact with each other. The right field superiority is reduced for concrete words; imageable words; high frequency words; and for nouns and verbs. Not all verbal stimuli are processed in the same way. Similarly, although there is generally a left visual field advantage for slopes of lines, patterns of dots, faces and nonsense figures, the advantage shifts to the right visual field if the faces are familiar, or the shapes are nameable.

In dichotic listening, there is generally a left hemisphere advantage for recognition and recall of verbal material and speech sounds, and a right hemisphere advantage for nonspeech sounds, melodies and pitch discrimination. Whatever the method employed, different subjects may adopt different strategies for coding or recoding stimulus material, and may evolve new strategies at different stages of practice. Recoding strategies therefore contribute both to inter-subject variability, and to intra-subject variability in the magnitude and direction of hemisphere asymmetries.

There is a further problem in identifying the source of asymmetries in performance. The observed hemisphere differences may originate at any stage intervening between stimulus input and response output, and experimental designs do not always allow the critical stage to be identified. Hemispheric asymmetries could be reflecting differences in perception, in analysis, in judgement, or in control of the voice or hand making the response. Asymmetries at the analysis stage and at the response stage may cancel each other out.

Figure 40 gives a diagrammatic representation of some alternative models for the recognition of faces, with either manual or vocal responses. Model A represents the way Geffen *et al.* (1971) interpreted their finding that reaction times for face recognition were faster for left field, right hemisphere presentation, when a manual response was required. They assumed that processing took place within the hemisphere of presentation, the right hemisphere being superior, and that the manual responses could be mediated by either hemisphere. Model B represents their interpretation of

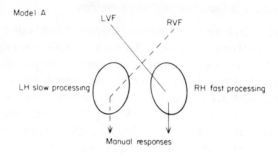

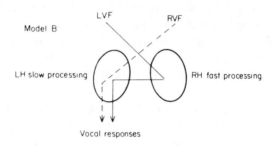

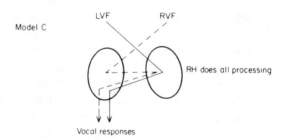

FIG. 40. *Models for processing and responding to faces. Model A—no crossing, LVF is faster; Model B—single crossing, LVF = RVF; Model C—double crossing, LVF is faster.*

the results obtained when a vocal response was required. Here the superiority of the right hemisphere at processing faces is cancelled out, because the results of the processing have to be transferred across to the left hemisphere, which has sole control of the vocal response mechanism. Model C represents another possibility whereby face processing is confined to the right hemisphere, and vocal responses to the left. This version is not consistent with the results obtained by Geffen *et al.* (1971), but is included here to illustrate the way in which models can be arbitrarily constructed to explain whatever experimental results are obtained. Most researchers assume that responses made with the whole hand can be mediated by either hemisphere, but that responses requiring fine control of individual fingers can only be mediated by the contralateral hemisphere. In the split-brain patients, however, the isolated hemispheres could not control ipsilateral responses made with the whole hand, so it may be wrong to assume, as in Model A, that the manual responses could be initiated equally well by either hemisphere. Since we cannot be certain whether the processing mechanisms, or the response mechanisms, are completely lateralized or only partially lateralized, the researcher is not constrained in his choice of assumptions. In consequence, a general weakness of this kind of model-building is that by making *ad hoc* assumptions about crossing, re-crossing and differences in processing efficiency, it is possible to "save" the hypothesis of lateralization of function whether the predicted asymmetry is found or not.

Models of Hemispheric Specialization

The models that have been proposed can be roughly divided into two kinds. These are fixed structural models, and dynamic process models. As can be seen in Figure 41 it is possible to construct a combined model, incorporating both structural and dynamic aspects into a single system.

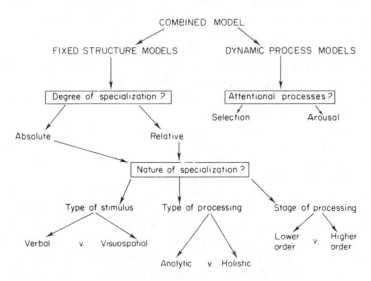

FIG. 41. *Models of hemispheric specialization.*

Structural models

According to a fixed structural model, asymmetries of cognitive function arise because the brain structures that mediate a given function are lateralized to one hemisphere, rather than the other. Observed hemisphere differences are attributed to the localization of the structures. The model predicts that when a stimulus is directed unilaterally performance will be superior if the hemisphere-of-entry is also the site of the structures specialized for processing that stimulus. This is sometimes known as the "direct pathway" explanation, and is common to different versions of the structural model.

Structural models are to some extent corroborated by the existence of neuroanatomical differences between the hemispheres that correlate with handedness. Witelson (1980) reviews evidence that the planum temporale is about 40% larger in the left hemisphere than in the right hemisphere in most right-handed individuals. This region of the temporal lobe is part of Wernicke's area which is known to be crucial for language comprehension. Structural models vary, however, in the degree of specialization that is assumed, and in the precise nature of the specialization.

The degree of specialization. Specialization of cognitive functions may be either absolute or relative. On an absolute specialization theory, a given function is considered to be absolutely reserved to one hemisphere and performance differences are attributed to crossing-over. On a partial specialization theory, a given function is considered to be performed more efficiently by one hemisphere, and performance differences are attributed to unequal efficiency. On the whole, the evidence from the damaged brain, the split brain and the intact brain is more consistent with a partial or relative specialization of some kind, than with absolute specialization, although some functions may be more strongly lateralized than others, and degree of lateralization may vary between individuals.

Recently a novel technique for monitoring regional changes in cerebral blood flow (rCBF) has been developed (Lassen *et al.*, 1978). During performance of a cognitive task, blood flow increases above the base level in the active regions of the brain. These changes in the pattern of density of blood flow are scanned and are reproduced as a visual display depicting the working brain with different colours representing the different densities of blood flow. The potential importance of this method, which allows us to observe the normal intact brain in operation, is obviously very great. Using this technique, Risberg (1980) found that, during verbal reasoning, blood flow increased in the left hemisphere more than the right in 32 out of 36 subjects. A nonverbal perceptual task produced the reverse pattern, although less consistently. Typically these studies reveal a large increase in blood flow in the hemisphere specialized for the ongoing task. So, for example, speech and reading produce evidence of increased activity in the left hemisphere. At the same time, there is a smaller increase in corresponding areas of the right hemisphere. This overall pattern is more consistent with relative specialization. Both hemispheres appear to be functionally interactive, with the specialist hemisphere making the larger contribution to the task.

The nature of the specialization. One way to explain why it is that performance asymmetries for verbal and nonverbal material do not always emerge as predicted, is to argue that the hemispheres are specialized not for particular kinds of stimuli, but more generally, for characteristic types of processing. According to this view, hemispheric differences originate from differences in *how* information is processed, not from *what* is processed. This hypothesis has considerable plausibility, but it has proved difficult to construct a model that is sufficiently tightly specified to be testable. Several versions of "type of processing" models have been proposed.

Specialization for analytic v. holistic processing. The most detailed account of this model is offered by Bradshaw and Nettleton (1981). According to their formulation, the left hemisphere processing mechanisms are sequential, analytic and time-dependent. The right hemisphere is characterised as a holistic, spatial processor. A substantial number of empirical findings can be assembled in support of the model. Left hemisphere superiority for judgements of duration, of temporal order, and for production of temporal sequences (Carmon and Nachshon, 1971; Lomas and Kimura, 1976) is cited in evidence. Since language skills such as syntactic analysis, speech and reading depend on temporal ordering, the superiority of the left hemisphere for most language tasks is considered as a secondary consequence of its control of sequencing mechanisms. Note, however, that left hemisphere superiority for temporal ordering does not seem to extend to haptic (touch and movement) processing, since Braille is usually read better with the left hand (Hermelin and O'Connor, 1971). Bradshaw and Nettleton claim that the serial/parallel processing distinction is a special case of the analytic/holistic one. So results that are consistent with a characterization of the left hemisphere as a serial processor, and the right hemisphere as a parallel processor, are considered as supporting their position. Cohen (1973) found that left hemisphere reaction times increased with the number of letters in an array—the typical serial processing function. Right hemisphere reaction times did not increase, and conformed to a parallel processing model. Patterson and Bradshaw (1975) also found evidence that the left hemisphere processed faces by a serial analytic feature match. However, Cohen's result did not hold good when the stimuli in the array were nonsense shapes instead of letters. It must also be remembered that evidence of parallel processing in the right hemisphere is not equivalent to holistic processing. Parallel processing is feature-analytic, with features being processed simultaneously rather than nonanalytically.

Clinical observations of drawings done by patients with left hemisphere lesions are also presented as evidence of the right hemisphere's holistic tendencies. These drawings typically preserve global outline, but lack detail and organization of the relationships of the parts. Nebes (1978) found that split-brain patients are better able to judge the size of a circle after palpating a segment of arc with the left hand, than with the right hand. He claims this ability to form a spatial representation from incomplete information is a right hemisphere speciality, but constructing wholes from parts does not seem to be an example of holistic processing.

Studies of ear differences in music perception also form part of the case for classifying the hemispheres as analytic and holistic processors. Bever and Chiarello (1974) found that musically untrained listeners showed a left ear advantage for recognition of musical sequences, while trained musicians showed a left hemisphere, right ear advantage. Post hoc interpretation of this finding produced the claim that musicians process analytically, and naive listeners holistically. In support of this interpretation, they noted that only the expert listeners were able to recognize single notes from the sequence, but this argument is weak because these same subjects failed to display any ear asymmetry for single note recognition. Although musical chords, as opposed to sequences, are supposed to be perceived holistically by both naive and expert listeners and should therefore yield a left ear advantage, Gordon (1980) found that a group of professional musicians were equally divided. Half did better with the left ear and half with the right. On the whole, the interaction of expertise with ear differences in processing musical stimuli has not been very consistent.

The analytic/holistic model suffers because the terms of the dichotomy are ill-defined. An assorted set of abilities is arbitrarily labelled as holistic. What does it mean to process a musical sequence holistically? It is not good enough to classify a process as holistic or analytic without further justi-fication. Some right hemisphere abilities such as singing, drawing, and assembling block designs could just as easily be considered as sequential activities, rather than holistic ones.

Bever (1980) has recast the analytic/holistic distinction as relational/ holistic. Relational processing is defined as requiring a manipulation of a relation between two stimulus–response pairs and associated mental representations, whereas holistic processing involves only a single direct association of one mental representation to stimulus and response. According to Bever, syntax, semantics and music require relational processing; simple nonsense figures are processed holistically; and faces can be processed either relationally or holistically. Bever's distinction is better defined, but is still open to the same counter-examples. Constructing block designs and copying drawings involve manipulation of a number of elements, and so ought to be relational, but these tasks are right hemisphere specialities.

Specialization for descriptive systems. Goldberg and Costa (1981) proposed that the hemispheres differ in the type of "descriptive systems" they employ. A descriptive system is defined as a set of units for encoding, and transformation rules. According to Goldberg and Costa, the left hemisphere is specialized for unimodal, well-learned routinized codes; the right hemisphere for novel codes, and for cross-modal systems. This model has at least the merit of generating some clear predictions. The most important of these are that a shift from right hemisphere to left hemisphere superiority should be observable as competence in a task increases, and that left hemisphere damage should disrupt well-learned systems, while right hemisphere damage should inhibit acquisition of novel routines. As confirmation of these predictions, Goldberg and Costa cite developmental trends which typically reveal increasing left hemisphere superiority as language and reading skills improve. Support also comes from a study which reported larger right ear advantages in multilingual children than in monolingual children, attributed to their more developed language capacity (Starck *et al.*, 1980). Not all the available results can be fitted to this pattern. Tzavaras *et al.* (1981) tested matched groups of literate and illiterate peasants in Northern Greece. The illiterates had a larger right ear advantage for digit recognition in dichotic listening, although, according to the hypothesis, the more linguistically experienced literate subjects should have shown greater asymmetry.

The relationship between musical expertise and left hemisphere processing (insofar as this holds) is consistent with the model, and Goldberg and Costa also claim that right hemisphere damage produces stereotyped and repetitive responses in problem-solving, while left hemisphere damage produces more innovative solution attempts.

Yet another distinction between the type of processing characteristic of each hemisphere has been proposed by Luria and Simernitskaya (1977). Their studies of unilateral lesions suggested that conscious intentional memorizing is controlled by the left hemisphere, and passive, unconscious, incidental memorization is a right hemisphere function.

Specialization for stages of processing. Several models have been proposed suggesting that the two hemispheres are specialized for different *stages* of processing rather than for particular *types* of processing. Such models attempt to decompose tasks into functionally separate stages of processing, and to establish the presence or absence of laterality effects at different stages. The Information Processing model described below is an example. Any model of this kind will be difficult to verify since stages of processing are not necessarily sequentially arranged in such a way that asymmetries arising at a particular level of processing will be reflected in the subsequent stages, but absent in preceding stages. Current theories of cognitive processing emphasize the interactive heterarchical organization of stages and interactive effects are liable to blur the divisions between stages, and obscure the point at which asymmetries originate.

The component operations model. Cohen (1977) suggests that each of the component operations forming part of a complete task may be lateralized to one hemisphere or the other, to varying degrees. The overall performance asymmetries observed for the task are therefore the product of the component asymmetries which may, in a multistage task, interact so as to accumulate or cancel out. This model explains how small changes in the nature of the task, the stimuli, or the strategy employed could alter the relative contribution of different components, and so shift the overall asymmetry. In this way, it can explain some of the variability of experimental results.

Evidence consistent with lateralization of component operations comes from letter and word recognition experiments. A task originally devised by Posner and Mitchell (1967) allows the physical and nominal stages of letter recognition to be decomposed. When subjects are asked to judge whether a pair of letters is same or different, pairs in the same case (AA or aa) can be judged the same on the basis of physical shape (a physical identity match), but pairs in different cases like Aa can only be judged the same on the basis of name (a nominal identity match). The left hemisphere appears to be functionally specialized for the naming stage, since nominal identity matches have reliably produced a right visual field advantage, whereas physical identity matches yielded either no difference or a small left field advantage (Cohen, 1972; Geffen *et al.*, 1972; Ledlow *et al.*, 1972). These results are also compatible with findings reported by Cohen and Freeman (1976) in a lexical decision task. In this task, letter strings were displayed in left and right visual fields, and the subject was required to decide if a given string was a word or a nonword. Some of the nonwords were homophones of real words (e.g. mone, hirt, werk). It is usually assumed that homophones take longer to reject as nonwords if the subject is forming a phonological representation of the letter string. The phonological resemblance of homophonic nonwords to real words makes it more difficult to recognize them as nonwords. In Cohen and Freeman's experiment the homophones took longer to reject as nonwords when presented to the left hemisphere, but not when presented to the right, indicating that the misleading phonologial analysis occurred only in the left hemisphere.

Bradshaw (1974) showed that semantic information is extracted more readily from the right visual field. When a homographic word such as "palm" was displayed centrally, in between two peripherally located words (e.g. "tree" on the left and "hand" on the right), the subject's interpretation of the meaning of the homograph was more often influenced by the meaning of the flanking word in the right field. These results show that physical processing of language can be carried out by either hemisphere, but phonological and semantic processing are predominantly left hemisphere functions.

However, these conclusions are challenged by Simion *et al.* (1980) who found a right visual field advantage for letter matches, and a left visual field advantage for geometrical figures which persisted whether physical or name matches were required. The lateralization of the semantic stage is also not clear cut. Semantic disorders may arise with right sided lesions (Lesser, 1974) and split-brain patients can make some semantic judgements with the right hemisphere.

Applied to linguistic tasks, the component operations model, whereby hemispheres are specialized for particular stages, is more accommodating than a model that assumes all aspects of linguistic processing are lateralized to one hemisphere. Different component stages may be lateralized to different degrees, and the degree of lateralization at each stage may vary between individuals. However, not all of the evidence supports this model.

The Information Processing Model. Attempts to identify the locus of hemispheric asymmetries within a general model of information processing have tended to assign asymmetries to late, but not early stages of processing; to memory rather than perception; to postcategorical, but not precategorical stages; to higher order or central processes rather than lower order, peripheral processes. These overlapping distinctions are embraced within the model outlined by Moscovitch (1979) and diagrammed in Fig. 42. The main assumptions are that laterality effects will be absent from early stages such as sensory processes and iconic storage; and from judgements based on perceptual characteristics. Simultaneous comparisons of letters, shapes and faces based on physical appearance, are considered as precategorical and unlateralized. Successive comparisons, where the first presented item must be held in memory for matching to the second, are more likely to be lateralized. Moscovitch *et al.* (1976) found that visual field asymmetries in a face comparison task developed as the interval between the to-be-matched faces was extended. They also reported that peripheral masking (which disrupts early precategorical stages of processing) does not produce asymmetrical effects. Central masking which interrupts later categorical stages does affect the hemispheres asymmetrically. According to the Moscovitch model, masking has less effect on the hemisphere which is the locus of the specialist processors where rapid and efficient processing is more likely to be completed before the mask can interfere with it. In the nonspecialist hemisphere processing is more vulnerable. Moscovich himself provides a careful review of the evidence relating to his model. Given the difficulty of dividing cognitive processes into discrete stages and interrogating them separately, it is not surprising that some of the relevant studies fail to fit with the model. Nevertheless it provides a coherent and plausible account for a substantial number of observed asymmetries.

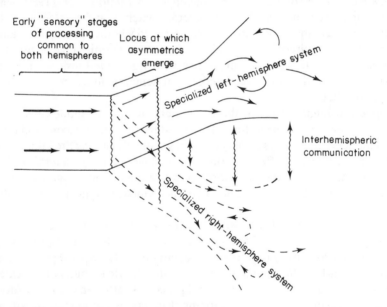

FIG. 42. *Moscovitch's Stage of Processing model.*

Dynamic models

None of the fixed structural models can explain the variability of observed hemisphere differences adequately. Specialization for types of stimulus, or types of processing may explain task-to-task variability, but the way in which within-task asymmetry can shift from trial to trial can only be explained by postulating some dynamic mechanism which may influence the functioning of the fixed structures. Dynamic models are therefore superimposed on structural models rather than replacing them. Some researchers have divided dynamic models into attentional and strategy models, but choice of strategy and change of strategy can both be regarded as attentional processes, and included within the attentional model.

The attentional model. Kinsbourne (1970, 1973, 1975) argues that asymmetries would be more robust and more consistent if they were governed only by a structural determinant such as functional specialization. Kinsbourne also maintains that the observed asymmetries are too large to be accounted for by crossing time, which he estimates at 4 ms. According to his theory, a basic asymmetry arising out of the functional specialization of the left hemisphere for verbal material, and of the right hemisphere for nonverbal material, may be either enhanced, obscured, or reversed by attentional factors. For example, when the left hemisphere is primed or activated, its superiority in processing verbal material becomes more marked, but if the right hemisphere is activated, its advantage diminishes. Concurrent verbal activity or the expectation of verbal stimuli activates the left hemisphere, while concurrent nonverbal activity or the expectation of nonverbal stimuli serves to activate the right. Whenever one hemisphere is more highly activated than the other, there is an attentional bias toward the contralateral side of space, resulting in enhanced processing of material presented on that side. The theory also postulates that activation of one hemisphere exerts an inhibitory influence on the functioning of the other. Thus, observed asymmetries may shift in accordance with the subject's expectations or cognitive "set", and with whether or not he is engaging in concurrent covert verbalization. Empirical tests of these predictions have yielded mixed results.

Priming for stimulus type: Several studies confirm that foreknowledge of the type of stimulus to be presented can prime the appropriate hemisphere and enhance its performance. Spellacy and Blumstein (1970) reported that when subjects were expecting speech sounds, there was a right ear, left hemisphere advantage for identification of dichotically presented vowels, but if the subjects were expecting nonspeech sounds, there was a left ear advantage. Cohen (1975) also found that no visual field differences were evident when words, digits and dots were presented in a randomly mixed sequence, but when the subject received a pre-trial cue, indicating which kind of stimulus would follow, a clear right field advantage for words, and a small, though not significant, left field advantage for dots, were obtained.

It is not clear whether these effects arise because expectancy causes the subject to pre-select the best strategy for the task; or whether expectancy increased the capacity of the appropriate hemisphere by arousal; or whether, as Kinsbourne claims, it produces a perceptual orientation to the side contralateral to the appropriate hemisphere. The exact nature and locus of the priming effect are uncertain.

Priming by practice or repetition: The effects of practice are particularly inconsistent. Asymmetries that are absent in the early stages of practice may appear at later stages (Pearl and Haggard, 1975), but sometimes an initial asymmetry disappears as practice is prolonged (Kallman and Corballis, 1975; Ward and Ross, 1977). Or, instead of disappearing, the initial asymmetry may reverse with practice. Sidtis and Bryden (1978) found that in a dichotic listening task, the ear superiority for tones shifted from right to left, while the ear superiority for words changed from left to right. These shifts may be caused by changes of strategy as the task is prolonged, or by changes in capacity as the hemispheres are differentially activated or fatigued.

Priming by concurrent task: Again the pattern of results is complex. Kinsbourne found that when subjects were required to locate the position of a gap in a square, no difference between left and right visual field presentation was obtained, but when a concurrent verbal task load (holding a set of words in memory) was imposed, the left hemisphere was primed and a right field advantage emerged. A left field advantage appeared when the right hemisphere was loaded by requiring subjects to hold a melody in mind. However, an attempt to replicate this experiment (Gardner and Branski, 1976) failed. Moscovitch and Klein (1980) studied the effect of requiring subjects to identify a centrally placed item in addition to recognizing a pair of items peripherally placed in the left or right visual field. According to Kinsbourne's model asymmetries should increase if the central and peripheral items are both of the same class (both words or both faces) because both would prime the same hemisphere. Moscovitch and Klein found that the right field superiority for words, and left field superiority for faces were unaffected by the nature of the central item, though there was an overall decrement in performance when it was the same class as the peripheral items. Instead of being primed, recognition of peripheral faces was poorer when the central item was also a face, than when it was a word or a nonsense syllable. They interpreted this finding as evidence for interference within the limited capacity mechanisms of the specialist hemisphere.

Whether secondary tasks will prime or interfere seems difficult to predict in advance. Hellige and Cox (1976) showed that the difficulty and the modality of the concurrent task both affected the result. They varied the difficulty of the secondary task by giving the subjects two, four or six words to hold in memory. Left hemisphere performance on the primary task of recognizing nonsense shapes was facilitated with small verbal memory loads, but deteriorated as the size of the load increased and the hemisphere was overloaded. This overload effect occurred even with small loads if the primary task was word recognition, so that both primary and secondary tasks involved the same processing mechanisms.

Concurrent tasks can affect the performance of both hemispheres. Kinsbourne (1975) suggests that the two hemispheres are in a relationship of reciprocal balance, so that a see-saw effect should be observable. Thus, for example, if the left hemisphere is activated by a verbal memory load so that performance improves, the right hemisphere should be correspondingly depressed. Hellige *et al.* (1979) reported a variety of different patterns of shift. Sometimes, in their experiments, the primed hemisphere improved and the unprimed one was unchanged; sometimes both improved. If the left hemisphere was overloaded by a concurrent verbal memory task so that performance worsened, then the right hemisphere might either improve, deteriorate or be unchanged. The predicted see-saw effect is only one of several possible patterns of shift. Hellige *et al.* have suggested that a combination of general and hemisphere-specific effects can account for the results. According to their model, general arousal affects the entire cognitive system in both hemispheres, while at the same time selective activation, or selective interference effects are confined to one hemisphere. Assumptions of this kind make it possible to explain almost any pattern of variability in hemispheric asymmetry.

The weakness of the attentional model is that, because the model is insufficiently constrained, it is too difficult to predict results in advance, and too easy to explain them in retrospect. To sum up, although there is some experimental evidence which favours the attentional theory, it is not clear how strong attentional effects are, relative to the effects of the underlying functional specialization; it is not clear at what point a concurrent task ceases to activate and starts to overload, or at what point activation degenerates into fatigue. Because of these uncertainties, the effects of attentional determinants of hemispheric asymmetry are unpredictable.

A combined model incorporating both structural and dynamic elements is nevertheless more powerful than either alone. A structural model can explain the existence of asymmetries in cerebral organization, but a dynamic model is necessary to explain the variability of the hemisphere differences observed in the performance of normal intact subjects. As yet, this combined model lacks precision and is too underdetermined to be considered adequate in its present form. It is simultaneously both complex and vague. However, in spite of the methodological criticisms that can justifiably be made of experimental techniques, and in spite of the lack of a theoretical explanation that can satisfactorily account for all of the findings, the convergence of results from a wide variety of different sources has provided a solid empirical basis of evidence for functional specialization of the hemispheres. The development of new techniques such as the monitoring of cerebral blood flow should make it possible to extend and confirm the findings and generate more satisfactory models.

Recommended reading

Gazzaniga's book *The Bisected Brain* is a readable introduction to the split-brain studies and Newcombe's *Missile Wounds of the Brain* gives a detailed account of the effects of unilateral lesions. Moscovitch provides an excellent review and critique in his chapter in Gazzaniga's *Handbook of Neurobiology*. Herron's edited volume on the *Neuropsychology of Left-Handedness* is packed with interesting information. To get the flavour of current debates in this area, read the articles and commentaries by McGlone (*The Behavioral and Brain Sciences* 3, 1980) and Bradshaw and Nettleton (*The Behavioral and Brain Sciences* 4, 1981). Not to be missed is the striking account of blood flow studies in *Scientific American*, 1978, by Lassen *et al*.

References

Albert, M. L. and Obler, L. K. (1978). *The Bilingual Brain*. Academic Press, New York.

Allport, D. A. (1980). Patterns and actions; cognitive mechanisms are content specific. In G. Claxton (Ed.) *Cognitive Psychology: New Directions*. Routledge and Kegan Paul, London.

Allport, D. A. (1970). Conscious and Unconscious Cognition: a computational metaphor for the mechanism of attention and integration. In L. G. Nillson (Ed.) *Perspectives on Memory Research*. Lawrence Erlbaum Associates, Hillsdale, NJ.

Anderson, J. A. (1977). Neural models with cognitive implications. In D. Laberge and S. J. Samuels (Eds) *Basic Processes in Reading: Perception and Comprehension*. Lawrence Erlbaum Associates, Hillsdale, NJ.

Anderson, J. R. (1976). *Language, Memory and Thought*. Lawrence Erlbaum Associates, Hillsdale, NJ.

Anderson, J. R. (1978). Arguments concerning representations for mental imagery. *Psychological Review* **85**, 249–277.

Anderson, J. R. and Bower, G. H. (1973). *Human Associative Memory*. Winston–Wiley, Washington and New York.

Anderson, R. C. and Ortony, A. (1975). On putting apples into bottles—a problem of polysemy. *Cognitive Psychology* **7**, 167–180.

Anglin, J. M. (1976). Les premiers termes de reference de l'enfant. In S. Ehrlich and E. Tulving (Eds) *La mémoire sémantique*. Bulletin de Psychologie, Spécial Annuel, Paris.

Anglin, J. M. (1977). *Word, object and conceptual development*. W. W. Norton, New York.

Atwood, G. (1971). An experimental study of visual imagination and memory. *Cognitive Psychology* **2**, 290–299.

Atwood, M. E. and Polson, P. G. (1976). A process model for water jug problems. *Cognitive Psychology* **8**, 191–216.

Baddeley, A., Grant, S., Wight, E. and Thompson, N. (1975). Imagery and visual working memory. In P. M. A. Rabbitt and S. Dornics, Eds. *Attention and Performance* Vol. 5. Academic Press, London and New York.

Bahrick, H. P., Bahrick, P. O. and Wittlinger, R. P. (1975). Fifty years of memory for names and faces: a cross sectional approach. *Journal of Experimental Psychology General* **104**, 54–75.

Bakker, D. J. (1970). Ear asymmetry with monoaurual stimulation: relations to lateral dominance and lateral awareness. *Neuropsychologia* **8**, 103–117.

Barr, A. and Feigenbaum, E. (1981). *Handbook of Artificial Intelligence*. Pitman, London.

Banks, W. P., Clark, H. H. and Lucy, P. (1975). The locus of the semantic congruity effect in comparative judgements. *Journal of Experimental Psychology, Human Perception and Performance*, **104** (1) 35–47.

Bartlett, F. C. (1932). *Remembering: A Study in Experimental and Social Psychology*. Cambridge University Press, Cambridge.

Baylor, G. W. (1972). A treatise on the mind's eye: an empirical investigation of visual mental imagery. Doctoral dissertation, Carnegie-Mellon University, Ann Arbor, Michigan.

Beaumont, J. S. (1982). Studies with verbal stimuli. In J. G. Beaumont (Ed.) *Divided Visual Field Studies of Cerebral Organization*. Academic Press, London and New York.

Beech, J. R. and Allport, D. A. (1978). Visualization of compound scenes. *Perception* **7**, 129–138.

Bellugi, U. and Fischer, S. (1972). A comparison of sign language. *Cognition* **1**, 173–200.

Bellugi, U., Klima, E. S. and Siple, P. (1974–1975). Remembering in signs. *Cognition* **3**, 93–125.

Berkeley, G. (1710). *The Principles of Human Knowledge* (reprinted 1901). Clarendon Press, Oxford.

Berlin, C. (1977). Hemispheric asymmetry in auditory tasks. In S. Harnad, R. W. Doty, L. Goldstein, J. Jaynes and G. Krauthamer (Eds) *Lateralization in the Nervous System*. Academic Press, New York and London.

Bernstein, B. B. (1971). *Class Codes and Control*. Paladin, St Albans.

Bernstein, B. B. (1972). A sociolinguistic approach to socialization with some reference to educability. In J. J. Gumperz and D. Hymes (Eds) *Directions in Sociolinguistics*. Holt, Rinehart and Winston, New York.

Bever, T. G. and Chiarello, R. J. (1974). Cerebral dominance in musicians and nonmusicians. *Science, NY* **185**, 537–539.

Bever, T. G. (1980). Broca and Lashley were right: cerebral dominance is an accident of growth. In D. Caplan (Ed.) *Biological Studies of Mental Processes*. MIT Press, Cambridge, Mass.

Bloom, L. M. (1973). *One word at a time: the use of single word utterances before syntax*. Mouton, The Hague.

Bobrow, D. G. and Collins, A. (1975). *Representation and Understanding*. Academic Press, New York and London

Boden, M. (1977). *Artificial Intelligence and Natural Man*. Harvester Press, Hassocks, Sussex.

Bolton, N. (1972). *The Psychology of Thinking*. Methuen, London.

Bourne, L. E. (1966). *Human Conceptual Behaviour*. Allyn and Bacon, Boston.

Bourne, L. E. (1974). An inference model for conceptual rule learning. In R. L. Solso (Ed.) *Theories in Cognitive Psychology*. The Loyola Symposium. Lawrence Erlbaum, Potomac, Maryland.

Bourne, L. E. and Restle, F. (1959). Mathematical theory of concept identification. *Psychological Review* **66**, 278–296.

Bower, G. H. and Trabasso, T. R. (1964). Concept identification. In R. C. Atkinson (Ed.) *Studies in Mathematical Psychology* Stanford University Press.

Bower, G. H. and Winzenz, D. (1970). Comparison of associative learning strategies. *Psychonomic Science* **20**, 119–120.

Bowerman, M. (1975). The acquisition of word meaning: an investigation of some current conflicts. Paper presented at the Third International Child Language Symposium, London.

Bowerman, M. (1979). Systematizing semantic knowledge: changes over time in the child's organization of word meaning. *Child Development* **49**, 977–987.

Bradshaw, J. L. (1974). Peripherally presented and unreported words may bias the perceived meaning of a centrally fixated homograph. *Journal of Experimental*

Psychology **103**, 1200–1202.

Bradshaw, J. L. and Nettleton, N. C. (1981). The nature of hemispheric specialization in Man. *The Behavioral and Brain Sciences* **4**, 51–91.

Brainerd, C. J. (1978). The stage question in cognitive developmental theory. *The Behavioral and Brain Sciences* **1**, 173–213.

Bransford, J. D. and Johnson, M. K. (1973). Considerations of some problems of comprehension. In W. G. Chase (Ed.) *Visual Information Processing*. Academic Press, New York and London.

Bransford, J. D., Barclay, J. R. and Franks, J. H. (1972). Sentence memory: a construct versus interpretive approach. *Cognitive Psychology* **3**, 193–209.

Braun, H. W., Patton, R. A. and Barnes, H. W. (1952). Effects of electro-shock convulsions upon learning performance of monkeys: I. Object-quality discrimination learning. *Journal of Comparative Physiological Psychology* **45**, 231–238.

Brewer, W. H. and Lichtenstein, E. H. (1974). Memory for marked semantic features versus memory for meaning. *Journal of Verbal Learning and Verbal Behaviour* **13**, 172–180.

Broca, P. (1865). Sur la faculté du langage articulé. *Bulletin Société Anthropologie, Paris* **6**, 493–494.

Bronowski, J. and Bellugi, U. (1970). Language, name and concept. *Science, N.Y.* **168**, 669–673.

Brooks, L. R. (1968). Spatial and verbal components of the act of recall. *Canadian Journal of Psychology* **22**, 349–368.

Brooks, L. R. (1978). Nonanalytic concept formation and memory for instances. In E. Rosch and B. B. Lloyd (Eds) *Cognition and Categorization*. Lawrence Erlbaum, Hillsdale, NJ.

Brown, R. W. (1958). How shall a thing be called? *Psychological Review* **65**, 14–21.

Brown, R. W. (1970). *Psycholinguistics*. The Free Press, New York.

Brown, R. W. and Lenneberg, E. H. (1954). A study in language and cognition. *Journal of Abnormal and Social Psychology* **49**, 454–462.

Bruner, J. S. (1960). *The Process of Education*. Harvard University Press.

Bruner, J. S. (1974–1975). From communication to language: a psychological perspective. *Cognition* **3** (3), 255–287.

Bruner, J. S., Goodnow, J. J. and Austin G. A. (1956). *A Study of Thinking*. John Wiley, New York.

Bruner, J. S., Olver, R. R. and Greenfield, P. M. (1966). *Studies in Cognitive Growth*. John Wiley, New York.

Bryant, P. H. and Trabasso, T. (1971). Transitive inferences and memory in young children. *Nature, Lond.* **232**, 456–458

Byrnne, B. (1970). Referred to in J. R. Anderson and G. Bower, *Human Associative Memory*, p.459. V. H. Winston, Washington, DC.

Campbell, B. (1971). The roots of language. In J. Morton (Ed.) *Biological and Social Factors in Psycholinguistics*. Logos Press, in association with Elek Books, London.

Carmichael, L., Hogan, H. P. and Walter, A. A. (1932). An experimental study of the effect of language on reproduction of visually perceived form. *Journal of Experimental Psychology* **15**, 73–86.

Carmon, A. and Rachshon, I. (1971). Effects of unilateral brain damage on perception of temporal order. *Cortex* **7**, 410–418.

Carramazza, A., Gordon, J., Zurif, E. G. and De Luca, D. (1976). Right hemispheric damage and verbal problem solving behaviour. *Brain and Language* **3**, 41–46.

Carroll, J. B. (1979). Psychometric approaches to the study of language. In C. J. Fillmore, D. Kempler and W. S-Y. Wang (Eds) *Individual Differences in Language Ability and Language Behaviour*. Academic Press, New York.

Carroll, J. B. and Casagrande, J. B. (1958). The function of language classification. In E. E. Maccoby, T. M. Newcomb and E. L. Hartley (Eds) *Readings in Social Psychology*. Holt, Rinehart and Winston, New York.

Carroll, J. B. and White, M. N. (1973). Word frequency and age of acquisition as determiners of picture naming latency. *Quarterly Journal of Experimental Psychology* **25**, 85–95.

Case, R. (1974). Structures and Strategies: some functional limitations on the course of cognitive growth. *Cognitive Psychology* **6**, 544–574.

Charness, N. (1976). Memory for chess positions: resistance to interference. *Journal of Experimental Psychology*: Human Learning and Memory, **2**, 641–653

Chase, W. G. and Simon, H. A. (1974). The mind's eye in chess. In W. G. Chase (Ed.) *Visual Information Processing*. Academic Press, London and New York.

Chi, M. T. H. (1978). Knowledge structures and memory development. In R. S. Siegler (Ed.) *Children's Thinking: What Develops?* Lawrence Erlbaum Associates, Hillsdale, NJ.

Chiang, A. and Atkinson, R. C. (1976). Individual differences and interrelationships among a select set of cognitive skills. *Memory and Cognition* **4**, 661–672.

Chomsky, N. (1965). *Aspects of the Theory of Syntax*. MIT Press, Cambridge, Massachusetts.

Chomsky, N. (1967). The general properties of language. In C. H. Millikan and F. L. Darley (Eds) *Brain Mechanisms underlying Speech and Language*. Grune and Stratton, New York and London.

Chomsky, N. (1967). The formal nature of language. In E. H. Lenneberg (Ed.) *Biological Foundations of Language*. John Wiley, New York.

Chomsky, N. (1980). Rules and Representations. *The Behavioral and Brain Sciences*, **3**, 1–61.

Clark, H. H. (1969a). Linguistic processes in deductive reasoning. *Psychological Review* **76**, 387–404.

Clark, H. H. (1969b). The influence of language in solving three term series problems. *Journal of Experimental Psychology* **82**, 205–215.

Clark, H. H. and Chase, W. G. (1972). On the process of comparing sentences against pictures. *Cognitive Psychology* **3**, 472–517.

Clark, H. H. and Clark, E. V. (1977). *Psychology and Language: An Introduction to Psycholinguistics*. Harcourt Brace Jovanovich, New York International Edition.

Clark, H. H. and Lucy, P. (1975). Understanding what is meant from what is said: a study in conversationally conveyed requests. *Journal of Verbal Learning and Verbal Behaviour* **14**, 56–72.

Clark, H. J. (1965). Recognition memory for random shapes as a function of complexity, association value and delay. *Journal of Experimental Psychology* **69**, 590–595.

Clark, E. V. (1973). What's in a word? On the child's acquisition of semantics in his first language. In T. E. Moore (Ed.) *Cognitive development and the acquisition of language*. Academic Press, New York.

Cohen, G. (1967). Conservation of quantity in children: the effect of vocabulary and participation. *Quarterly Journal of Experimental Psychology* **19**, 150–154.

Cohen, G. (1972). Hemisphere differences in a letter classification task. *Perception and Psychophysics* 11, 139–142.

Cohen, G. (1973). Hemisphere differences in serial versus parallel processing. *Journal of Experimental Psychology* **97**, 349–356.

Cohen, G. (1975). Hemisphere differences in the effects of cueing. *Journal of Experimental Psychology*: Human Perception and Performance **1**, 366–373.

Cohen, G. (1977). *The Psychology of Cognition*. First edition. Academic Press, London and New York.

Cohen, G. and Freeman, R. H. (1978). Individual differences in reading strategies in relation to handedness and cerebral asymmetry. In J. Requin (Ed.) *Attention and Performance VII*. Lawrence Erlbaum Associates, Hillsdale, NJ.

Cohen, G. and Martin, M. (1975). Hemisphere differences in an auditory stroop task. *Perception and Psychophysics* **17**, 79–83.

Colbourn, C. J. (1978). Can laterality be measured? *Neuropsychologia* **16**, 283–289.

Cole, M. (1977). An ethnographic psychology of cognition. In P. N. Johnson-Laird and P. C. Wason (Eds). *Thinking: Readings in Cognitive Science*. Cambridge University Press, Cambridge.

Collins, A., Warnock, E., Aiello, N. and Miller, M. (1975). Reasoning from incomplete knowledge. in D. G. Bobrow and A. Collins (Eds) *Representation and Understanding*. Academic Press, London and New York.

Collins, A. M. and Loftus, E. F. (1975). A spreading activation theory of semantic processing. *Psychological Review* **82**, 407–428.

Collins, A. M. and Quillian, M. R. (1969). Retrieval time from semantic memory. *Journal of Verbal Learning and Verbal Behaviour* **8**, 240–247.

Conrad, C. (1972). Cognitive economy in semantic memory. *Journal of Experimental Psychology* **92**, 149–154.

Conrad, R. (1964). Acoustic confusions in immediate memory. *British Journal of Psychology* **55**, 75–84.

Cooper, L. A. and Shepard, R. N. (1973). Chronometric studies of the rotation of mental images. In W. G. Chase (Ed.) *Visual Information Processing*. Academic Press, London and New York.

Corsi, P. (1971). Cited by Milner, B., in Interhemispheric differences and psychological processes. *British Medical Bulletin Supp.* **27**, 272–277.

Craik, K. J. W. (1943). *The Nature of Explanation*. Cambridge University Press, Cambridge.

Curtiss, S. (1977). *Genie: A Psycholinguistic Study of a Modern-Day "Wild Child"*. Academic Press, New York and London.

Deese, J. (1962). On the structure of associative meaning. *Psychological Review* **69**, 161–175.

De Laguna, G. (1927). *Speech: its Function and Development*. Yale University Press.

Dennis, M. and Whitaker, H. A. (1977). Hemispheric equipotentiality and language acquisition. In S. J. Segalowitz and F. A. Gruber (Eds) *Language Development and Neurological Theory*. Academic Press, New York.

Dennis, M. (1980). Language acquisition in a single hemisphere: semantic organization. In D. Caplan (Ed.) *Biological Studies of Mental Processes*. MIT Press, Cambridge, Mass.

Dominowski, R. L. (1974). How do people discover concepts? In R. L. Solso (Ed.) *Theories in Cognitive Psychology*. The Loyola Symposium. Laurence Erlbaum,

Potomac, Maryland.
Donaldson, M. and Balfour, G. (1968). Less is more: a study of language comprehension in children. *British Journal of Psychology* **59**, 461–471.
Dresher, B. E. and Hornstein, N. (1976). On some supposed contributions of artificial intelligence to the scientific study of language. *Cognition* **4**, 321–398.
Dreyfus, H. L. (1972). *What Computers Can't Do*. Harper and Row, New York.
Eifermann, R. R. (1961). Negation: a linguistic variable. *Acta Psychologica* **18**, 258–273.
Ekstrand, B. R. and Dominowski, R. L. (1965). Solving words as anagrams. *Psychonomic Science* **2**, 239–240.
Elio, R. and Anderson, J. R. (1981). The effects of category generalizations and instance similarity on schema abstraction. *Journal of Experimental Psychology: Human Learning and Memory* **4**, 397–417.
Engelkampf, J. and Hörmann, H. (1974). The effect of non-verbal information on the recall of negation. *Quarterly Journal of Experimental Psychology* **26**, 98–105.
Entus, A. K. (1977). Hemispheric asymmetry in processing of dichotically presented speech and nonspeech stimuli by infants. In S. J. Segalowitz and F. A. Gruber (Eds) *Language Development and Neurological Theory*. Academic Press, New York.
Erickson, J. R. Research on syllogistic reasoning (1978). In R. Revlin and R. E. Mayer (Eds) *Human Reasoning*. V. H. Winston, Washington, DC.
Erickson, J. R., Zajkowski, M. M. and Ehrmann, E. D. (1966). All or none assumptions in concept identification: analysis of latency date. *Journal of Experimental Psychology* **72**, 690–697.
Ericsson, K. A. and Simon, H. A. (1980). Verbal reports as data. *Psychological Review* **87**, 215–251.
Ernest, C. H. (1977). Imagery ability and cognition: a critical review. *Journal of Mental Imagery* **1**, 181–216.
Ervin-Tripp, S. (1964). An analysis of the interaction of language, topic and listener. *American Anthropologist* **66**, 94–100.
Evans, J. St B. T. (1972). On problems of interpreting reasoning data. *Cognition* **1**, 373–384.
Fairweather, H. (1976). Sex differences in cognition. *Cognition* **4**, 231–280.
Fillmore, C. J. (1968). The case for case. In E. Bach and R. T. Harms (Eds) *Universals of Linguistic Theory*. Holt, Rinehart and Winston, New York.
Fillmore, C. J., Kempler, D. and Wang, W. S-Y. (1979). *Individual Differences in Language Ability and Language Behaviour*. Academic Press, New York.
Flavell, J. H. (1963). *The Developmental Psychology of Jean Piaget*. Van Nostrand, Princeton, New Jersey.
Fodor, J. A. (1981). The mind-body problem. *Scientific American*, **244**, No. 1, 124–132.
Fodor, J. A., Bever, T. G. and Garrett, M. F. (1974). *The Psychology of Language: An Introduction to Psycholinguistic and Generative Grammar*. McGraw-Hill, New York.
Foorman, B. R. and Kinoshita, Y. (1982). Linguistic effects on children's encoding and decoding performance in Japan, the United States and England. In press.
Fouts, R., Shapiro, G. and O'Neil, C. (1978). Studies of linguistic behavior in apes

and children. In P. Siple (Ed.) *Understanding Language through Sign Language Research.* Academic Press, New York and London.

Frederiksen, C. H. (1975). Effects of context induced processing operations on semantic information acquired from discourse. *Cognitive Psychology* **7**, 139–166.

Frisch, K. von (1967). *The Dance Language and Orientation of the Bees.* Harvard University Press, Cambridge, Massachusetts.

Furth, H. G. (1966). *Thinking without Language.* The Free Press, New York.

Gardner, B. T. and Gardner, R. A. (1975). Evidence for sentence constituents in the early utterances of child and chimpanzee. *Journal of Experimental Psychology: General* **104**, 244–267.

Gardner, E. and Branski, D. (1976). Unilateral cerebral activation and perception of gaps: a signal detection analysis. *Neuropsychologia* **14**, 43–53.

Gardner, R. A. and Gardner, B. T. (1969). Teaching sign language to a chimpanzee. *Science, N.Y.* **165**, 664–672.

Garrity, L. I. (1977). Electromyography: a review of the current status of subvocal speech research. *Memory and Cognition* **5**, 615–622.

Gazzaniga, M. S. (1970). *The Bisected Brain.* Appleton Century Crofts, New York.

Gazzaniga, M. S. and Sperry, R. W. (1967). Language after sectioning the cerebral commissures. *Brain* **90**, 131–148.

Geffen, G., Bradshaw, J. L. and Wallace, G. (1971). Interhemispheric effects on reaction times to verbal and nonverbal stimuli. *Journal of Experimental Psychology* **87**, 415–422.

Geffen, G., Bradshaw, J. L. and Nettleton, N. C. (1972). Hemisphere asymmetry: verbal and spatial encoding of visual stimuli. *Journal of Experimental Psychology* **95**, 25–31.

Geffen, G., Bradshaw, J. L. and Nettleton, N. C. (1973). Attention and hemispheric differences in reaction times during simultaneous audio-visual tests. *Quarterly Journal of Experimental Psychology* **25**, 404–412.

Glass, A. L. and Holyoak, K. J. (1975). Alternative conceptions of semantic theory. *Cognition* **3**, 313–339.

Glanzer, M. and Duarte, A. (1971). Repetition between and within languages in free recall. *Journal of Verbal Learning and Verbal Behaviour* **10**, 625–630.

Gleitman, L. R., Gleitman, H. and Shipley, E. (1972). The emergence of the child as a grammarian. *Cognition* **1**, 137–164.

Glucksberg, S. (1962). The influence of strength of drive on functional fixedness and perceptual recognition. *Journal of Experimental Psychology* **63**, 36–51.

Goggin, J. and Wickens, D. (1971). Proactive interference and language change in short term memory. *Journal of Verbal Learning and Verbal Behaviour* **10**, 453–458.

Goldberg, E. and Costa, L. D. (1981). Hemispheric differences in the acquisition and use of descriptive systems. *Brain and Language* **14**, 144–173.

Gopnik, A. (1982). Words and Plans: early language and the development of intelligent action. *Journal of Child Language* **9**, 303–318.

Gordon, H. W. (1980). Degree of ear asymmetries for perception of dichotic chords and for illusory chord localization in musicians of different levels of competence. *Journal of Experimental Psychology*: Human Perception and Performance **6**, 516–527.

Green, R. T. and Laxon, V. J. (1970). The conservation of number, mother, water and a fried egg chez l'enfant. *Acta Psychologica* **32**, 1–30.

Greene, J. (1970). The semantic function of negatives and passives. *British Journal of Psychology* **61**, 17–22.

Greenfield P., Reich, L. and Olver, R. (1966). On culture and equivalence, 2. In P. Greenfield, L. Reich and R. Olver (Eds) *Studies in Cognitive Growth*. John Wiley, New York.

Greeno, J. L. (1978). The nature of problem solving abilities. In W. K. Estes (Ed.) *Handbook of Learning and Cognitive Processes* Vol. 5. Human Information Processing. Lawrence Erlbaum Associates, Hillsdale, NJ.

Griggs, R. A. (1978). Drawing inferences from set inclusion information given in text. In R. Revlin and R. E. Mayer (Eds) *Human Reasoning*. V. H. Winston, Washington, DC.

Gruenberger, F. (1962). *Benchmarks in Artificial Intelligence* p. 2586. The RAND Corporation.

Haber, R. N. (1979). Twenty years of haunting eidetic imagery: where's the ghost? *The Behavioral and Brain Sciences* **2**, 583–619.

Harlow, H. F. (1949). The formation of learning sets. *Psychological Review* **56**, 51–65.

Hayes, C. (1951). *The Ape in our House*. Harper, New York.

Hayes, J. R. (1974). On the function of visual imagery in elementary mathematics. In W. G. Chase (Ed.) *Visual Information Processing* pp. 177–211. Academic Press, London and New York.

Hayes, K. J. and Nissen, C. H. (1971). Higher mental functions of a home-raised chimpanzee. In A. M. Schrier and F. Stollnitz (Eds) *Behaviour of Nonhuman Primates* Vol. 4. Academic Press, New York and London.

Hayes-Roth, B., and Hayes-Roth, F. (1979). A cognitive model of planning. *Cognitive Science* **3**, 275–310.

Hayes-Roth, F. (1979). Distinguishing theories of representation: a critique of Anderson's Arguments concerning mental imagery. *Psychological Review* **86**, 376–392.

Haygood, R. C. and Bourne, L. E. (1965). Attribute and rule learning, aspects of conceptual behaviour. *Psychological Review* **72**, 175–195.

Hebb, D. O. (1968). Concerning imagery. *Psychological Review* **75**, 466–477.

Hellige, J. B. and Cox, P. J. (1976). Effects of concurrent verbal memory on recognition of stimuli from left or right visual fields. *Journal of Experimental Psychology*: Human Perception and Performance, **2**, 210–221.

Hellige, J. B., Cox, P. J. and Litvac, L. (1979). Information processing in the cerebral hemispheres: selective activation and capacity limitations. *Journal of Experimental Psychology*: General, **108**, 251–279.

Henle, M. (1962). On the relation between logic and thinking. *Psychological Review* **69**, 366–378.

Hermelin, B. and O'Connor, N. (1971). Functional asymmetry in the reading of Braille. *Neuropsychologia* **9**, 431–435.

Herrman, D. J. and Neisser, U. (1978). An inventory of everyday memory experiences. In M. M. Gruneberg, P. E. Morris, and R. N. Sykes (Eds) *Practical Aspects of Memory*. Academic Press, London and New York.

Herron, J. (1980). *Neuropsychology of Left-Handedness*. Academic Press, London and New York.

den Heyer, K. and Barrett, B. (1971). Selective loss of visual and verbal interpolated tasks. *Psychonomic Science* **25**, 100–102.

Hockett, C. F. (1960). The origin of speech. *Scientific American* **203**, 89–96.

Homa, D., Sterling, S. and Trepel, L. (1981). Limitations of exemplar based generalization and the abstraction of categorical information. *Journal of Experimental Psychology*: Human Learning and Memory **4**, 418–439.

Hughes, J. (1975). Acquisition of a non-vocal 'language' by aphasic children. *Cognition* **3**, 41–55.

Hughlings Jackson, J. (1880). On aphasia with left hemiplegia. *Lancet* **i**, 637–638.

Hunt, E. B. (1978). Mechanics of verbal ability. *Psychological Review* **85**, 109–130.

Hunt, E. B. (1980). The borders of cognition. *The Behavioral and Brain Sciences* **3**, 140.

Hunt, E. B. and Hovland, C. I. (1960). Order of consideration of differential types of concepts. *Journal of Experimental Psychology* **59**, 220–225.

Hunt, E. B., Frost, N. and Lunneborg, C. L. (1973). Individual differences in cognition: a new approach to intelligence. In G. Bower, (Ed.) *Advances in Learning and Motivation* Vol. 7. Academic Press, New York and London.

Hunt, E. B., Lunneborg, C. and Lewis, J. (1975). What does it mean to be a high verbal? *Cognitive Psychology*, **7**, 194–227.

Hunter, I. M. L. (1957). The solving of three term series problems. *British Journal of Psychology* **48**, 286–298.

Huttenlocher, J. (1963). Growth and the organization of inference. Centre for Cognitive Studies Annual Report, Cambridge, Massachusetts.

Huttenlocher, J. (1968). Constructing spatial images: a strategy in reasoning. *Psychological Review* **75**, 550–560.

Huttenlocher, J. (1974). The origins of language comprehension. In R. L. Solso (Ed.) *Theories in Cognitive Psychology*. The Loyola Symposium. Lawrence Erlbaum. Potomac, Maryland.

Jarrard, L. and Moise, S. (1971). Short term memory in the monkey. In L. Jarrard (Ed.) *Cognitive Processes of Nonhuman Primates*. Academic Press, London and New York.

Jeffries, R., Polson, P. G., Razran, L. and Atwood, M. (1977). A process model for missionaries and cannibals and other river crossing problems. *Cognitive Psychology* **9**, 412–440.

Johnson, M. K., Bransford, J. D., Nyberg, S. E. and Cleary, J. J. (1972). Comprehension factors in interpreting memory for concrete and abstract sentences. *Journal of Verbal Learning and Verbal Behaviour* **11**, 451–454.

Johnson-Laird, P. N. (1981). Comprehension as the construction of mental models. *Philosophical Transactions of the Royal Society, London* **295B**, 353–374.

Johnson-Laird, P. N. (1980). Mental models in cognitive science. *Cognitive Science* **4**, 71–115.

Jonides, J., Kahn, R. and Rozin, P. (1975). Imagery instructions improve memory in blind subjects. *Bulletin of the Psychonomic Society* **5**, 424–426.

Kahneman, D. and Tversky, A. (1973). On the psychology of prediction. *Psychological Review* **80**, 237–251.

Kahneman, D. and Tversky, A. (1974). Subjective probability: a judgement of representativeness. In C-A. S. Stael von Holstein, (Ed.) *The Concept of Probability in Psychological Experiments*. Academic Press, London and New York.

Kallman, H. J. and Corballis, M. C. (1975). Ear asymmetry in reaction times to musical sounds. *Perception and Psychophysics* **17**, 368–370.

Keenan, J. M. and Moore, R. E. (1979). Memory for images of concealed objects: a re-examination of Neisser and Kerr. *Journal of Experimental Psychology*:

Human Learning and Memory **5**, 374–385.

Kendler, H. H. and Kendler, T. S. (1962). Vertical and horizontal processes in problem solving. *Psychological Review* **69**, 1–16.

Keil, F. C. (1979). *Semantic and conceptual development*. Harvard University Press, Cambridge, Mass.

Kimura, D. (1961). Cerebral dominance and the perception of verbal stimuli. *Canadian Journal of Psychology* **15**, 166–171.

Kimura, D. (1966). Dual functional asymmetry of the brain in visual perception. *Neuropyschologia* **4**, 275–285.

Kimura, D. (1967). Functional asymmetry of the brain in dichotic listening. *Cortex* **3**, 163–178.

Kinsbourne, M. (1970). The cerebral basis of asymmetries in attention. *Acta Psychologica* **33**, 193–210.

Kinsbourne, M. (1971). The minor hemisphere as a source of aphasic speech. *Archives of Neurology* **25**, 302–306.

Kinsbourne, M. (1973). The control of attention by interaction between the cerebral hemispheres. In S. Kornblum (Ed.) *Attention and Performance* Vol. 4. Academic Press, New York.

Kinsbourne, M. (1975). The mechanism of hemispheric control of the lateral gradient of attention. In P. M. A. Rabbitt and S. Dornic (Eds) *Attention and Performance* Vol. 5. Academic Press, New York.

Kintsch, W. (1972). Abstract nouns; imagery versus lexical complexity. *Journal of Verbal Learning and Verbal Behaviour* **11**, 59–65.

Kintsch, W. (1976). Memory for Prose. In C. N. Cofer (Ed.) *The Structure of Human Memory*. W. H. Freeman, San Francisco.

Kirsner, K., Brown, H. L., Abrol, S., Chadha, N. K. and Sharma, N. K. (1980). Bilingualism and lexical representation. *Quarterly Journal of Experimental Psychology* **32**, 585–594.

Klahr, D. (1978). Goal formation, planning and learning by pre-school children or My Socks are in the Dryer. In R. S. Siegler (Ed.) *Children's Thinking: What Develops?* Lawrence Erlbaum Associates, Hillsdale, NJ.

Klatt, D. H. (1977). Review of the ARPA speech understanding project. *Journal of the Accoustical Society of America* **62**, 1345–1366.

Klatt, D. H. (1980). Speech perception: a model of acoustic-phonetic analysis and lexical access. In R. A. Cole (Ed.) *Perception and Production of Fluent Speech*. Lawrence Erlbaum Associates, Hillsdale, NJ.

Kolers, P. A. (1965). Bilingualism and bicodalism. *Language and Speech* **8**, 122–126.

Kossan, N. E. (1981). Developmental differences in concept acquisition strategies. *Child Development* **52**, 290–298.

Kosslyn, S. M. and Pomerantz, J. R. (1977). Imagery, propositions and the form of internal representations. *Cognitive Psychology* **9**, 1977, 52–76.

Kosslyn, S. M. and Shwartz, S. P. (1977). A simulation of visual imagery. *Cognitive Science* **1**, 265–295.

Kosslyn, S. M., Pinker, S., Smith, G and Shwartz, S. P. (1979). On the demystification of mental imagery. *The Behavioral and Brain Sciences* **2**, 535–581.

Kosslyn, S. M. (1980). *Image and Mind*. Harvard University Press, Cambridge, Mass.

Kosslyn, S. M. (1981). The medium and the message in mental imagery: a theory. *Psychological Review* **88**, 46–65.

Kuenne, M. R. (1946). Experimental investigation of the relation of language to transposition behaviour in young children. *Journal of Experimental Psychology* **36**, 471–490.

Labov, W. (1966). *The Social Stratification of English in New York City*. Center for Applied Linguistics, Washington, DC.

Lachman, J. L. and Lachman, R. (1979). Theories of memory organization and human evolution. In C. R. Puff (Ed.) *Memory Organization and Structure*. Academic Press, New York.

Lakoff, G. (1972). Hedges: a study in meaning criteria and the logic of fuzzy concepts. Chicago Linguistics Society. Eighth regional meeting, Chicago.

Lambert, W. E. and Preston, M. S. (1967). The interdependencies of the bilingual's two languages. In K. Salzinger and S. Salzinger (Eds) *Research in Verbal Behaviour and Some Neurophysiological Implications* Academic Press, New York and London.

Landauer, T. K. and Meyer, D. E. (1972). Category size and semantic memory retrieval. *Journal of Verbal Learning and Verbal Behaviour* **11**, 539–549.

Lassen, N. A., Ingvar, D. H. and Skinhoj, E. (1978). Brain function and blood flow. *Scientific American*, **239**, October, 50–59.

Ledlow, A. (1976). A reaction time and evoked potential investigation of lateral asymmetries in a stimulus classification task. Unpublished doctoral dissertation, University of Texas, Austin.

Ledlow, A., Swanson, J. M. and Carter, B. (1972). Specialization of the hemispheres for physical and associational memory comparisons. Paper presented at the Convention of the Midwestern Psychological Association, Cleveland.

Lenneberg, E. H. (1967). *Biological Foundations of Language*. John Wiley, New York and London.

Lesser, R. (1974). Verbal comprehension in aphasia: an English version of three Italian tests. *Cortex* **10**, 247–263.

Lesser, V. R. and Erman, L. D. (1979). An experiment in distributed interpretation. Report No. CMU-CS 79–120, Computer Science Dept., Carnegie Mellon University, Pittsburgh, Pa.

Levelt, W. J. M. (1981). The speaker's linearization problem. *Philosophical Transactions of the Royal Society London* **295**, 305–315.

Levine, M. (1962). Cue neutralization: the effects of random reinforcements upon discrimination learning. *Journal of Experimental Psychology* **63**, 438–443.

Levine, M. (1965). Hypothesis behaviour. In A. M. Schrier, H. F. Harlow and F. Stollnitz (Eds) *Behaviour of Nonhuman Primates* Vol. 1. Academic Press, London and New York.

Levine, M. (1966). Hypothesis behaviour by humans during discrimination learning. *Journal of Experimental Psychology* **71**, 331–338.

Levy, J. (1969). Possible basis for the evolution of lateral specialization of the human brain. *Nature, Lond.* **222**, 614–615.

Levy, J. and Reid, M. L. (1978). Variations in cerebral organization as a function of handedness, hand posture in writing and sex. *Journal of Experimental Psychology*: General, **107**, 119–144.

Levy, J. and Trevarthen, C. (1977). Perceptual, semantic and phonetic aspects of elementary language processes in split-brain patients. *Brain* **100**, 105–118.

Lieberman, P. and Crelin, E. S. (1971). On the speech of Neanderthal man. *Linguistic Inquiry* **2**, 203–222.

Loftus, E. F. (1975). Leading questions and the eyewitness report. *Cognitive*

Psychology **7**, 560–572.

Loftus, E. F. and Palmer, J. P. (1974). Reconstruction of automobile destruction: an example of the interaction between language and memory. *Journal of Verbal Learning and Verbal Behaviour* **13**, 585–589.

Loftus, E. F., Miller, D. G. and Burns, H. J. (1978). Semantic integration of verbal information into a visual memory. *Journal of Experimental Psychology: Human Learning and Memory* **4**, 19–31.

Lomas, J. and Kimura, D. (1976). Intrahemispheric interaction between speaking and sequential manual activity. *Neuropsychologia* **14**, 23–33.

Luchins, A. S. (1942). Mechanization in problem solving: the effect of Einstellung. *Psychological Monographs* **54**, 6, Whole No. 248.

Luria, A. R. (1967). The regulative function of speech in its development and dissolution. In K. Salzinger and S. Salzinger (Eds) *Research in Verbal Behaviour and Some Neurophysiological Implications*. Academic Press, New York and London.

Luria, A. R. (1968). *The Mind of a Mnemonist*. Basic Books, New York.

Luria, A. R. and Simernitskaya, E. G. (1977). Interhemispheric relations and the functions of the minor hemisphere. *Neuropsychologia* **15**, 175–178.

Lyons, J. (1972). Human Language. In R. A. Hinde (Ed.) *Non-verbal communication*. Cambridge University Press, Cambridge.

McCartney, K. A. and Nelson, K. (1981). Children's use of scripts in story recall. *Discourse Processes* **4**, 59–70.

McCaulay, C., Weil, C. M. and Sperber, R. D. (1976). The Development of memory structure as reflected by semantic priming effects. *Journal of Experimental Child Psychology* **22**, 511–518.

McCloskey, M. E. and Glucksberg, S. (1978). Natural categories: well defined or fuzzy sets? *Memory and Cognition*, **6**, 462–472.

McGlone, J. (1980). Sex differences in human brain organization. *The Behavioral and Brain Sciences* **3**, 215–263.

Mackay, D. G. (1973). Aspects of a theory of comprehension, memory and attention. *Quarterly Journal of Experimental Psychology* **25**, 22–40.

McKeever, W. (1979). Handwriting posture in left-handedness: sex, familial sinistrality and language laterality correlates. *Neuropsychologia* **17**, 429–444.

McKenna, P. and Warrington, E. K. (1980). Testing for nominal dysphasia. *Journal of Neurology, Neurosurgery and Psychiatry* **43**, 781–788.

MacLeod, C. M., Hunt, E. B. and Matthews, N. N. (1978). Individual differences in the verification of sentence-picture relationships. *Journal of Verbal Learning and Verbal Behavior* **17**, 493–507.

Macnamara, J. (1972). The cognitive basis of language learning in infants. *Psychological Review* **27**, 1–13.

Maier, N. R. F. (1930). Reasoning in humans, I. On direction. *Journal of Comparative Psychology* **10**, 115–143.

Mandler, G. (1967). Organization and memory. In K. W. Spence and J. T. Spence (Eds) *The Psychology of Learning and Motivation* Vol. 1. Academic Press, New York and London.

Marmor, G. S. and Zaback, L. A. (1976). Mental rotation by the blind: does mental rotation depend on imagery? *Journal of Experimental Psychology: Human Perception and Performance* **2**, 515–521.

Marr, D. (1976). Early processing of visual information. *Philosophical Transactions of the Royal Society* **275B**, 483–519.

Marshall, J. C. (1970). The Biology of communication in man and animals. In J. Lyons, (Ed.) *New Horizons in Linguistics.* Penguin Books, Middlesex.

Marshall, J. C. (1977). Minds, machines and metaphors. *Social Studies of Science* **7**, 475–488.

Mattingley, I. G. (1972). Speech cues and sign stimuli. *American Scientist* **60**, 327–337.

Medin, D. L. and Smith, E. E. (1981). Strategies and classification learning. *Journal of Experimental Psychology: Human Learning and Memory* **4**, 241–253.

Melton, A. W. and Martin, E. (1972). *Coding Processes in Human Memory.* Winston, Washington, DC.

Mervis, C. B. and Pani, J. R. (1980). Acquisition of basic object categories. *Cognitive Psychology* **12**, 496–522.

Mervis, C. B. and Rosch, E. (1981). Categorization of natural objects. *Annual Review of Psychology* **32**, 89–115.

Meyer, D. E. (1970). On the representation and retrieval of stored semantic information. *Cognitive Psychology* **1**, 242–300.

Millar, S. (1975). On the nature and functioning of spatial representations: experiments with blind and sighted subjects. Paper presented at the International meeting of the Experimental Psychology Society, Cambridge, July, 1975.

Miller, G. A. (1971). Empirical methods in the study of semantics. In D. D. Steinberg and L. A. Jakobovits (Eds) *Semantics: An Interdisciplinary Reader.* Cambridge University Press, Cambridge.

Miller, G. A. and McKean, K. O. (1964). A chronometric study of some relations between sentences. *Quarterly Journal of Experimental Psychology* **16**, 297–308.

Milner, B. (1971). Interhemispheric differences and psychological processes. *British Medical Bulletin* **27**, 272–277.

Milner, B. and Taylor, L. (1972). Right hemisphere superiority in tactile pattern recognition after cerebral commissurotomy: evidence for nonverbal memory. *Neuropsychologia* **10**, 1–15.

Moeser, S. D. and Bregman, A. S. (1973). Imagery and language acquisition. *Journal of Verbal Learning and Verbal Behaviour* **12**, 91–98.

Mosher, F. A. (1962). Strategies for information gathering. Paper read at the Eastern Psychological Association, Atlantic City, New Jersey.

Morton, J. (1971). *Biological and Social Factors in Psycholinguistics.* Logos Press, in association with Elek Books, London.

Morton, J. and Byrne, R. (1975). Organization in the kitchen. In P. M. A. Rabbitt and S. Dornics (Eds) *Attention and Performance* Vol. 5. Academic Press, London and New York.

Moscovitch, M. (1979). Information processing and the cerebral hemispheres. In M. S. Gazzaniga (Ed.) *Handbook of Neurobiology* Vol. 2. Neuropsychology. Plenum Press, New York and London.

Moscovitch, M. and Klein, D. (1980). Material specific perceptual interference for visual words and faces: Implications for models of capacity limitations, attention and laterality. *Journal of Experimental Psychology*: Human Perception and Performance, **6**, 590–604.

Moscovitch, M., Scullion, D. and Christie, D. (1976). Early versus late stages of processing and their relation to functional hemispheric asymmetries in face recognition. *Journal of Experimental Psychology*: Human Perception and Performance, **2**, 401–416.

Mynatt, C. T., Doherty, M. E. and Tweney, R. D. (1977). Confirmation bias in a simulated research environment: an experimental study of scientific inference. *Quarterly Journal of Experimental Psychology* **29**, 85–95.

Nebes, R. D. (1971). Perception of part-whole relations in commissurotomized man. *Cortex* **4**, 333–349.

Nebes, R. D. (1978). Direct examination of cognitive function in the right and left hemispheres. In M. Kinsbourne (Ed.) *Asymmetrical Function of the Brain.* Cambridge University Press, New York.

Neisser, U. (1963). Imitation of man by machine. *Science, N.Y.* **139**, 193–197.

Neisser, U. (1963). The multiplicity of thought. *British Journal of Psychology* **54**, 1–14.

Neisser, U. (1972). A paradigm shift in psychology. *Science, N. Y.* **176**, 628–630.

Neisser, U. (1976). *Cognition and Reality: principles and implications of cognitive psychology.* Freeman, San Francisco.

Neisser, U. (1978). Memory: what are the important questions? In M. M. Gruneberg, P. E. Morris and R. N. Sykes (Eds) *Practical Aspects of Memory.* Academic Press, London and New York.

Neisser, U. and Kerr, N. (1973). Spatial and mnenomic properties of visual images. *Cognitive Psychology* **5**, 138–150.

Nelson, K. (1974). Concept, word and sentence: interrelations in acquisition and development. *Psychological Review*, **81**, 267–285.

Nelson, K. (1977). The syntagmatic-paradigmatic shift revisited: a review of research and theory. *Psychological Bulletin* **84**, 93–116.

Nelson, K. (1978). How children represent knowledge of their world in and out of language: a preliminary report. In R. S. Siegler (Ed.) *Children's Thinking: What Develops?* Lawrence Erlbaum, Hillsdale, NJ.

Nelson, K. (1981). Individual differences in language development: Implications for development and language. *Developmental Psychology* **17**, 170–187.

Newcombe, F. (1969). *Missile Wounds of the Brain.* Oxford University Press, Oxford.

Newcombe, F. (1975). From a paper presented at a conference in the Department of Educational Studies, University of Oxford.

Newcombe, F. and Ratcliff, G. (1973). Two Brains: Independence or Interaction? Paper presented at the British Association for the Advancement of Science.

Newell, A., Shaw, J. C. and Simon, H. A. (1958). Elements of a theory of general problem solving. *Psychological Review* **65**, 151–166.

Newell, A., Shaw, J. C. and Simon, H. A. (1959). Report on a general problem solving programme. In *Proceedings of the International Conference on Information Processing.* Unesco House, Paris.

Newell, A., Shaw, J. C. and Simon, H. A. (1963). Empirical explanations with the logic theory machine: a case study in heuristics. In E. A. Feigenbaum and J. Feldman (Eds) *Computers and Thought.* McGraw-Hill, New York.

Nickerson, R. S. (1977). Some comments on human archival memory as a very large data base. In *Proceedings of the Third International Conference on Very Large Data Bases.* Tokyo, Japan, Oct. 1977.

Nisbett, R. E. and Wilson, T. D. (1977). Telling more than we can know: verbal reports on mental processes. *Psychological Review* **84**, 231–259.

Norman, D. A. and Rumelhart, D. E. (1975). *Explorations in Cognition.* W. H. Freeman, San Francisco.

Norman, D. A. (1973). Memory, knowledge and the answering of questions. In R.

L. Solso (Ed.) *Contemporary Issues in Cognitive Psychology*. The Loyola Symposium. V. H. Winstons, Washington.

Norman, D. A. (1980). Copycat science or does the mind really work by table look-up? In R. A. Cole (Ed.) *Perception and Production of Fluent Speech*. Lawrence Erlbaum Associates, Hillsdale, NJ.

Norman, D. A. (1980). Twelve issues for cognitive science. *Cognitive Science* **4**, 1–32.

Oleron, P. (1953). Conceptual thinking of the deaf. *American Annals of the Deaf* **98**, 304–310.

Olson, D. (1970). Language and Thought: aspects of a cognitive theory of semantics. *Psychological Review* **77**, 257–273.

Ornstein, P. A. and Corsale, K. (1979). Organizational factors in children's memory. In C. R. Puff (Ed.) *Memory Organization and Structure*. Academic Press, New York.

Osgood, C. E. (1952). The nature and measurement of meaning. *Psychological Bulletin* **49**, 197–237.

Osherson, D. N. and Smith, E. E. (1981). On the adequacy of prototype theory as a theory of concepts. *Cognition*, **9**, 35–58.

Paige, J. M. and Simon, H. A. (1966). Cognitive processes in solving algebra word problems. In B. Leinmuntz (Ed.) *Problem Solving: Research, Method and Theory*. John Wiley, New York.

Paivio, A. (1969). Mental imagery in associative learning and memory. *Psychological Review* **76**, 241–263.

Palmer, S. F. (1978). Fundamental aspects of cognitive representation. In E. H. Rosch and B. B. Lloyd (Eds) *Cognition and Categorization*. Lawrence Erlbaum, Hillsdale, NJ.

Patterson, K. and Bradshaw, J. L. (1975). Differential hemispheric mediation of non-verbal stimuli. *Journal of Experimental Psychology*: Human Perception and Performance, **1**, 246–252.

Perl, N. and Haggard, M. (1975). Practice and strategy in a measure of cerebral dominance. *Neuropsychologia*, **13**, 347–354.

Phillips, W. A. and Baddeley, A. D. (1971). Reaction time and short term visual memory. *Psychonomic Science* **22**, 73–74.

Piaget, J., Inhelder, B. and Szeminska, A. (1960). *The Child's Conception of Geometry*. Routledge and Kegan Paul, London.

Podgorny, P. and Shepard, R. N. (1978). Functional representation common to visual perception and imagination. *Journal of Experimental Psychology: Human Perception and Performance* **4**, 21–35.

Polich, J. M. and Schwartz, S. H. (1974). The effect of problem size on representation in deductive problem solving. *Memory and Cognition* **2**, 683–686.

Posner, M. I. (1973). *Cognition: An Introduction*. Scott, Foresman, Glenview, Illinois.

Posner, M. I. (1980). Orienting of attention. *Quarterly Journal of Experimental Psychology* **32** 3–25.

Posner, M. I. and Keele, S. W. (1968). On the genesis of abstract ideas. *Journal of Experimental Psychology* **77**, 353–363.

Posner, M. I. and Keele, S. W. (1970). Retention of abstract ideas. *Journal of Experimental Psychology* **83**, 304–308.

Posner, M. I. and Mitchell, R. F. (1967). Chronometric analysis of classification.

Psychological Review **74**, 392–409.

Posner, M. I. and Snyder, C. R. (1975). Attention and cognitive control. In R. L. Solso (Ed.) *Information Processing and Cognition*. Lawrence Erlbaum, Hillsdale, NJ.

Posner, M. I., Boies, S. J., Eichelman, W. H. and Taylor, R. L. (1969). Retention of name and visual codes of single letters. *Journal of Experimental Psychology* **79**, Monogr. Supp. 1–16.

Potts, G. R. and Scholz, K. W. (1975). The internal representation of a three term series problem. *Journal of Verbal Learning and Verbal Behaviour* **14**, 439–452.

Premack, D. A. (1970). A functional analysis of language. *Journal of Experimental Analysis of Behaviour* **14**, 107–125.

Premack, D. A. and Woodruff, G. (1978). Does the chimpanzee have a theory of mind? *The Behavioral and Brain Sciences* **1**, 515–526.

Pylyshyn, Z. W. (1973). What the mind's eye tells the mind's brain: a critique of mental imagery. *Psychological Bulletin* **80**, 1–24.

Pylyshyn, Z. W. (1975). Minds, machines and phenomenology: some reflections on Dreyfus's 'What computers can't do'. *Cognition* **3**, (1), 57–77.

Pylyshyn, Z. W. (1979). Validating computational models: a critique of Anderson's indeterminacy of representation claim. *Psychological Review* **86**, 383–394.

Pylyshyn, Z. W. (1980). Computation and cognition: issues in the foundations of cognitive science. *The Behavioral and Brain Sciences* **3**, 111–169.

Pylyshyn, Z. W. (1981). The imagery debate: analogue versus tacit knowledge. *Psychological Review* **88**, 16–45.

Quillian, M. R. (1968). Semantic memory. In M. Minsky (Ed.) *Semantic Information Processing* MIT Press, Cambridge, Mass.

Quine, W. V. O. (1960). *Word and Object*. John Wiley, New York.

Reddy, R. (1980). Machine models of speech perception. In R. A. Cole (Ed.) *Perception and Production of Fluent Speech*. Lawrence Erlbaum, Hillsdale, NJ.

Reed, S. K. (1974). Structural descriptions and the limitations of visual images. *Memory and Cognition* **2**, 329–336.

Renzi, E. de, Faglioni, P. and Spinnler, H. (1968). The performance of patients with unilateral brain damage on face recognition tasks. *Cortex* **4**, 17.

Restle, F. (1962). The selection of strategies in cue learning. *Psychological Review* **69**, 329–343.

Revlin, R. and Leirer, V. O. (1978). The effects of personal biases on syllogistic reasoning: rational decision for personalized representations. In R. Revlin and R. E. Mayer (Eds) *Human Reasoning*. V. H. Winston, Washington, DC.

Revlin, R. and Mayer, R. E. (1978). *Human Reasoning*. V. H. Winston, Washington, DC.

Richardson, J. T. E. (1975). Imagery, concreteness and lexical complexity. *Quarterly Journal of Experimental Psychology* **27**, 211–223.

Rips, L. J. (1975). Quantification and semantic memory. *Cognitive Psychology* **7**, 307–340.

Rips, L. J., Shoben, E. J. and Smith, E. E. (1973). Semantic distance and the verification of semantic relations. *Journal of Verbal Learning and Verbal Behaviour* **12**, 1–20.

Risberg, J. (1980). Regional cerebral blood flow measurements by $133X^e$-inhalation methodology and applications in neuropsychology and psychiatry. *Brain and Language* **9**, 9–34.

Roberts, J. and Engle, A. (1974). Family background, early development and intelligence of children 6–11 years. National Health Survey, series 11, No. 142. Washington, DC.

Rosch, E. (1975). Cognitive reference points. *Cognitive Psychology* 7, 532–547.

Rosch, E. (1978). Principles of categorization. In E. Rosch and B. B. Lloyd (Eds), *Cognition and Categorization.* Lawrence Erlbaum, Hillsdale, NJ.

Rosch, E. and Mervis, C. B. (1975). Family Resemblances: studies in the internal structure of categories. *Cognitive Psychology* 7, 573–605.

Rosch, E., Mervis, C. B., Gray, W., Johnson, D. and Boyes-Braem, P. (1976). Basic objects in natural categories. *Cognitive Psychology* 8, 382–439.

Rossi, G. F. and Rosadini, G. (1965). In F. L. Darley and Millikan (Eds) *Brain Mechanisms Underlying Speech and Language* , Grune and Stratton, New York and London.

Rumbaugh, D. M. (1977). *Language Learning by a Chimpanzee: The Lana Project.* Academic Press, London and New York.

Rumbaugh, D. M., von Glaserfeld, E., Warner, H., Pisani, P. and Gill, T. V. (1974). Lana (chimpanzee) learning language: a progress report. *Brain and Language* 1, 205–212.

Rumelhart, D. E. (1975). Notes on a schema for stories. In D. G. Bobrow and A. M. Collins (Eds) *Representation and Understanding: studies in Cognitive Science.* Academic Press, New York.

Rumelhart, D. E. and Norman, D. A. (1975). The Computer Implementation. In D. A. Norman and D. E. Rumelhart (Eds) *Explorations in Cognition.* W. H. Freeman, San Francisco.

Rumelhart, D. E., Lindsay, P. H. and Norman, D. A. (1972). A process model for long term memory. In E. Tulving and W. Donaldson (Eds) *Organization of Memory.* Academic Press, New York.

Ryle, G. (1949). *The Concept of Mind.* Barnes and Noble, New York.

Sachs, J. S. (1967). Recognition memory for syntactic and semantic aspects of connected discourse. *Perception and Psychophysics* 2, 437–442.

Salthouse, T. A. (1974). Using selective interference to investigate spatial memory representations. *Memory and Cognition* 2, 749–757.

Sasanuma, S. (1974). Kanji versus Kana processing alexia with transient agraphia. *Cortex* 10, 89–97.

Savage-Rumbaugh, E. S., Rumbaugh, D. M. and Boysen, S. (1978). Linguistically mediated tool use and exchange by chimpanzees. *The Behavioral and Brain Sciences* 1, 539–554.

Savage-Rumbaugh, E. S., Rumbaugh, D. M., Smith, S. T. and Lawson, J. (1980). The linguistic essential. *Science, NY.* 210, 922–925.

Schaeffer, B. and Wallace, R. (1970). The comparison of word meanings. *Journal of Experimental Psychology* 86, 144–152.

Schank, R. C. (1972). Semantics in conceptual analysis. *Lingua* 30, 101–140.

Schank, R. C. (1972). Conceptual dependency: a theory of natural language understanding. *Cognitive Psychology* 3, 552–631.

Schank, R. C. (1980). An artificial intelligence perspective on Chomsky's view of language. *The Behavioral and Brain Sciences* 3, 35.

Schank, R. C. and Abelson, R. (1976). *Scripts, Plans, Goals and Understanding.* Lawrence Erlbaum, Hillsdale, NJ.

Scheerer, M. (1963). Problem solving. *Scientific American* 208, 118–128.

Schlesinger, I. M. (1971). The grammar of sign language and the problems of language universals. In J. Morton, (Ed.) *Biological and Social Factors in*

Psycholinguistics. Logos Press, in association with Elek Books, London.

Scribner, S. (1977). Modes of thinking and ways of speaking: culture and logic reconsidered. In P. N. Johnson-Laird and P. C. Wason (Eds) *Thinking: Readings in Cognitive Science*. Cambridge University Press, Cambridge.

Searleman, A. (1977). A review of right hemisphere linguistic capabilities. *Psychological Bulletin* **84**, 503–528.

Sebeok, T. (1968). *Animal Communication: Techniques and Study of the Results of Research*. Indiana University Press, Bloomington and London.

Sellars, W. F. (1963). *Science, Perception and Reality*. The Humanities Press, New York.

Seyfarth, R. M., Cheney, D. L. and Marler, P. (1980). Monkey responses to three different alarm calls: evidence of predation classification and semantic communication. *Science, NY.* **210**, 801–803.

Shaver, P., Pierson, L. and Lang, S. (1975). Converging evidence for the functional significance of imagery in problem solving. *Cognition* **3/4**, 359–375.

Shepard, R. N. (1975). Form, formation and transformation of internal representations. In R. L. Solso (Ed.) *Information Processing and Cognition*. The Loyola Symposium. Laurence Erlbaum, Hillsdale, NJ.

Shepard, R. N. (1978). Externalization of mental images and the act of creation. In B. S. Randhawa and W. E. Coffman (Eds) *Visual Learning, Thinking and Communication*. Academic Press, London and New York.

Shepard, R. N. and Chipman, S. (1970). Second order isomorphism of internal representations: shapes of states. *Cognitive Psychology* **1**, 1–17.

Shepard, R. N. and Metzler, J. (1971). Mental rotation of three-dimensional objects. *Science, N.Y.* **171**, 701–703.

Shepard, R. N., Kilpatric, D. W. and Cunningham, J. P. (1975). The internal representation of numbers. *Cognitive Psychology* **7**, 82–138.

Shiffrin, R. M. and Schneider, W. (1977). Controlled and automatic human information processing: perceptual learning, automatic attending and a general theory. *Psychological Review* **84**, 127–190.

Shortliffe, E. H. (1976). *Computer based medical consultations: MYCIN*. Elsevier, New York and Amsterdam.

Sidtis, J. J. and Bryden, M. P. (1978). Asymmetric perception of language and music: evidence for independent processing strategies. *Neuropsychologia* **16**, 627–632.

Siegler, R. S. (1978). The origin of scientific thinking. In R. S. Siegler (Ed.) *Children's Thinking: What Develops?* Lawrence Erlbaum, Hillsdale, NJ.

Simion, F., Bagnara, S., Bisiachi, P., Roncato, S. and Umilta, C. (1980). Laterality effects, levels of processing and stimulus properties. *Journal of Experimental Psychology*: Human Perception and Performance, **6**, 184–195.

Simon, H. A. (1979). Information processing models of cognition. *Annual Review of Psychology* **30**, 363–396.

Simon, H. A. and Gilmartin, K. (1973). A simulation of memory for chess positions. *Cognitive Psychology* **5**, 29–46.

Simon, H. A. and Hayes, J. R. (1976). The Understanding process: problem isomorphs. *Cognitive Psychology* **8**, 165–190.

Simon, H. A. and Reed, S. K. (1976). Modelling strategy shifts in a problem solving task. *Cognitive Psychology* **8**, 86–97.

Sinclair-de-Zwart, H. (1969). Developmental psycholinguistics. In D. Elkind and J. Flavell (Eds) *Studies in Cognitive Development*. Oxford University Press, New

York.

Siple, P. (1978). Linguistic and psychological properties of ASL: an overview. In P. Siple (Ed.) *Understanding language through Sign Language Research.* Academic Press, New York and London.

Slamecka, N. J. A. (1968). A methodological analysis of shift patterns in human discrimination learning. *Psychological Bulletin* **69**, 423–438.

Smedslund, J. (1961). Acquisition of conservation of substance and weight in children. *Journal of Scandinavian Psychology* **2**, 71–84.

Smith, E. E. (1978). Theories of semantic memory. In W. K. Estes (Ed.) *Handbook of Learning and Cognitive Processes; Linguistic Functions in Cognitive Theory.* Vol. 6. Lawrence Erlbaum, Hillsdale, NJ.

Smith, E. E., Shoben, E. J. and Rips, L. J. (1974). Structure and process in semantic memory: a featural model for semantic decisions. *Psychological Review* **81**, 214–241.

Smith, S. M., Brown, H. O., Toman, J. E. P. and Goodman, L. S. (1947). The lack of cerebral effects of d-tubercurarine. *Anesthesiology* **8**, 1–14.

Spearman, C. (1927). *The Abilities of Man: Their Nature and Measurement.* Macmillan, London.

Spellacy, F. and Blumstein, S. (1970). The influence of language set on ear preference in phoneme recognition. *Cortex* **6**, 430–439.

Standing, L. (1973). Learning 10,000 pictures. *Quarterly Journal of Experimental Psychology* **25**, 207–222.

Starck, R., Genesee, F., Lambert, W. E. and Seitz, M. (1980). In D. Caplan (Ed.) *Biological Studies of Mental Processes.* MIT Press, Cambridge, Mass.

Starkey, D. (1981). The origins of concept formation: object sorting and object preference in early infancy. *Child Development* **52**, 489–497.

Staudenmayer, H. and Bourne, L. E. (1978). The nature of denied propositions in the conditional sentence reasoning task: interpretation and learning. In R. Revlin and R. E. Mayer (Eds) *Human Reasoning.* V. H. Winston, Washington, DC.

Sternberg, R. J. (1977). *Intelligence, information processing and analogical reasoning: the componential analysis of human abilities.* Lawrence Erlbaum, Hillsdale, NJ.

Sutherland, N. S. (1974). Computer simulation of brain function. In S. C. Brown (Ed.) *Philosophy of Psychology.* Macmillan, London.

Taylor, I. (1971). How are words from two languages organized in bilinguals' memory? *Canadian Journal of Psychology* **25**, 228–240.

Terrace, H. S., Pettito, L. A., Sanders, R. J. and Bever, T. G. (1979). Can an ape create a sentence? *Science, N.Y.* **206**, 891–902.

Teuber, H-L. (1962). Effects of brain wounds implicating right and left hemispheres. In V. B. Mountcastle (Ed.) *Interhemispheric Relations and Cerebral Dominance.* John Hopkins Press, Baltimore.

Thomas, J. C. (1971). An analysis of behaviour in the hobbits-orcs problem. University of Michigan, Human Performance Center, Technical Report No. 31.

Thompson, C. R. and Church, R. M. (1980). An explanation of the language of a chimpanzee. *Science, N.Y.* **208**, 313–314.

Thompson, J. R. and Chapman, R. S. (1975). Who is "Daddy"? The status of two-year olds' overextended words in use and comprehension. Papers and Reports on Child Language Development (Stanford University) **10**, 59–68.

Thorpe, W. H. (1972). The comparison of vocal communication in animals and man.

In R. A. Hinde (Ed.) *Non-verbal Communication*. Cambridge University Press, Cambridge.

Tinklepaugh, O. L. (1928). An experimental study of representative factors in monkeys. *Journal of Comparative Psychology* **8**, 197–202.

Townsend, J. T. (1973). A note on the identifiability of serial and parallel processes. *British Journal of Mathematical and Statistical Psychology* **25**, 168–199.

Trabasso, T. R. (1963). Stimulus emphasis and all or none learning in concept identification. *Journal of Experimental Psychology* **65**, 398–406.

Trabasso, T. R., Rollins, H. and Shaughnessy, E. (1971). Storage and verification stages in processing concepts. *Cognitive Psychology* **2**, 239–289.

Tulving, E. (1972). Episodic and semantic memory. In E. Tulving and W. Donaldson (Eds) *Organization of Memory*. Academic Press, New York.

Tulving, E. and Colotla, V. A. (1970). Free recall of trilingual lists. *Cognitive Psychology* **1**, 86–98.

Tulving, E. and Pearlstone, Z. (1966). Availability versus accessibility of information in memory for words. *Journal of Verbal Learning and Verbal Behaviour* **5**, 381–391.

Turing, A. M. (1950). Computing machinery and intelligence. *Mind* **59**, 433–460.

Tversky, B. (1969). Pictorial and verbal encoding in a short-term memory task. *Perception and Psychophysics* **6**, 225–233.

Tweney, R. D., Doherty, M. E., Warner, W. J., Pliske, D. B., Mynatt, C. R., Gross, K. A. and Arkkelin, D. L. (1980). Strategies of rule discovery in an inference task. *Quarterly Journal of Experimental Psychology* **32**, 109–123.

Tzavaras, A., Kaprinis, G. and Gatzoyas, A. (1981). Literacy and hemispheric specialization for language: digit dichotic listening in illiterates. *Neuropsychologia* **19**, 4, 565–570.

Vygotsky, L. S. (1962). *Thought and Language*. MIT Press, Cambridge, Mass. (First published in 1934.)

Wales, R. J., Garman, M. A. G. and Griffiths, P. D. (1976). More or less the same: a markedly different view of children's comparative judgements in three cultures. In R. J. Wales and E. Walker (Eds) *New Approaches to Language Mechanisms*. North-Holland, Amsterdam.

Waltz, D. L. (1979). On the function of mental imagery. *The Behavioral and Brain Sciences* **2**, 579.

Wapner, W., Hamby, S., and Gardner, H. (1981). The role of the right hemisphere in the apprehension of complex linguistic materials. *Brain and Language* **14**, 15–33.

Ward, T. B. and Ross, L. E. (1977). Laterality differences and practice effects under central backward masking conditions. *Memory and Cognition* **5**, 221–226.

Warrington, E. K. (1975). The selective impairment of semantic memory. *Quarterly Journal of Experimental Psychology* **27**, 635–657.

Warrington, E. K. and Rabin, P. (1970). Perceptual matching in patients with cerebral lesions. *Neuropsychologia* **8**, 474.

Wason, P. C. (1960). On the failure to eliminate hypotheses in a conceptual task. *Quarterly Journal of Experimental Psychology* **12**, 129–140.

Wason, P. C. (1965). The contexts of plausible denial. *Journal of Verbal Learning and Verbal Behaviour* **4**, 7–11.

Wason, P. C. and Johnson-Laird, P. N. (1972). *The Psychology of Reasoning: Structure and Content*. Batsford, London.

Watson, J. (1930). *Behaviorism*. Norton, New York.

Weinstein, B. (1941). Matching from sample by rhesus monkeys and by children. *Journal of Comparative Psychology* **31**, 195.

Weisberg, R. W. (1980). *Memory, thought and behaviour.* Oxford University Press. New York and Oxford.

Weizenbaum, J. (1968). Contextual understanding by computers. In P. A. Kolers and M. Eden (Eds). *Recognizing Patterns: Studies in Living and Automatic Systems.* MIT Press, Cambridge, Mass.

Whorf, B. (1941). The relation of habitual thought and behaviour to language. In L. Spier (Ed.) *Language, Culture and Personality: Essays in Memory of Edward Sapir.* University of Utah Press.

Wickens, D. D. (1970). Encoding categories of words; an empirical approach to meaning. *Psychological Review* **77**, 1–15.

Wilkins, A. T. (1971). Conjoint frequency, category size and categorization time. *Journal of Verbal Learning and Verbal Behaviour* **10**, 382–385.

Wilks, Y. (1976). Dreyfus's Disproofs. *British Journal of the Philosophy of Science* **27**, 177–185.

Winograd, T. (1972). Understanding natural language. *Cognitive Psychology* **3** (1), 1–191.

Winograd, T. (1975). Frame representations and the declarative/procedural controversy. In D. G. Bobrow and A. Collins (Eds) *Representation and Understanding.* Academic Press, New York.

Winston, P. (1973). Learning to identify toy block structures. In R. L. Solso (Ed.) *Contemporary Issues in Cognitive Psychology.* The Loyola Symposium. Winston–Wiley, Washington, DC.

Witelson, S. F. (1980). Neuroanatomical asymmetry in left-handers: a review and implications for functional asymmetry. In J. Herron (Ed.) *Neuropsychology of Left-Handedness.* Academic Press, London and New York.

Wittgenstein, L. (1953). *Philosophical Investigations.* Basil Blackwell, Oxford.

Wood, D. J. (1969). The nature and development of problem solving strategies. Unpublished D. Phil. thesis, University of Nottingham.

Woodruff, G. and Premack, D. (1979). Intentional communication in the chimpanzee: the development of deception. *Cognition* **7**, 333–362.

Woodruff, G. and Premack, D. (1981). Primitive mathematical concepts in the chimpanzee: proportionality and numerosity. *Nature, Lond.* 293–295.

Woodruff, G., Premack, D. and Kennel, K. (1978). Sarah can conserve liquid and quantity. *Science, N.Y.* **202**, 991–994.

Woods, W. A. (1980). Multiple theory formation in speech and reading. In R. J. Spiro, B. C. Bruce and W. F. Brewer (Eds) *Theoretical Issues in Reading Comprehension.* Lawrence Erlbaum, Hillsdale, NJ.

Yamadori, A. and Albert, M. L. (1973). Word category aphasia. *Cortex* **9**, 112–125.

Young, R. M. (1976). *Seriation by Children: a Production System Approach.* Birkhauser Verlag.

Subject Index